SOVEREIGNS OF THE SEA

The Quest to Build the
Perfect Renaissance Battleship

Angus Konstam

WILEY

John Wiley & Sons, Inc.

To Peter Konstam, FRCS, OBE (1908–1995), born a century ago, into a very different world. Surgeon, refugee from the Nazis, man of culture, all-round European, and an inspirational father.

CONTENTS

ATLAS

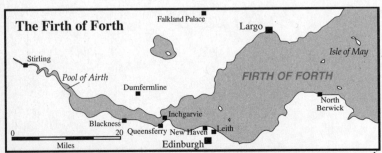

The Firth of Forth

Falkland Palace

Largo

Isle of May

Stirling

FIRTH OF FORTH

Pool of Airth

Dumfermline

North Berwick

Inchgarvie

Blackness

Queensferry   New Haven   Leith

Edinburgh

0   20
Miles

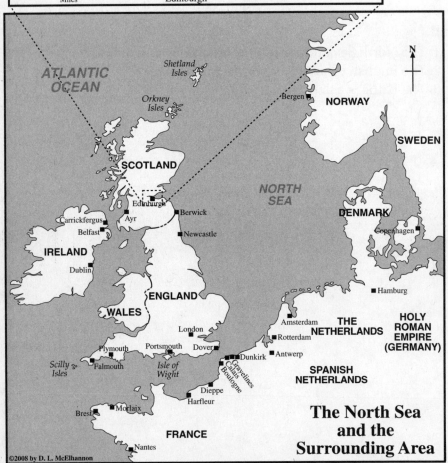

ATLANTIC OCEAN

Shetland Isles

Bergen

NORWAY

Orkney Isles

SWEDEN

SCOTLAND

NORTH SEA

DENMARK

Edinburgh   Berwick

Carrickfergus   Ayr

Copenhagen

Belfast

Newcastle

IRELAND

Dublin

Hamburg

ENGLAND

WALES

Amsterdam   **THE NETHERLANDS**

HOLY ROMAN EMPIRE (GERMANY)

London

Rotterdam

Plymouth   Portsmouth   Dover

Antwerp

Scilly Isles   Falmouth   *Isle of Wight*

Dunkirk

Gravelines
Calais
Boulogne

SPANISH NETHERLANDS

Dieppe

Brest   Morlaix

Harfleur

FRANCE   Nantes

The North Sea and the Surrounding Area

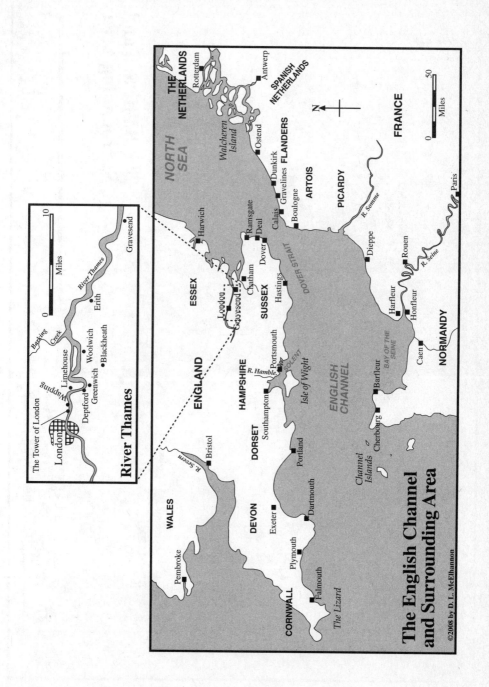

The English Channel and Surrounding Area

©2008 by D. L. McElhannon

River Thames

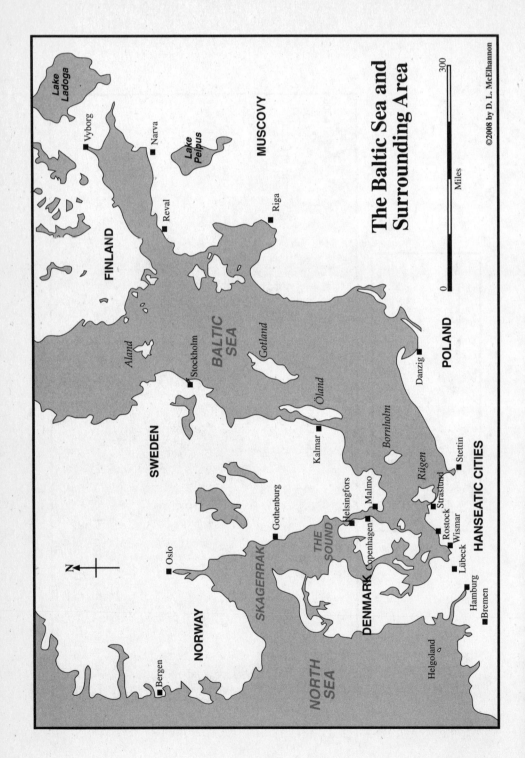

The Baltic Sea and Surrounding Area

©2008 by D. L. McElhannon

Lake Ladoga

Vyborg

Narva

Lake Peipus

MUSCOVY

FINLAND

Reval

Riga

Åland

BALTIC SEA

Gotland

Stockholm

SWEDEN

Öland

Kalmar

Bornholm

POLAND

Danzig

Rügen

Stettin

Gothenburg

Helsingfors

Malmö

Strasund

Oslo

SKAGERRAK

THE SOUND

Copenhagen

Rostock

Wismar

DENMARK

Lübeck

HANSEATIC CITIES

NORWAY

Hamburg

Bremen

Helgoland

NORTH SEA

Bergen

N

Miles

0   300

x

PREFACE

This book was almost a quarter century in the making. Back in the summer of 1983 I had just left the Royal Navy and was busy thinking about what to do next. I was visiting my parents in Orkney, Scotland, when a magazine came in the mail. An old aunt had died, and while my mother was sorting out her estate, the mail was being redirected. My aunt was a graduate of St. Andrews University, and they were still sending her their annual graduates' journal. One day I was idly flicking through it when I came across an article about the foundation of a new department: the Scottish Institute of Maritime Studies, run by Dr. Colin Martin. It was one of those career-defining moments. The postgraduate course it planned to run involved a combination of maritime archaeology and historical research. It sounded custom-made for me. After all, I had dived in the navy and studied history at Aberdeen University. Amazingly, my reading of the article was followed a week later by a visit to my father by an academic who was touring Orkney— Dr. Geoffrey Parker, then professor of modern history at St. Andrews. He praised the course and recommended that I apply.

Three months later I was a student again, and immersing myself quite literally in the world of maritime archaeology. It was all fascinating stuff, but while I found the ships of the ancient world engrossing enough, my real interest lay a little later—the era of the Age of Discovery and the early days of the sailing battle fleets. When the time came to write the thesis for my master's degree, I opted for exactly that period, and over the next year or so I wrote a thesis with the less than snappy title of "Naval Artillery to 1550: Its Design, Evolution, and Employment." Another part of the appeal

was that this was virgin territory—despite Dr. Martin's excavations
of Spanish Armada shipwrecks and the recent raising of the *Mary
Rose*, very few people had really looked at the way guns played a
major part in the evolution of the Renaissance warship.

Although it sounded glamorous enough, my subsequent career
as a maritime archaeologist lasted less than a year. In the summer
of 1985 I was hired by the Royal Armouries at the Tower of London
to help organize a two-week archaeological dig. I stayed for ten
years, having discovered a whole new career as a museum curator.
Naturally enough, my main field was artillery, and over that decade
I met hundreds of archaeologists and divers, museum professionals
and academics—all of whom added something to my understand-
ing of guns and ships. In 1995 I left for a new job in Florida, where
I was immersed in a whole new world of Spanish shipwrecks,
sunken treasure, and yet more guns lying on the seabed. More than
a decade later I found myself back in Scotland, surrounded by the
piles of notes, books, photos, and drawings accumulated during
this twenty-five-year quest to find out more about the ships of the
Renaissance. I thought it might be time to put some of it down on
paper. This is the result.

ACKNOWLEDGMENTS

This project took so long to come to fruition that I couldn't begin to list all the people who helped along the way, or even the places I visited in my search for evidence of ships, guns, or both. An awful lot of people have pointed me in the right direction, or told me when I was making an idiot of myself, including curators, archivists, maritime archaeologists, metalworkers, shipbuilders, historians, academics, librarians, salt-encrusted sailors, and gung-ho divers. The best I can do is mention a few of them.

I would particularly like to express my gratitude to the staff of the National Maritime Museum, the British Library, the Royal Armouries at the Tower of London, and the Public Record Office, all in London; the Mel Fisher Maritime Museum in Key West, Florida; the Mariners' Museum in Newport News, Virginia; the *Vasa* Museum and the Swedish Maritime Museum in Stockholm, Sweden; the *Mary Rose* Trust and Fort Nelson Museum of Artillery in or near Portsmouth, Hampshire, England; the National Library of Scotland, the United Services Museum, and the Scottish National Archives in Edinburgh, Scotland; the Archives of the Indies in Seville, Spain; the Museo Naval and the Army Museum in Madrid; the Nederlands Scheepvaartmuseum in Amsterdam; the Dutch Army Museum in Delft, Netherlands; the Musée de l'Armée in Paris; the Musée National de la Marine in Brest and Port-Louis, France; the Deutsches Schiffahrtsmuseum in Bremerhaven, Germany; and the Germanishes Museum in Nuremberg, Germany. There are too many people in these institutions to mention by name, so please accept my profuse thanks.

However, I would like to single out a handful of individuals who have been especially helpful over the years and who have inspired me to keep up the quest. Dr. Colin Martin and Dr. Robert Prescott of St. Andrews University are at the top of the list, for pointing me in the right direction. Then there's Ruth Rhynas Brown and Robert Smith of the Royal Armouries, who let me into their museum and introduced me to experts such as John F. Guilmartin Jr. and Joe Simmons III of the United States, Jeremy Green of Australia, Jan Piet Puype of Holland, and Adrian Carruana of the United Kingdom. Then there were the rest of the staff at the Royal Armouries— A. V. B. Norman, Guy Wilson, Graeme Rimer, and Nick Hall, who put up with my artillery obsession. I also owe a special debt to Dr. Margaret Rule, Andrew Fielding, Chris Dobbs, and Alex Hildred of the *Mary Rose* Trust. Alex in particular knows more about Tudor guns and gunnery than anyone since the sixteenth century, and she guided me past the obvious pitfalls. The late David Lyon and Teddy Archibald of the National Maritime Museum walked me through their painting collection, argued with me over a beer about minor points of ship design, and generally showed me how little I really knew. I miss them both. Finally I have to thank my late father for all his translation work; my mother for her long-suffering patience; and, of course, Aunt May, that old St. Andrews graduate whose magazine started me off on this long quest.

INTRODUCTION

The Quest

This book tells the story of Renaissance rulers, their guns, and their ships. It describes the first attempts by naval designers to introduce guns onto warships, and it reveals the consequences of this groundbreaking innovation. This was a time when the technologies of gunfounding and shipbuilding were both rapidly changing. When these two parallel lines of development touched, the result was a technical revolution that helped change world history. The introduction of heavy guns to naval warfare came when fresh innovations in sailing ship technology were creating a type of ship that could carry these new weapons. While combining the two technologies wasn't an easy process, it produced the breakthrough that allowed mariners to conquer new worlds, and their royal masters to enrich themselves from the wealth of the Indies and the Americas.

More than forty years ago an eminent economic historian, the late Carlo M. Cipolla, wrote a book called *Guns, Sails, and Empires*. In it he argued that in the fifteenth and sixteenth centuries the world was transformed by European sailors who pioneered new sea routes to the Americas and the Far East. The period also saw the establishment of the world's first transatlantic empire and the beginnings of European colonial domination over the peoples they came into contact with. They achieved this because of two inter-linked technical innovations: the development of the sailing ship and the invention of shipborne artillery. Rather touchingly, Profes-sor Cipolla claimed that he was an inveterate landlubber and paci-fist, but the conclusions were the inescapable result of his research into Renaissance history. Today it seems obvious, but only because other historians have pushed forward along the path blazed by the Italian-born scholar.

Of course, this is only part of the picture—the past seen from the perspective of trade. While there certainly was a major leap forward in the design of ships during the Renaissance, and the introduction of guns into ships transformed the ability of these ships to fight, these two great developments also led in other directions. The most important was probably the establishment of national navies—an institution pioneered by the English and the French. The creation of national fleets also led to the possibility of waging a new kind of war. Rather than just maintaining ships to transport an army across the sea or to raid an enemy coast, the owners of a powerful fleet could attempt to gain control of the seas. Although the whole idea of sea power is a more modern concept, the notion of maintaining a fleet with which a country could protect its sea lanes and coasts, and deny the enemy this protection, was first developed during the Renaissance.

This was an incredible period in history, when small states of Europe finally broke out of their Continental confines and expanded their influence across the globe. However, it also was an era of great political upheaval, as the nation-states we know today were forged in battle, or through the imposition of central power by a monarch or a city-state. Above all, the Renaissance is remembered as a time of cultural rebirth, when for the first time since the collapse of the Roman Empire people were able to look at the world around them in a new way. This was the age of the great humanist schol-ars and of poets, architects, painters, inventors, scientists, sculp-tors, and doctors. Today we think of the Renaissance in terms of Michelangelo, Raphael, Titian, or Donatello. We tend to forget that these great artists worked for secular patrons, many of whom were engaged in brutal wars against neighboring states. We gloss over the uncomfortable fact that Leonardo da Vinci trained as a military engineer, and he spent almost as much time designing weapons of war and improving siege techniques as he did creating works of artistic beauty. This was the other side of the cultural coin—the same impetus for advancement also led to far-reaching changes in the way warfare was fought, both on land and at sea.

In his book of the same name, the British-born historian Geoffrey Parker introduced the phrase "The Military Revolution" to encompass the effects that the invention of gunpowder had on military abilities and tactics. He argued that by maintaining control of gunpowder weapons the monarchs of Europe were finally able to establish their military supremacy over their feudal nobles, and this inevitably led to the creation of a national standing army. These gunpowder weapons—handguns and artillery—also transformed the way battles were fought, which led to a change in both battlefield tactics and campaign strategy. This gave these European armies an edge over enemies who hadn't gone through the same process and were therefore technologically inferior.

Exactly the same transformation was taking place at sea. The introduction of artillery into warships didn't lead to any immediate improvement in fighting ability. It took time to work out how best to mount these new weapons in the ships and how to use them effectively. This means that while the great military captains of the day were experimenting with the rock, scissors, and paper of sixteenth-century military technology, trying to work out how to use cavalry, infantry, and artillery on the battlefield, naval captains were going through much the same process. At first, artillery was seen as an auxiliary weapon that could augment but not replace the traditional tools of naval warfare. For much of the sixteenth century, two schools of naval thought existed: one based on a traditional approach to naval warfare, the other centered on the destructive potential of the gun. When the inevitable showdown came in 1588, the advocates of firepower were the unequivocal winners.

From that point on, naval artillery was seen as the arbiter of victory at sea, and the maritime powers of Europe embarked on an arms race, trying to build a standing navy that could hold its own in this new maritime arena. Consequently, while the size of most navies increased, so too did the size of the warships within

A carrack under sail, after Breugel the Elder

each fleet. The only limitation on the size of these fleets was the depth of the national coffers. The real winners in this naval arms race were the nations that had already developed extensive overseas trade routes and whose mercantile wealth allowed rulers to indulge themselves to the full. By the start of the seventeenth century, only one limiting factor remained. The technological developments and design innovations that had transformed the business of shipbuilding seemed to have run their course.

There were technical limitations on the size of wooden sailing ships and on the weight of ordnance they could carry. This problem had plagued rulers and shipbuilders since the early fifteenth century. Meanwhile, the technology of gunfounding continued to develop, and it was inevitable that designers would try to throw caution to the wind and create floating fortresses that were as technically unstable as they were powerful. While the main theme of this book is the quest to create the perfect warship, a major subtheme is the way this resulted in designers trying to "push the envelope." The challenge was simple enough. If you accepted that recent innovations in shipbuilding allowed the creation of larger and more effective ships than ever before, and that the future of naval warfare lay in the introduction of heavy guns onto ships, then the task was clear. If only a warship could be designed that was large enough to dwarf its rivals, and that carried an overwhelming amount of firepower, then victory at sea would be assured. At least that was the theory.

Of course, this was only part of the impetus. For rulers such as Henry VIII of England, James IV of Scotland, and Francis I of France, the international prestige to be gained from building a floating leviathan was probably just as important as the naval firepower it offered. A ship of this kind would be a floating symbol that the nation whose flag it flew had mastered the new technology and was a country that was going places. It suggested that its ruler was a man who embraced progress and who would make either a powerful ally or a formidable adversary. By commissioning such a ship he also showed himself to be a true Renaissance prince, a man who looked toward the future: in other words, a combination of personal ego and international prestige lay behind the building of these great ships. That means that the stories of these great warships and the rulers who ordered their construction were closely intertwined.

While Renaissance shipbuilders also built large merchant ships, the requirements were completely different. The introduction of heavy guns meant that for the first time warship design had become highly specialized. While at the start of our period some monarchs charted their royal ships to merchants in an attempt to recoup some of their building costs, this practice tended to die out as the sixteenth century progressed. Put simply, heavy guns took up space that would otherwise be devoted to cargo, and you couldn't design a ship to carry grain as well as guns. Of course, these small fleets of specialized warships could be augmented by armed merchantmen in time of war, but this was immaterial. During the Spanish Armada campaign of 1588 the Spaniards included some huge hired merchantmen in their armada, but these were largely unsuited to the rigors of naval warfare. As Dr. Colin Martin once put it, their hulls were designed to keep grain in, not cannonballs out. He claimed that their hulls were like eggshells—strong in some places, but easy to crack if you knew where to squeeze.

One of the most fascinating things about the story of the great Renaissance leviathans is that they didn't live up to all those high expectations. They represented a hefty investment of what were often very limited resources, yet rulers seemed obsessed by this quest for size, power, and prestige. However, the English *Henri Grace à Dieu* was too large to enter most of the Channel ports, the *Michael* all but bankrupted the Scots but achieved nothing, and the giant Portuguese carrack *Santa Catarina do Monte Sinai* did little apart from impressing visitors to Lisbon Harbor. Apart from the prohibitive costs involved in building and maintaining these ships, the desire to load them with as much weaponry as possible meant that they were prone to be top-heavy. Two mighty Renaissance warships—the English *Mary Rose* and the Swedish *Vasa*—both capsized because they carried too many guns. Others proved too lumbering and cumbersome to perform well under sail. However, as shipbuilding technology progressed, European rulers kept trying out new solutions to the problem of finding the optimum balance between warship and gun. The quest would continue.

By the later sixteenth century most ship designers had realized that size wasn't everything. A more agile warship could run rings around a more lumbering opponent. After all, sailing ships can only fire to the side, so by keeping out of the enemy arc of fire while bringing your own guns to bear, you could outshoot the enemy ship with impunity. This lesson was demonstrated fairly spectacularly during the Spanish Armada campaign, when the Spaniards found themselves outsailed by their English opponents. However, many historians also ignored another, less obvious lesson. Many of the bigger Spanish ships took an incredible pounding, but the English were unable to damage them enough to deflect them from their goal of sailing in formation along the English Channel to their rendezvous at Calais. Consequently Europe's rulers took another look at big ships, only this time they wanted them to be well armed and maneuverable.

This book is called *Sovereigns of the Sea* for good reason. These great Renaissance warships represented the quest to find the perfect

Aftermath of the sinking of the Mary Rose

balance among warship size, firepower, and operational effectiveness. It was a quest that led to several dead ends and included
its fair share of failures. However, a third of the way through the
seventeenth century—a time that many historians claim marks
the end of the Renaissance—someone finally got the balance right.
In 1637 the English shipbuilder Phineas Pett supervised the launch
of Charles I's giant warship *Sovereign of the Seas*. She might have
been ornate and gilded, but she was also an extremely potent fighting ship—so much so that the Dutchmen who faced her in battle
dubbed her the "Golden Devil." She would become the model for
a whole new generation of warships, the forerunner of the ships
of the line that would dominate naval warfare until the advent of
steam power. In her the Renaissance "battleship" had finally come
of age. This book follows the quest to achieve this perfect balance

among the aspirations of the rulers, the design of warships, and the changing requirements of naval firepower.

Old Tongues and Past Times

Spelling was a haphazard business in the sixteenth and seventeenth centuries, and words were often written in more than one way within the same sentence. Where possible I've tried to retain the original spelling in a quote. However, in some cases I've had to resort to a modern equivalent to render the passage even vaguely intelligible. Grammar and the names of ships, people, and places also have been standardized. Any errors in the translation of passages into modern English are entirely my own fault.

Where possible or appropriate I have adopted the Julian (or "Old Style") calendar, which began its year on March 25 and counted every fourth year as a leap year. In 1582 Pope Gregory XIII introduced the Gregorian (or "New Style") calendar, and this system was rapidly adopted by most of Europe. True to form, the British clung to the older calendar until 1752. As most of the book is set in the period before the new calendar came into effect, I decided to follow the British example and stick with the Old Style throughout the book. After so many centuries the difference of about ten days between the two calendars seems less important than it might have been at the time.

1

Europe Comes of Age

The Flowering of the Renaissance

It seems strange to label a historical period after a cultural move-ment. The spread of ideas is not something that can be neatly pigeon-holed and dated. The Renaissance was first and foremost a revival of classical learning, a rebirth of interest in knowledge in all its forms. This led to the cultural phenomena that most people associate with the period—the paintings of Raphael, the statues of Michelangelo, and the buildings of Brunelleschi. However, the Renaissance was so much more. It led to significant political and economic changes within Europe, while the thirst for knowledge was harnessed to the desire for profit to produce the voyages of exploration and discovery that revealed a world beyond Europe's shores.

It is also virtually impossible to date. Once again, historians seem to come up with dates and events that help pin a historical era together but that don't really embrace the whole picture. Europe was just too large and diverse for that. If you date the Renaissance by the spread of ideas, then you could claim it all began with the growth of universities in the second half of the fifteenth century. Followers of the world of literature would tend to agree, as the first printed book—the Gutenberg Bible—was produced in 1455. Art historians cite the works of Donatello and Masaccio in the 1420s, or else jump forward to the paintings of Botticelli or Leonardo da Vinci from the late 1470s onward. For their part, historians use the fall of Constantinople (1453), the Spanish conquest of Moorish Granada (1492), or the French invasion of Italy (1494) as their benchmarks. However, few can argue with maritime historians when they claim that the world changed forever in 1492, when Columbus discovered the New World.

We have the same problem when we try to work out when the Renaissance ended. The turn of the seventeenth century is often cited, as it marked the end of several political eras, including the end of Elizabethan England, Huguenot France, and the Spain of Philip II. The death of artists such as Tintoretto and Veronese marked the end of the high Renaissance of Italian art, while the Reformation had already divided Europe along religious lines, which meant a new political order in Europe, where allegiances were decided by religion rather than dynastic rivalry. Others argue that the Renaissance continued well into the new century, particularly in northern Europe, where religion gave a fresh impetus to cultural and artistic endeavor. This was the age of Rembrandt and the Dutch masters, of scientists such as Galileo and Bacon, writers such as Shakespeare, and architects such as Inigo Jones.

On the wider stage the sixteenth century had seen the establishment of Spanish colonies in the Americas, while the Portuguese carved out their own overseas trading empire in India and the East Indies. For much of the period these overseas empires remained firmly in Iberian control, but the Spanish monopoly fell apart in the wake of a series of attacks by English sea dogs and French corsairs. By the end of the sixteenth century the maritime powers of northern Europe—the English, the French, and the Dutch—had all gained their own colonial foothold in North America and were set to challenge the southern Europeans for control of the riches of the Americas. This shift in power became even more marked during the early seventeenth century, when the Dutch and English East India companies began to oust the Portuguese from India, and the American colonies became permanent fixtures on the newly drawn map of the world. Smaller European nations—the Swedes, the Danes, and even the Scots—tried to establish their own overseas colonies, but by that stage the others were too well entrenched to allow the interlopers any chance of success.

Whichever way you define it, the Renaissance also was marked by a series of wars that may not have embraced the whole Continent but that seemed never-ending. In northwestern Europe the Hundred Years' War (1337–1453) between England and France caused widespread devastation but also led to the rise of national governments. Similarly, the Scandinavian countries fought a series of wars for independence that ended only with the emergence of Sweden as a power in the Baltic. Then came the Hapsburg-Valois wars between the French king and the Holy Roman emperor, a conflict that used Italy as a battleground. In the Mediterranean the longest-running conflict was between Christians and Muslims. Although the Moors were driven from Spain in 1492, the Ottoman Turks were victorious in the eastern Mediterranean, and throughout the sixteenth century the two religions remained at loggerheads. This meant that the great cultural, artistic, religious, and economic developments of the period were set against a backdrop of nearly constant warfare.

However, this book isn't about art, literature, architecture, or science. Our focus is on the maritime world, particularly the revolution in the design and fighting ability of sailings ships of war. Although the great age of discovery plays a part in this story, it is a secondary one, as are the cultural and religious changes that characterized the Renaissance as a period of rebirth. Even the nearly endless succession of wars is secondary, except where they involved naval warfare, or encouraged the development of artillery that could be used at sea. What remains are the political and economic changes that helped shape the naval policies of Europe's rulers, that saw the creation of national fleets, and that witnessed the rise of European powers whose strength was drawn from sea power and maritime trade rather than from terrestrial affairs. Among these powers the quest to build bigger and better warships became an obsession, as did the desire to arm fleets with the latest weaponry. Therefore our view of the Renaissance is influenced by the key events in this naval revolution and by the way the rulers of Europe embraced sea power to ensure their own power and prestige.

The Princes of the West

During the last half of the fifteenth century major changes transformed the Continental map and established the political landscape of modern Europe. If Italy was the epicenter of the Renaissance, it is somewhat disappointing that none of this political upheaval had any lasting effect on the region. It had long been divided into small city-states and petty states, and while the fifteenth century might have witnessed a cultural upheaval of global importance, in political terms it remained business as usual in Italy, where intercity warfare was endemic. The arrival of the French in 1494 did little to change all this, while it also turned northern Italy into a battleground as allegiances formed and re-formed, and battles achieved little lasting political unity. The conflict reached a peak when the Spanish intervened, and the last decade of the Italian wars saw the conflict become a struggle between the Holy Roman emperor and the French crown.

While the Battle of Pavia in 1525 might have decided the struggle for Italy in favor of the emperor, the Hapsburg-Valois wars would continue for another two decades, by which time France was embroiled in its own internal war while the emperor faced religious unrest within his own realm. The only two maritime powers of any real note in Italy were the city-states of Genoa and Venice. However, by the end of the fifteenth century both cities were in decline, and Genoa became little more than a mercenary supplier of fleets to the French. Venice was on the front line in the bar against the Turks, and much of its efforts were devoted to preserving the Venetian trading empire in the central and eastern Mediterranean. A string of naval campaigns would be fought between Christian and Muslim as the sixteenth century unfolded, but the rest of the time war galleys and corsairs alike raided the coastline of their religious rivals, and piracy became a way of life.

It was a similar story in the western Mediterranean. Although the Spanish had succeeded in driving the Moors from Spain in 1492, these Muslims retained control of the North Africa seaboard, an area known as the Barbary Coast. The Spanish, the Knights of Malta, the French, the Genoese, and the smaller Italian powers all devoted considerable energy to trying to quash these Muslim corsairs, but little was achieved. The region would remain a pirate hot spot until well into the seventeenth century, and resources that could be spent elsewhere were devoted to the protection of Mediterranean trade. It also meant that the rulers of Spain and France had more to worry about than the creation of fleets of sailing ships of war, as they had to maintain powerful galley fleets in the Mediterranean. The galley itself would remain largely a Mediterranean phenomenon. Although war galleys were used in the waters of the English Channel and the Baltic, they never challenged the supremacy of the sailing warship. Therefore, as this story is concerned more with sailing ships than with oared warships, the Mediterranean plays a relatively minor part in this book.

The Spanish were something of a maritime enigma. After the success of the Reconquista, which united Spain under the Christian rulers Ferdinand and Isabella, they continued their campaign against the Moors of Africa, but they also looked west, across the Atlantic Ocean. Although the exploration phase continued for a few decades, by the mid-1520s regular shipments of gold and silver were being transported from the New World to Spain, and this naturally attracted the interest of others. After French corsairs began intercepting these shipments, the Spanish instituted a flota or convoy system, which would remain in operation for more than two centuries. The Spanish came to rely on this regular American windfall, and they devoted a lot of time and effort to ensure that the flotas arrived home safely. This meant that while the Spanish still prosecuted their war against the Barbary pirates in the Mediterranean, their efforts in the Atlantic were concentrated on the New World rather than on the establishment of a fleet designed to operate in northern European waters.

During the reign of King Philip II (1556–1598) this would change dramatically as the Spanish became embroiled in a costly war with the Dutch rebels of the Netherlands and a cold war with Elizabethan England. Spanish frustration would lead to a massive reallocation of resources as Philip created a powerful armada or fleet designed to carry an army of invasion to England. Although this expedition proved a costly failure, it demonstrated that Spain was still a maritime power of considerable importance that still could alter the strategic naval balance in northern Europe if its ruler wished. While the failure of the Spanish Armada has long been lauded as a triumph of English ship design and gunnery, the truth is that however good a few of the English ships were, they were unable to break up the armada's defensive formation as it advanced up the English Channel, and the only Spanish ships to fall victims to the English lagged behind the rest of the fleet.

During the last decade of his life Philip II also was distracted by war with the French. After the Spanish-led victory over the French at Pavia in 1525, the two sides maintained an uneasy peace, broken by short periods of open warfare. However, from 1562 to 1598, the French were distracted by an intermittent civil war known as the French Wars of Religion. The religious violence reached a peak in the St. Bartholomew's Day Massacre of 1572, a slaughter of Protestants that was applauded by both the pope and Philip II of Spain. Many Protestants—Huguenots—responded by waging their own war against Catholic Spain in the waters of the Americas. During the reign of King Henry IV (ruled 1589–1610), decrees of religious tolerance effectively ended the war, but following his death the monarchy resumed its persecution of the Protestant minority, and once more France became a resolutely Catholic country.

Francis I of France

The result of this century of conflict meant that from the mid-sixteenth century the French monarchs were more concerned with maintaining military control of their own country than with the creation of a national fleet. The exception was in the Mediterranean, where the French continued to maintain a powerful galley fleet throughout the sixteenth and early seventeenth centuries. Francis I (reigned 1515–1547) was therefore the last French king of the Renaissance to devote his energies toward the creation of a fleet of sailing warships. This fleet last saw action in 1545, and in the years that followed its ships rarely put to sea, and they were eventually decommissioned or allowed to rot at their moorings. It wasn't until the accession of King Louis XIV to the French throne in 1643 that a French royal fleet was again considered a strategic necessity. Still, the meager French fleet still boasted an occasional gem, such as the *Saint Louis* of 1625, built in Holland in response to the launch of the English warship *Prince Royal*. This powerful French warship carried forty-eight heavy guns mounted on two continuous gun decks. However, she remained the exception to the rule, and throughout this period the French punched well below their weight.

The situation was markedly different in the Netherlands, where in 1568 the Dutch rebelled against Spanish rule. The region was already heavily engaged in maritime trade, and consequently the Dutch rebels could draw on a pool of experienced sailors and sea captains. The Dutch relied on these men—the "Sea Beggars"—to defend the coastal cities of Holland and to harass the Spanish on the high seas. Throughout the first phase of this war the Dutch never created a powerful national navy like their Protestant allies in England. However, from 1597 the Dutch Republic began raising its own fleet of medium-size warships, and by the resumption of the war with Spain in 1621 these were used to launch attacks on Spanish and Portuguese colonies in the Americas and the East Indies. This culminated in the destruction of a Spanish treasure flota off the coast of Cuba in 1628, a victory that comprehensively demonstrated the decline of Spain's maritime effort and the rise of the Dutch as a maritime power.

Just as important to Dutch national interests were the armed merchantmen of the Vereenigde Oostindische Compagnie (VOC)—the Dutch East India Company. Formed in 1602 to develop trade routes with the Indies, the "VOC" was the world's first true multinational corporation, and by the mid-seventeenth century it had broken the Portuguese monopoly on the spice trade. This success was based on a combination of aggressive mercantile dealing and the creation of a fleet of powerful East Indiamen capable of holding their own against just about any attacker they might encounter. These ships had to be built according to very rigid specifications—shallow enough to navigate the Dutch waterways and coastal waters of India or the East Indies, but commodious enough to carry a substantial cargo. They also had to be fast, as a speedy voyage meant a profitable one. The result was an effective warship that also was a well-designed merchant vessel, and in time of war the Dutch would eventually be able to double their naval strength by drawing on surplus East Indiamen.

Of all the future maritime powers of northern Europe, the English were among the first to embrace sea power. They were prepared to take full advantage of the shipbuilding and gunfounding revolutions of the late fifteenth and early sixteenth centuries, and in the process they laid the groundwork for a national fleet that would be the envy of the maritime world throughout the age of sail and beyond. Henry V—Shakespeare's warrior king—was one of the first English monarchs to realize the importance of controlling his territorial waters. He ordered the building of the first European "super ship," the *Grace Dieu*—a warship so big and powerful that it could single-handedly dominate the sea lanes of the English Channel. While the notions of a national navy and a naval leviathan might have been forgotten after Henry's death in 1422, they would return, and would remain an important theme in English foreign policy throughout the rest of the Renaissance.

The foundation of an English national navy is usually credited to Henry VII, who seized the English throne in 1485. While he inherited a small navy from his predecessor Richard III—Shakespeare's evil hunchback—his real achievement was to build two heavily armed warships, the foundation of the Tudor Navy Royal. The *Regent* and the *Sovereign* both carried a mixture of heavy and light pieces of ordnance, making them the first purpose-built gun-armed warships in northern Europe. Other warships would follow, and by the time Henry VIII succeeded his father in 1509, the fleet was considered one of the cornerstones of Tudor power. The young king would build on this, creating powerful gun-armed modern warships such as the *Mary Rose*. The monarch was also responsible for commissioning England's next great "super ship," the *Henri Grace à Dieu*. The fleet he built survived his death and was passed on intact, first to his son Edward, and then to his daughters Mary and Elizabeth.

The Tudor Navy Royal really came into its own during the reign of Queen Elizabeth I (reigned 1558–1603). Under her elder sister Mary, English shipwrights had been introduced to aspects of Spanish ship design, and shortly after Elizabeth's succession the first of a new type of English warship appeared, a combination of the best of English and Spanish design. These vessels were far more maneuverable than earlier English ships, and better suited to making long Atlantic voyages. However, unlike Spanish galleons, their English counterparts were designed primarily to be mobile gun platforms possessing a level of firepower that put them into a class all of their own. These "race-built" galleons would later play a major part in England's defensive victory during the Spanish Armada campaign of 1588, and would serve as the flagships of Elizabethan sea dogs such as Francis Drake, John Hawkins, and Martin Frobisher.

However, Elizabethan ship design continued to evolve, and the last years of the virgin queen's reign saw a move toward the creation of warships that carried a more homogeneous armament of heavy guns. Warships began to be built or converted to carry heavy guns in two or more full gun decks. One possible influence for these new ships was the commodious armed trading vessels built for the Honourable East India Company, England's answer to the VOC. By the second decade of the seventeenth century the English were producing an entirely new type of warship, typified by the *Prince Royal* of 1610, which carried fifty-six heavy guns mounted on three full gun decks. During her life she was rebuilt twice, and adapted to carry a further thirty-four pieces of heavy ordnance. She was designed by Phineas Pett, the man who would go on to build the *Sovereign of the Seas*.

A quick glance at a map will show why the English were so anxious to integrate a national fleet into their policy of national defense. The English Channel created a natural barrier to an invader, and the Spanish Armada campaign of 1588 demonstrated that a powerful navy could prevent the landing of an enemy invasion fleet on the English coast. The Achilles heel of England was its land border with Scotland, so resources had to be devoted to the protection of northern England by fortified garrisons and a network of militias. This threat was made even more potent because the Scots were often openly hostile to the English, even when the two countries were ostensibly at peace. This animosity drew the Scots into an alliance with France, which raised the specter of a two-pronged attack—a Scottish invasion while England was embroiled in a land war with the French. Fortunately for the English this invasion threat rarely materialized, and when it did, the Scots proved singularly unsuccessful on the battlefield.

It was also fortunate for the English that their northern neighbors lacked the resources to build up a powerful navy. The one exception came during the reign of King James IV of Scotland (reigned 1488–1513). He created a small navy from scratch, and amazingly he built a flagship—the *Michael*—which for a few short years was the most powerful sailing warship in the world. It was an incredible achievement for such a small and impoverished country, and ultimately it turned out to be a monumental folly. After the king's death on the battlefield of Flodden in 1513, the *Michael* passed into obscurity, and all dreams of a Scottish navy were abandoned. Ironically, one legacy of the *Michael* was that her building spurred Henry VIII into creating his own even larger super warship—the *Henri Grace à Dieu*.

For much of James IV's reign his closest European ally was King Hans (or John) of Denmark (1481–1513), who spent much of his life fighting to control the rest of Scandinavia, particularly Sweden, which he conquered in 1497. This war against Swedish rebels and their Hanseatic allies involved a struggle for naval control of the Baltic Sea, and Hans built up a small but effective fleet during the last decade of his reign. His son Christian II continued this struggle with the Swedes, which culminated in his temporary reconquest of these rebel territories in 1520 and the brutal massacre of his Swedish opponents in Stockholm. Like his father, he recognized that Danish power relied on control of the sea, and consequently he built up a powerful fleet. Unfortunately, Christian ended up a prisoner of his uncle Frederick of Holstein, who used this golden opportunity to seize the crown. Ultimately this drive for regional naval supremacy

The "WA" carrack

came to nothing, and ultimately it was Denmark's main rival that would control the cold waters of the Baltic.

The Swedes had managed to regroup after the "Stockholm Bloodbath" of 1520, and in 1523 the twenty-four-year-old nobleman Gustav Vasa was elected as the new Swedish king. The previous summer the Swedish Riksdag (Parliament) purchased several ships from their major ally, the German Baltic port of Lübeck, a member of the once-powerful Hanseatic League. These formed the basis of a new national navy. Gustav I and his successors realized that Swedish independence depended on the maintenance of a Baltic fleet, and shortly after the temporary cessation of hostilities with Denmark in 1524, the Swedes set about building an even larger fleet. The flagship of this new fleet was the *Elefant*, built in Stockholm in 1532.

She was reputedly a warship of about 750 tons, which made her bigger than anything the Danes could send against her.

This Swedish obsession with size would return almost a century later, after a succession of Baltic wars that saw the country's navy gradually gain the ascendancy in the Baltic. However, resources were limited, and the Swedes rarely did more than achieve temporary control of the region. Then in 1625 King Gustavus Adolphus (reigned 1611–1632) ordered the building of four new warships, the largest of which was called the *Vasa*. She was designed along the lines of the English *Prince Royal*, with two full gun decks augmented by a few more guns on her upper deck. This ornate and stately sixty-four-gun warship was launched in Stockholm, and began her maiden voyage in August 1628. She had barely sailed a mile before a sudden gust of wind forced her to heel over. Water poured into her open gunports and she sank in minutes, taking thirty of her crew with her. This disaster proved that while rulers such as Gustavus Adolphus now realized the potential of modern heavy guns to influence a naval battle, ship designers were still trying to figure out the best way to carry all this weaponry within the hull of a sailing man-of-war.

Within six years of this disaster King Charles I of England and Scotland visited the shipbuilder Phineas Pett in the royal shipyard in Woolwich, just outside London. Charles ordered the building of his own super warship, the largest vessel built in Europe since Henry V's *Grace Dieu*. Naval experts swore it couldn't be done and that this vessel—the *Sovereign of the Seas*—would be unmanageable under sail and would be too large to navigate the coastal waters of Britain. Charles I and Phineas Pett proved them wrong. When the *Sovereign of the Seas* was launched in 1637, she was the biggest and most powerful warship in Europe, a naval leviathan with more than a hundred heavy guns, and the most heavily decorated ship anyone had ever seen. Ultimately she would cost Charles I his kingdom and his head, but that is another story.

His designer, Phineas Pett, had finally achieved what European ship designers had been striving for since the early fifteenth century: he had built the ultimate Renaissance "battleship," a warship so well armed and so well designed that she could well have stood alongside the British fleet at the Battle of Trafalgar almost two centuries later. If we decided to begin our own naval Renaissance as early as 1418, when Henry V's *Grace Dieu* became the first European super ship, the launch of the *Sovereign of the Seas* provides us with the perfect point at which to end the Renaissance. The two centuries between would be remembered for their contribution to culture, science, religion, and politics. They should also be recognized as the time when the great quest to find the ultimate gun-armed warship would run its course.

2

Knights of the Sea

The Grace of God

If this journey has a clear beginning, it probably was on St. Crispin's Day in 1415, amid the mud and blood of Agincourt. That was when—on October 25—a small, bone-tired, and dispirited English force led by King Henry V was cornered by a far larger French army commanded by Charles d'Albret, the constable of France. The French held almost all the advantages, including overwhelming numbers, all the supplies they needed, and a large contingent of feudal knights—the elite of the French nobility. However, Henry had one battle-winning edge: the majority of his ragged troops were armed with the longbow. In the late Middle Ages the English longbowman was a force to be reckoned with.

The battle that followed lasted less than three hours, and by its end the French dead littered the battlefield in their thousands. The French constable was one of the casualties, killed by an arrow as he led a desperate charge against the English ranks. Perhaps the greatest casualty of this small battle was the whole chivalric ethos that had dominated Europe for centuries. From that point on, the

French monarch—along with most other European rulers—would place far less emphasis on chivalry and knightly glory. Instead he would put his faith in the new arbiters of victory: the missile power of lowly infantry, and the ability to keep those men supplied and armed. The Age of Chivalry died on that muddy, rain-soaked battlefield, and what followed was a military revolution.

Of course, Henry V of England—Shakespeare's "Good King Harry"—was well aware that the rules were changing. The twenty-eight-year-old monarch was unable to match the manpower or the money available to his rival, Charles VI of France. The two countries had been locked in conflict for almost eight decades—an intermittent struggle for territorial control of French soil that was later dubbed the Hundred Years' War. Since the war began in 1337, the fortunes of both sides had waxed and waned, but by the time Henry was born in 1387 the protagonists had fought each other to a standstill and had declared a truce. However, as soon as he ascended the throne in 1413, Henry planned to renew the fight.

He hoped that a popular war would lead to the conquest of territory that could boost his treasury, as could the income generated by plunder raids (*chevauchées*) and the ransoming of noble prisoners. Besides, Charles VI was half insane, and Henry hoped the French would be unable to put an army into the field that could threaten him. The English already held lands in southern France, but instead of consolidating this foothold, Henry coveted the Duchy of Normandy, the hereditary lands of his forebears. On August 13, 1415, he landed at Harfleur, at the mouth of the River Seine. Before he took it, Henry spent six weeks besieging the port, where Shakespeare later had Henry cry, "Once more unto the breach, dear friends, once more; Or close the wall up with our English dead." By that time his army was riddled by disease, so he decided to march overland to the English-held fortress town of Calais, some 250 miles to the north. It was during this march that his starving, ragtag army destroyed the flower of French chivalry at Agincourt.

To the victor went the spoils. Henry consolidated his hold over much of northern France, not just Normandy, and was even recognized as the official heir to the French throne. The French lost access to the sea, apart from their Mediterranean ports and a little toehold on the coast of Gascony near St. Rochelle. Most of Charles

VI's fleet had been in Harfleur when the English arrived, and these ships were captured along with the port. However, Henry now had a problem: to maintain his grip on his French lands, he had to make sure he retained control of the "Narrow Seas"—the English Channel. For the moment he enjoyed mastery of the seas, but there was no guarantee that this would last. He began by ordering construction of a new warship in the English-controlled port of Bayonne, in southwestern France. This was only the start. He decided to build a new "super warship," one so large and so powerful that it would guarantee his continued control over his vital lines of communication between Dover and Calais. Given his recent spectacular and unexpected victory on the battlefield, it seemed appropriate to call the new ship *Grace Dieu* (Grace of God).

What records we have of this mighty ship tell us everything and nothing. They speak of how much the timbers cost to build her, or the number of iron fasteners used in her construction. They don't tell us how she was built or how impressive she would have looked—a floating cathedral among the lesser shipping of the English Channel. However, we do have the description of an experienced Florentine sea captain, Luca di Maso degli Albizzi, who saw her in 1530 as she lay at anchor in the River Hamble, near Southampton. He even dined on board as a guest of her captain, William Soper. Luca di Maso described the ship as being about 1,500 or even 1,650 tons, with a length along her deck of 184 feet, and a 50-foot beam. Her forecastle soared some 52 feet above the river, and that wasn't even its full height, as an extra level was added in wartime. The mainmast was almost 7 feet in diameter and was 200 feet high. Luca di Maso described her as the largest and most beautiful construction he had ever seen—high praise from a man who had sailed throughout the Mediterranean as well as the seas of northern Europe. Clearly the *Grace Dieu* was something special.

She was laid down in 1416 in Southampton, under the supervision of Soper, the keeper of the king's ships. The shipbuilder was named as John Hoggekyns, while Robert Berd helped Soper manage the finances. The work was carried out in a specially built dock, surrounded by an enclosure of wooden stakes to provide security for the site. From the accounts it seems as if this shipyard was built from scratch, the wood-lined dock dug from a piece of low-lying ground on the edge of the city, and protected from the sea by a temporary seawall. When the ship was ready this wall would be breached, sea-water would flood in, and the *Grace Dieu* would float free. Beside the dock Soper also built a long, wooden storehouse with a tiled roof, and a blacksmith's shop, where the nails needed to build the ship would be made. Wood—mostly elm—was transported to the site from the nearby forest, and work progressed surprisingly quickly, given that nobody in England had built a ship quite so large before. She remained the biggest ship ever built in the British Isles for more than two hundred years—until the very end of our story, when she was finally overtaken by the *Sovereign of the Seas*.

It helped that the *Grace Dieu* was "clinker-built": the planks on the side of the hull overlapped each other like small steps, with each one overlapping the plank below it. This was the type of boatbuild-ing used by the Vikings for their longships, and it had remained the standard method of constructing ship hulls in northern Europe ever since. The men who built her would have known exactly what they were doing, even though they'd never worked on a ship of her scale. Many historians doubted that such a large clinker-built ship could have been built. The ship drew its strength from the way the outer hull was fastened together, rather than from a series of rigid internal frames. It seemed that a ship the size of the *Grace Dieu* would have pushed clinker-built ship construction beyond its technical limits. However, these experts were proved wrong.

As late as the 1870s the skeletal remains of a wooden ship lay protruding from the mudbed of the River Hamble. In 1875 these timbers were sawed away during an attempt to widen and dredge the river. Fortunately the attempt was abandoned, and the wreck was left alone. It was always thought that it was the remains of an old Viking longship, and a section of the hull was even taken and displayed in a local museum, where the curator declared that it dated from the tenth century A.D. It wasn't until 1933 that archae-ologists looked at the wreck properly, surveying it at low tide, tak-ing samples of her timbers, and looking at the way she was put together. It soon became clear that the wreck was no Viking ship but something much larger, and five centuries later. Despite the mud and the fast-flowing river they found that their wreck had a keel about 130 feet long, and the ship once had a beam of at least 50 feet.

Remains of the Grace Dieu

This meant that she would have once been a ship of about 1,500 tons. When the archaeologists began looking through the historical records they found only one contender for a ship of her size. They had found the wreck of the *Grace Dieu*.

While there was little left of her apart from her lower hull timbers, they revealed that she was clinker-built. Normally a clinker-built hull was made up of single planks, each one overlapping the one below, and the two were then pinned together using wooden or iron fasteners. In the *Grace Dieu* the shipbuilders used three planks rather than one, a sandwich of wood designed to make the hull far thicker and stronger than usual. The whole thing was riveted together using iron bolts, the washers of which gave the outside of the hull a hobnailed appearance. That was the way the shipbuilders got around the technical limitations of the clinker-built design. Given the limited technology available to William Soper and his shipbuilders, the building of such a large and complex structure was an incredible achievement. It was little wonder that Luca di Maso was so impressed.

Since her identification the shipwreck has been examined several times, first by a team from the National Maritime Museum in Greenwich, and then by the University of Southampton. The development of underwater archaeology allowed more detailed surveys, and recently the site has been investigated using sonar. Support work has also been carried out at nearby Bursledon, where Henry V and his successors established a small royal dockyard and where the *Grace Dieu* spent most of her working life. Finally her planking has been measured, her construction methods analyzed in detail, and the historical archives scoured for any new information. Unfortunately, all this still can't tell us exactly what she looked like when Luca di Maso had dinner on board her, or how she would have performed as a warship. For instance, although we suspect she was three-masted, this cannot be proved. All we can say with any certainty was that she dwarfed all other warships of her age. However, we do know how she ended up as a forgotten shipwreck in a Hampshire river.

It took less than two years to build her, and in 1418 the dock wall was demolished and she floated free. After being fitted out she was christened by the bishop of Bangor in a ceremony that would have drawn hundreds to Southampton to see history being made. Unfortunately she was a warship without a war. While she was being built, Henry V formed an alliance with the Genoese, who kept the small French fleet pinned in the Mediterranean. This left the English free to control the English Channel, and the *Grace Dieu* was left with nobody to fight. However, she did go to sea in 1420, under the command of William Soper, one of Henry V's most experienced sea captains. The cruise achieved little, and was notable more than anything else for the discontent of the ship's crew, who complained of poor victuals, a lack of pay, and the denial of shore leave. By the end of the year the great English ship was back at Bursledon, its new base on the River Hamble.

In theory the *Grace Dieu* would have been the perfect warship. If her mast was as high as Luca di Maso claimed, then a lookout two hundred feet above the warship's deck would have been able to spot a ship on the horizon sixteen miles away. When she was built a small flotilla of support ships were built with her, and if they sailed in consort they could have been used to investigate suspicious sails and to delay the enemy until the *Grace Dieu* arrived to fight them. Once a sea battle started she would have been in her element. Her towering forecastle and sterncastle would have been almost impossible to capture, and with a full complement of archers she would have been able to outshoot any ship she encountered, as long as she was within bow range. She was designed to carry exactly the kind of troops who had stood in the English ranks at Agincourt—longbowmen, supported by men at arms with weapons such as bills and half-pikes ready to be used in hand-to-hand combat.

However, the *Grace Dieu* also embraced the future. An inventory drawn up at the time of her maiden voyage in 1420 reported that when she went to sea she carried three pieces of artillery, which would almost certainly have been wrought-iron breech-loading guns, as they were listed in the accounts, together with their powder chambers. These would have been carried in her waist and fired over the top of the gunwale, although how exactly this would have been worked is still a matter of conjecture. One theory is that the three guns were designed to be moved around the deck so they could be fired from either side of the ship. If so, the guns couldn't have been particularly large or heavy, and would have done little more than augment the antipersonnel fire of the ship's archers.

Geoffrey Chaucer, the late-fourteenth-century English author of *The Canterbury Tales*, described how a late medieval sea battle would have been fought. In his description of the ancient sea battle of Actium, the firing of "the great gone" was set amid the general mayhem caused by a storm of arrows, the hurling of large stones from the fighting tops in the mastheads, the throwing of grappling hooks, the shredding of sails, and the throwing of pots filled with burning lime. Then came the boarding action—"in with the pole-axe"—until the enemy fled behind the mainmast and were driven overboard. This was a brutal close-quarters slugging match fought in a similar way to a land battle. It would be the best part of a century before naval commanders realized that artillery gave them the ability to fight the enemy at a distance.

After her voyage of 1420 there is no evidence that the *Grace Dieu* ever left her berth at Bursledon, an anchorage she shared with Henry V's other royal ships the *Jesus*, the *Trinity Royal*, and the

Holigost. These ships would have been stripped of all unnecessary stores and equipment, which would have been kept in one of the Bursledon storehouses. In modern naval parlance the ships would have been mothballed, and just a skeleton crew would have been retained to maintain the ship. The aim would have been to reduce the running costs of the ships. In wartime they would have been fitted out, crewed, and sent on active service. The orders never came. Henry V died in August 1422, and the regents who looked after his nine-month-old son, Henry VI, lacked the naval enthusiasm of the late king. The *Grace Dieu* was still anchored off Bursledon ten years later, when Luca di Maso saw her in late January 1430.

In June 1431 her mainmast was removed and stored ashore, an operation supervised by Peter Johnson, master mariner of Sandwich. That seemed to mark the beginning of the end, part of a general running down of the whole fleet. In 1434 she was towed upstream, where an anchorage was dredged in the mud of the River Hamble by thirty laborers. By that time she was probably little more than a hulk, stripped of everything important. Then on the night of January 6–7, 1439, the *Grace Dieu* was struck by lightning and caught fire. By the time the flames were extinguished she was burned beyond repair. Although some seven tons of metalwork were salvaged, the wooden hull itself was deemed worthless, and she remained where she lay until her rediscovery five centuries later. It was a sad end to what was probably the greatest ship ever seen in northern European waters during the Middle Ages.

By the time the *Grace Dieu* was lost, the English were on the defensive in France. Largely thanks to the efforts of Joan of Arc, the French were able to drive the English from much of their country, leaving the invaders with just two small toeholds, in Normany and Gascony. By the time Henry VI gained his majority in 1439, the Hundred Years' War was all but lost. By 1453 the English were finally driven from French soil, with the sole exception of Calais, which would remain in English hands for another century. Then in 1455 a growing political and dynastic crisis in England led to the outbreak of civil war—the start of the Wars of the Roses, which would turn the country into a battleground for the best part of three decades. While the war lasted, the English king and his leading nobles would forget any dreams of creating a navy of powerful royal warships. The situation was much the same in France, where Charles VII was too busy trying to control both his nobles and his son to worry about the luxury of building a fleet. It would be another half century before Europe saw a warship that would even come close to matching the power and majesty of the *Grace Dieu*.

The *Sovereign* and the *Regent*

Henry Tudor must have considered himself one of the most fortunate men in England. At dawn on August 22, 1485, he was nothing more than a rebel whose luck seemed to be running out. By nightfall he was the future king of England—the last man standing in a brutal contest for supremacy we now know as the Wars of the Roses. For a while it seemed that this great medieval orgy of regicide and bloodletting had run its course. For decades the rival claimants— represented by the great houses of York and Lancaster—had fought and died in a seemingly endless succession of battles. Then in the spring of 1471 the Yorkist king, Edward IV, defeated his rivals in two decisive battles just three weeks apart. First he beat his former ally Richard, Earl of Warwick, in a battle at Barnet, just north of London. Edward then marched his army northwest to Tewkesbury, where on May 4 he defeated and killed the Lancastrian heir presumptive, Edward, prince of Wales. The prince's father, the deposed King Henry VI, was already held prisoner in the Tower of London. The Yorkist king celebrated his victory by having his royal prisoner quietly murdered.

With his Lancastrian rivals dispatched, King Edward was free to enjoy the spoils of victory. The peace lasted for just over a decade— until April 1483, when the king died peaceably in his bed in Windsor Castle. His crown passed to his twelve-year-old son, Edward, who was duly crowed Edward V. He would reign for just two months. When Edward IV died he named his brother Richard, Duke of Gloucester, as regent, charged with ruling in the name of the young king until he came of age. Uncle Richard grasped this heaven-sent opportunity by having the young king taken to the Tower of London for his own safety, along with his young brother, Richard of Shrewsbury. The two "princes in the Tower" were never seen in public again. Richard was ultimately blamed for the deaths of the two princes (Shakespeare being the most famous finger-pointer). The truth of exactly what went on behind those dark walls may never be known.

In June 1483 Richard proclaimed himself the legitimate king, and the following month he was crowned King Richard III of England. While the country remained at peace, Richard's spies in France reported that a new rival planned to take advantage of the controversy surrounding Richard's accession to launch his own bid for power. This new contestant was the twenty-eight-year-old Henry Tudor, the Welsh-born son of Edmund Tudor and Lady Margaret Beaufort. His mother was a vague relative of the murdered King Henry VI, and so in theory Henry Tudor was related to the last Lancastrian king. Given that everyone else had been killed, by the end of 1483 young Henry was the closest there was to a Lancastrian claimant to the throne.

In July 1485 he landed a small mercenary army in Pembrokeshire, the area of his birthplace in the southwestern corner of Wales. He realized he had to move fast and raise a larger force before Richard III caught up with him. Henry marched north through Wales and into the midlands of England. By the time the two armies met in the middle of Leicestershire, Henry had five thousand men at his back. Although he was still outnumbered by Richard III's nine thousand men, at least he had a fighting chance of success. After all, Henry Tudor had a secret ally. Sir William Stanley and Thomas, Lord Stanley, had answered their king's call to army by putting a force of six thousand men into the field, but when they reached the battlefield the Stanleys decided to stay out of the fight. That meant that while two armies decided the fate of England, the Stanleys would wait to see who seemed to be winning. After all, backing the wrong side in the Wars of the Roses inevitably involved some form of grisly death.

The battle began soon after dawn on August 22. Richard III had deployed his army on Ambion Hill, although he kept one wing back a little, as he didn't trust the Stanley brothers. Although he had the smaller army, Henry Tudor decided to attack, and the battle soon settled into a brutal slugging match. However, Richard had weight of numbers, and after an hour or so the Tudor army began to give ground. Henry realized that his only chance of victory was to lead his reserves into the fray. Richard was watching all this from the hilltop, and when he saw his rival's standard move forward, he decided to charge. He led his own elite mounted reserve in a whirlwind charge that crashed into Henry's unit. Richard must have been certain of victory. However, Sir William Stanley then made his move. He charged his own force into Richard's reserve, and within moments the king found himself surrounded. His men formed a ring around him, but one by one they were cut down and killed. By the time the dust settled, Richard III lay dead—the last king of England to die on a battlefield. His crown was pulled out of the mud and handed to the victorious Henry Tudor.

On October 30, 1485, the victor was crowned Henry VII of England, the first in a line of Tudor monarchs who would include his son Henry VIII and his granddaughter Elizabeth I. While there

Henry VII

was no national standing army, he did acquire control of Richard III's small Navy Royal of nine ships, most of which were based on the River Thames by the Tower of London. The Yorkist kings didn't bother with their navy very much, and all their ships were converted merchantmen rather than purpose-built warships. To make matters worse, in 1483 Edward IV's Admiral Sir Edward Woodville defected to Henry Tudor, taking two of his ships—the *Falcon* and the *Trinity*—with him. He even filled their holds with gold from the Tower of London before he left. Richard responded by buying and converting two replacement warships, which he used to patrol the English Channel, keeping watch for signs of the Tudor invasion. Clearly it didn't prove much of a deterrent, and Woodville was able to land Henry Tudor on the Pembrokeshire coast without difficulty.

After Henry VII's coronation, Sir Edward kept his title of admiral of the Narrows and the Channel. He also helped recruit a group of captains whose loyalty to the new Tudor monarch could be ensured. Another official who kept his job was Thomas Rodgers, the keeper of the king's ships. His first job was to draw up a detailed report that laid out the condition of all nine ships and commented on their effectiveness as warships. The report couldn't have made particularly good reading for Henry. Many of the warships on the list were old and rotten beyond repair, while others were suffering badly from lack of maintenance. Of these nine ships, two were sold to a London merchant; three more were mothballed in the River Hamble near Southampton; and another was given to Sir Richard Guildeford, the new master of the ordnance at the Tower of London.

That left Henry with just three active warships—the *Trinity* and the *Bonaventure*, plus the 180-ton *Carvel of Ewe*, which was bought in 1487. Of the three mothballed ships, one was sold within a year, while another—named the *Grace Dieu* like her early-fifteenth-century predecessor—was broken up and her timbers and fittings used to build two brand-new warships. Henry realized that while he could deal with any Yorkist rising in England itself, he was vulnerable to an invasion launched from across the English Channel—just like the one he carried out in 1485. He realized that his small navy was in no condition even to police England's coastal waters, let alone stop an invasion. Of course, part of the problem was Henry's own fiscal prudence. He sold most of his ships to avoid spending a small fortune on their repair, and now that his control of the country's finances was assured, he probably regretted the decision. He needed more ships.

Given his general policy of fiscal prudence, what Henry VII did next seemed somewhat out of character. In early 1486 he ordered his trusted lieutenant Sir Richard Guildeford to draw up plans for building two purpose-built great ships—a special project that would cost the royal treasury more than £1,000. It would be the largest shipbuilding venture in Europe and would result in the first royal vessels to be designed from the keel up as warships since the laying down of the original *Grace Dieu* almost seventy years before. The royal directive called for building the ships in two locations. The first, the *Grace Dieu*, was to be built on Reding Creek, a small tidal waterway that flowed into the River Rother a few miles above Rye, on the Sussex coast. The second vessel—the *Trinity Sovereign*—would be built in Southampton, a hundred miles to the west, along the English southern coast.

We know a little about the building of these two ships from the records kept by Sir Richard. He also delegated part of the work, as Sir Reginald Bray supervised the building of the 450-ton *Trinity Sovereign*, although Guildeford remained in overall control of both shipbuilding projects. Sir Richard also took direct control over the building of the 600-ton *Grace Dieu*. Strangely enough, while Thomas Rodgers, the clerk of ships, should have been named as project manager, King Henry decided to have his own man supervise the work. This might have been an attempt to maintain a tight grip on the enterprise, or it might have reflected Rodgers's poor health, as the naval administrator died just two years later. Sir Richard Guildeford was certainly the man for the job—both ships were completed in record time, and entered service in 1489. While the larger vessel was being fitted out she was renamed the *Regent*, while her smaller companion had her name shortened to *Sovereign*. However, just to confuse things she also was sometimes referred to as the *Trinity*, probably because her other name might cause confusion. In the naval records the word "sovereign" was sometimes used when speaking about the fleet flagship, the principal—or sovereign—warship in the fleet.

One of the first of Rodgers's records—a payment authorization dated April 1487—directs the royal treasurer to pay "for the building of a ship which he has the oversight in the County of Kent of 600 tons, like a ship called the *Colombe* of France." Unfortunately, a lot of France's medieval documents were destroyed during the French Revolution, so we know nothing about this French ship, the inspiration for Henry VII's *Regent*. Presumably it was a vessel that had impressed him during his years in exile, while he was a guest of Francis, Duke of Brittany. One historian has suggested it was a ship Henry Tudor had seen during a visit to Rouen, which meant that she was possibly one of the royal warships of King Louis XI or even Charles VIII, who succeeded him in the summer of 1483. However, as we shall see later, King Charles did not see the need for large, powerful royal warships, and he preferred to hire suitable merchantmen and fit them out in wartime. The *Colombe* could well have been one of these armed merchantmen.

Another interesting document claims that before work started on the *Trinity Sovereign*, Sir Richard supervised the breaking up of Richard III's *Grace Dieu*, one of the three warships that Henry VII had ordered mothballed on the River Hamble. That meant that this former merchant carrack brought into service fourteen years earlier would have been demolished close to the rotting timbers of her namesake, Henry V's groundbreaking leviathan. The new shipyard in Southampton was only a short wagon journey away from the breaker's yard. The shipwrights certainly could use all the good-quality timber they could lay their hands on. A ship the size of the *Sovereign* would have needed approximately sixteen hundred tons of oak to build, a mixture of seasoned and unseasoned timber. That was the equivalent of twenty acres of prime, mature woodland, and all that timber would have to be cut, trimmed, stacked while it seasoned, then transported to the shipyard. That was exactly why Sir Richard chose Southampton. The port lay close to the New Forest, a vast expanse of woodland that covered much of the surrounding county of Hampshire.

Throughout 1487 the two ships gradually took shape, and despite other distractions Henry VII made sure that Sir Richard Guild-eford was given all the men and supplies he needed to finish the job. The biggest distraction was a rebellion: the Yorkist uprising Henry had been expecting. It was led by John, the Earl of Lincoln, who joined the banner of Lambert Simnel, a ten-year-old bogus claimant to the English throne. The rebellion was launched from France, and to dodge Henry's warships the expedition first headed to Ireland, where Simnel was proclaimed King Edward VI. The rebels finally landed in Lancashire, on England's western coast, then marched inland. However, Henry was ready for them, and he finally tracked the rebel army down at Stoke Field on June 16. Within three hours the rebellion had been crushed, and Lincoln and most of his army of Irish volunteers and French mercenaries lay dead on the field. In a rare act of clemency Henry VII pardoned young Lambert Simnel and gave him a job as a cook in the royal kitchens.

By the spring of 1488, construction work on the *Sovereign* was completed, and the business of fitting her out began—with masts shipped to Southampton from Scandinavia, and guns from the Tower of London. Being the larger ship, the *Regent* took a little longer to build, and it would be another six months before she reached the same stage. However, by late autumn both ships were finished, and they were officially commissioned into the Navy Royal. To the untrained eye both would have looked impressive, but they wouldn't have appeared much different from other large ships of the period. However, what made these two warships special was not so much their design and appearance but what they carried. Both were fitted out with as many pieces of artillery as they could sensibly carry, and when all the guns were run out or fixed in place they would have resembled floating fortresses bristling with guns.

We really don't know for sure how big the *Regent* was. While many of the contemporary records claim she had a cargo capacity of 600 tons, she was variously described as being an 800-ton and even a 1,000-ton vessel. Similarly, the *Sovereign* could have been 450 to 800 tons. It all depends on how you calculate tonnage, and the standard way in this period was very different from the one used from the seventeenth century on. Fortunately, we can work out roughly how big these vessels were by comparing them to the *Mary Rose*, which was built a quarter of a century later. As the *Sovereign* was still in service then, and the two ships were listed in Tudor records together, we can assume that the *Sovereign* would have been a little larger than her early-sixteenth-century successor, roughly 115 feet long in the keel, with a 45-foot beam and a depth from the waterline to the bottom of the keel of 14 feet.

If she was built in the same proportions the *Regent* would have been about 105 feet long in the keel, with a 40-foot beam and a depth of about 14 feet. That would make her fairly complementary in size to the *Mary Rose*, which was variously listed as being 600 to 800 tons, depending on whose records you go by. This meant that until the arrival of the *Mary Rose*, these two ships were the largest warships in the Tudor fleet, if not in Europe. Each warship was a carrack, the biggest ship type of the period, whose design had changed gradually throughout the century. By the time the *Regent* and the *Sovereign* were built, these ships were noted for their roomy hulls, their wide beam, and the permanent addition of substantial forecastle and sterncastle structures, which gave the ships a towering, majestic appearance. Both ships were also fitted with four masts—a foremast, a mainmast, a mizzenmast, and a bonaventure—as well as a bowsprit and possibly an outligger, the name for a small, stumpy, horizontal spar that stuck out from the stern of the ship.

Although no properly identified contemporary pictures of the ships have survived, a superb series of engravings from the period shows several late-fifteenth-century warships, and a couple of them are so large and impressive that we can say with some accuracy that they were based on Henry VII's new ships. *The Pageant of the Birth, Life, and Death of Richard Beauchamp, Earl of Warwick* is the imposing title given to a series of sketches illustrating incidents in the life of the English nobleman. However, most historians simply call them the *Warwick Roll*. Although Richard Beauchamp died in 1439, the sketches were produced much later, and may well have been drawn at the request of one of his children, possibly Anne, the Countess of Warwick, the wife of Henry IV's rival at the Battle of Barnet. She died in 1493, and the styles of armor and the ships all point to the illustrations being produced during the last decade of Anne's life. Alternatively it might have been produced for her daughter, who became Queen Anne after her husband, Richard, Duke of Gloucester, became King Richard III. She died in 1485, just five months before her husband was killed on the battlefield of Bosworth.

Twelve of the illustrations in the *Warwick Roll* show ships, and these can be divided into three groups. Some are clearly designed to show single-masted ships from earlier in the century, probably from when the earl was still alive. A few more show slightly later ships

Warwick Roll *ship*

with two or three masts, probably dating from the middle of the fifteenth century. Finally, a group of four-masted ships are clearly from the last part of the century. These vessels show large carracks with imposing forecastles and sterncastles, both pierced with numerous holes capable of housing swivel guns. They also carry a powerful battery of heavy guns in the waist. Two of the illustrations in particular show warships that would have been exactly the size of the *Sovereign* and the *Regent*. It seems too much of a coincidence that an artist would have come up with such accurate depictions of ships from his imagination. It seems far more likely that he based his drawings on sketches he made of the two Henrician warships as they swung at anchor off Portsmouth or in the River Thames.

Like the *Grace Dieu* before them, these ships were clinker-built, using the shipbuilding methods English shipwrights were used to.

However, in the Mediterranean a whole new form of shipbuilding evolved, where the planks were laid flush with each other, like the hulls of most modern wooden sailing craft. Of course, the difference between clinker-built and this new carvel-built form of construction didn't just end there. Traditionally clinker-built hulls were examples of shell-first construction, where the sides of the hull were built up without any internal supports, and frames were then added to the inside of the hulls to provide additional strength. Carvel-built ships followed the frame-first construction method, which is the type we automatically think of when we imagine the building of a wooden ship. A series of V-shaped frames were attached to the keel to form the basic wooden skeleton of the ship. The hull planking was then attached to these riblike frames.

What is so remarkable about the *Regent* and the *Sovereign* was that they were some of the last great wooden warships built in northern Europe using the older clinker method. The design followed a shipbuilding style that had been used in Europe for centuries, so construction of the ships would have been extremely straightforward. In fact, when they were built they were probably perfect—just the kind of ships Henry VII wanted. However, the ships were the last of their breed—large warships whose main armament was carried in their waist. If you wanted to add more guns you couldn't put them in the forecastle and sterncastle, as the ship would become top-heavy. The only place was lower in the hull, which meant cutting holes in the side of the ship. While this did not pose a problem for carvel-built ships, piercing the side of a clinker-built hull seriously weakened the ship. One or two holes might be acceptable, but a row of several gunports was nigh-on impossible.

It seems that Tudor shipbuilders had a solution. In 1911, workmen digging in the mud of the River Thames beside Roff's Wharf in Woolwich uncovered the remains of an old wooden ship. Experts dated it to the start of the sixteenth century, and on examining her remains they found that the vessel was a substantial one, and estimated her keel length at 115 to 120 feet and her beam at about 45 feet. Historians found only one likely candidate. The *Sovereign* was declared unfit for service, and was decommissioned at Woolwich in 1525. It was thought that her remains were left to quietly rot away. Fortunately it seems that the oozing anaerobic mud of the Thames preserved her lower hull timber for posterity. The ship had originally been clinker-built, as her frames showed signs of having been notched or stepped, a sure sign of clinker construction. However, the notches had subsequently been cut away to create a flat surface, and the hull timber was then replanked in the carvel style.

We know that the *Sovereign* was substantially rebuilt in 1509–1510, so it seems now that this involved replanking her hull in the new style. It seems that the *Regent* was never rebuilt, and remained a carvel-built ship throughout her life. There was only one reason to go to all the trouble and expense of a major rebuild like this: Henry VII wanted to increase the number of heavy guns his ship could carry. Unfortunately, the king died before he could see the result of all this effort, and the beneficiary would be his son Henry, Prince of Wales, who became Henry VIII in April 1509. This rebuilding also provides us with a perfect illustration of the changes in the two decades since the *Sovereign* was launched. She began life as a well-armed ship that relied for the most part on short-range weapons. She then turned into a floating gun platform capable of holding her own alongside the more modern ships of Henry VIII's navy.

When she first entered service, the *Sovereign* carried 32 heavy stone-shotted guns, almost certainly constructed from wrought iron, and 110 serpentines, swivel guns used primarily as close-range antipersonnel weapons. The stone-shotted guns were almost certainly designed to be used at close range, too, as the pieces would have lacked the velocity to fire much farther than about 75 yards— approximately the same distance that a contemporary longbowman could fire an arrow. We know that 20 of the larger guns were mounted in the waist of the *Sovereign*, while an additional 11 were carried farther aft, underneath the sterncastle. While the guns in the waist would probably have fired over the ship's gunwale, the *Warwick Roll* illustrations show that an extension of the upper deck running aft of the side of the hull was pierced with a series of large, arched apertures—perfect for the kind of guns carried on Henry VII's flagship.

Twenty-four swivel guns were carried inside the forecastle, firing out of smaller holes or arches in its side, while another 16 swivel pieces were mounted on the top of the forecastle itself. The term "swivel" was derived from its mounting—the weapon was mounted on a pintle that looked like the rowlock on a rowing boat, or the mounting for a modern vehicle machine gun. The same type of distribution was seen farther aft, where 20 swivel guns were mounted above the large stone guns, with an additional 4 mounted so they pointed astern. Another 25 serpentines were carried on the top of the sterncastle, and 20 more on the small poop deck. At first glance this seems an unbelievable number of guns. However, the term "serpentine" appears to have been a catch-all, covering anything from a gun firing a 1½-inch iron shot down to a piece the size of a large handgun. We know that the *Regent* carried 225 serpentines, 30 of which were made from bronze rather than wrought iron. It didn't appear that the smaller warship carried any larger guns.

By the time the armament of the ships was listed again, everything had changed. We know little about the later armament of the *Regent*, except that when she sailed into battle against the French in 1512 she still carried an armament consisting of swivel guns, supported by just 6 larger curtows, a type of large bronze gun. One source adds she was crewed by 80 soldiers and sailors supported by 100 gunners and 400 crossbowmen, but while the overall numbers seem right, the proportions don't reflect the manning of other ships in the fleet. She would have needed more sailors and fewer gunners.

The *Sovereign* emerged from her refit carrying a particularly impressive armament:

- 4 bronze muzzle-loading curtows
- 3 bronze muzzle-loading half-curtows
- 2 bronze muzzle-loading culverins
- 1 (bronze?) muzzle-loading culverin (without a stock)
- 7 wrought-iron breech-loading great pieces
- 2 bronze muzzle-loading falcons
- 4 bronze breech-loading serpentines
- 4 iron wrought-iron breech-loading slings
- 42 wrought-iron breech-loading serpentines (both great and small)
- 2 wrought-iron breech-loading stone guns (for the fighting tops)

The total of 16 large guns, 2 medium falcons, and 52 small swivel guns—70 guns in all—is far more impressive an armament than the 142 guns she carried before. While the great pieces might not have been much better than her original stone-shotted heavy guns, the other 10 muzzle-loading bronze guns were all the latest word in gunfounding—pieces capable of firing huge iron roundshot. A curtow fired a 60-pound shot, while the half-curtow (or demi-curtow) fired one half the size. A culverin was slightly smaller, and fired a 20-pound roundshot. These were true ship-smashing guns, and according to later-sixteenth-century tables they had an effective range of about 400 yards. While an inventory of 1497 lists a serpentine as firing a 6-pound shot and a falcon a 1-pound lead ball, it seems more likely that at sea the positions were reversed, and the falcon was marginally the bigger gun. Slings were almost certainly an improved version of the serpentine, as by the 1540s the term is closely associated with small swivel guns.

The change from a clinker-built hull to a carvel-built one meant that the hull of the *Sovereign* could be pierced with gunports without weakening the structure of the warship. Gunports, a relatively new invention, allowed guns to be carried lower in the hull, an improvement over a mere aperture in the hull in that the hole itself could be sealed by a gunport lid. Like many relatively simple technical developments, it opened up a whole range of new possibilities. In theory gunports would make the vessels less top-heavy. Given that the carrack was based around towering forecastles and sterncastles, this seemed like an excellent idea. It also meant that more heavy guns could be carried. The two ships therefore show that the general trend was toward using fewer guns, but larger ones. The only limitation was that these weapons were largely untested in combat, and with such an eclectic mixture of different gun types, methods of operation, and ranges, it is hardly surprising that few people really understood how to use all this firepower effectively.

As the naval commanders of the early sixteenth century still had to work out how best to use these new weapons, they made sure their ships could fight naval warfare according to the rules they understood. This meant that swivel guns would remain as a vital part of the firepower of the ship, because they could be fired at point-blank range to deter enemy boarding parties, or to sweep the decks of an enemy ship before the captain sent his own men aboard her. Tactics still revolved around taking the ship alongside that of the enemy and boarding it. This was why when the *Sovereign* sailed into battle in 1512 she carried 400 soldiers in addition to 260 sailors and 40 gunners. These troops were equipped with just about all the military hardware they could ever want—500 bows, 500 bills, 500 half-pikes, and 500 suits of infantrymen's armor. Like most military forces that went into battle in times of technological change, the Tudor navy was perfectly equipped to fight the last war rather than the next one.

It seems as if the French were not much better, although their commanders did have one significant advantage over their English counterparts: France maintained a standing galley fleet based on its Mediterranean coast, and the country had been involved in an intermittent war in Italy since 1494, which meant that France's galley fleet had already seen a lot of action. War galleys of the period could not mount broadside guns because of their banks of oars, so heavy weapons were limited to a small fighting platform mounted in the bows. However, French galleys regularly clashed with Spanish, Genoese, Papal, Venetian, and Ottoman adversaries, and the French captains came to understand the potential and the limitations of naval artillery. This meant that although the French might not have been as far advanced as the English about introducing heavy guns into their ships, at least they knew how they worked.

By the time Louis XII came to the French throne in 1492, the French already had a small navy divided between the English Channel and the Mediterranean. Although the Mediterranean fleet was predominantly a galley force, the French augmented this oared fleet with sailing vessels—warships, transports, and supply vessels. The royal fleet based at the mouth of the River Seine was smaller, but like their Tudor rivals the French could augment their fleet in wartime by hiring armed merchantmen. However, the king's predecessor, Charles VIII, cared little for naval power, and preferred to rely on mercenaries and pirates to harass the English in wartime. The navy, such as it was, consisted of no more than six poorly maintained warships of no great size.

Then in 1492 the French acquired the Duchy of Brittany, just seven years after Henry Tudor used the region as a springboard for his invasion of England. Not only did this give the French access to the ports of Brest, Morlaix, and St. Malo, it also provided the French king with a greater pool of ships and seamen to draw on. One of them was probably the 600-ton *Colombe*, which Henry Tudor reputedly had seen during his stay in Brittany. Given her name, she may well have originated in the region around Bordeaux, in southwestern France. If Henry was so impressed with her, she must have been particularly well armed, which suggests she was either a royal warship or a particularly well-armed merchantman. One suggestion is that she belonged to Duke Francis of Brittany, who certainly maintained his own small fleet. In 1495, three years after his coronation, Louis XII decided to build his own royal flagship. It seems entirely likely that this was a response to the building of the *Regent* and the *Sovereign*. Louis needed his own fleet to counter the threat of an English invasion and to maintain a French naval presence in the English Channel.

Work began on the flagship *Amiral Louise* in Rouen on the River Seine in late 1495. Although the records are scanty, it seems she took five years to complete—more than twice the time taken to build the *Sovereign* or the *Regent*. This probably reflects a less centralized system of funding and the procurement of supplies, as Louis lacked the experienced naval administration inherited by Henry VII. A contemporary depiction of the *Louise* shows a far less elegant vessel than the *Sovereign* or the *Regent*, which suggests she was a nef rather than a carrack. The main difference between the two was that while a carrack had a distinctively large forecastle and sterncastle, in France a nef was a development of a cog, an earlier type of trading vessel. Traditionally these vessels had the rounded hull shape of the late medieval cog, but the hull was surmounted by upper works similar to but less extensive than those of the carrack. Contemporary models and illustrations suggest that unlike the carrack, the sterncastle of the nef was not much bigger than the forecastle.

The largest nefs were four-masted, and all were carvel-built. In theory this made them suitable for carrying heavy ordnance, but what we know of the *Louise* suggests that she was not particularly well armed. One problem was that Louis XII intended to recoup the costs of building the ship by hiring her out as a merchantman. Although Henry did this with the *Sovereign* in the early 1490s, it seems that her French counterpart spent most of her time on trading voyages to the Mediterranean. Large guns would take up valuable cargo space, so her lighter armament compared with the *Sovereign* may well have been chosen for economic rather than naval reasons. However, the contemporary image of her shows a vessel with five large gun barrels protruding over her gunwale, while what could well be two more are shown sticking out of circular gunports on the level of her lower or orlop deck.

It may seem unlikely that she was pierced with gunports this far down her hull, but then unlike the carrack, the nef was particularly high-sided, so she may well have carried these extra-heavy guns on a lower tier without the guns being too close to the waterline to risk the safety of the ship. Certainly the *Louise* bears more than a passing resemblance to a model of a nef produced in Paris in 1527. Known as the Burghley nef, this model is now in the collection of London's

The Regent *and the* Cordelière

Victoria and Albert Museum. The hull is high and rounded, looking more like half a melon than the hull of a warship.

Another powerful French warship built during Louis XII's reign was the seven-hundred-ton *Marie de la Cordelière*, technically owned by the king's consort, Anne of Brittany. It seems that part of her wedding dowry in 1492 included the transfer of the ships of her father, Duke Francis of Brittany, to Louis XII. However, they officially remained the queen's property, as did subsequent warships built in Brittany during Anne's lifetime. That meant that the *Cordelière* remained a Breton rather than a French vessel. She was probably built in Brest, on the western edge of Brittany, and she entered service in 1508–1509. Unlike the *Louise*, she was described as a carrack, although given her armament, an English naval officer who encountered her on the high seas described the *Cordelière* and the *Louise* as being "the best with sail and furnished with artillery and men that was ever seen." It was high praise indeed. He went on to describe her armament: "15 great brass curtalls [bronze curtows] with some marvelous number of shot and other guns of every sort." This armament was even heavier and more homogenous than the *Sovereign's*, which suggests that the French were on par with, if not slightly ahead of, the English in employment of guns at sea.

The crew of the *Cordelière* was given as eight hundred soldiers and mariners, four hundred crossbowmen, and one hundred gunners. This is impossibly high, and it seems more likely that the total for the soldiers and sailors included the crossbowmen. In this case it makes the number of men carried on board similar to that of her large English counterparts. The large number of gunners also might reflect a different form of accounting. Instead of just including the gun captains of the heavier guns, the total might well include the men in charge of the ship's "marvellous number" of swivel guns. Unfortunately, no crew numbers exist for the *Louise*, although the total probably would have been very similar to that of the Breton ship. Apart from the fact that the French relied on crossbowmen and the English on longbowmen, the crew composition of both the French and the English ships suggests that both sides still viewed naval warfare in the same way. While both sides were increasingly willing to mount heavy guns on their ships, they were still fully prepared to fight a sea battle by closing with the enemy and fighting him in hand-to-hand combat. What the naval captains and ship designers needed now was the chance to test their new weapons and ships in action. Henry VII's young successor was anxious to give them just that opportunity.

Putting It to the Test

The big problem with new military technology is that people rarely know how it will work. The best way to try it out is in battle, preferably before too much has been invested in something that doesn't do what it should. While both King Henry VIII of England and King Louis XII of France had experimented with converting their principal warships to carry artillery, neither the monarchs nor their naval advisers were sure how effective these new weapons would be in combat, but hoped they could be employed so they made the most of their potential. Therefore the Anglo-French War of 1512–1514 provided everyone involved with the perfect opportunity to try these guns out in anger.

This was a war that Henry VIII didn't need to fight. He actively sought a conflict, first by joining the Holy League in December 1511—an anti-French alliance organized by Pope Julius II—and then by preparing his forces for a summer campaign in France. Naturally, Louis XII looked to his defenses, and ordered his fleet to prepare itself, while his commanders in northern France braced themselves to meet an English invasion. From the outset Henry had planned a two-pronged attack. First he would use his fleet to transport a small English army across the English Channel. Then it would protect its cross-Channel lines of communication by actively seeking out the French fleet and offering battle.

On April 7 Sir Edward Howard, lord admiral of England, was given his orders—"to keep and defend the sea . . . . After the fleet shall come to sea, the Admiral shall take his course, if wind and weather wills serve, toward the Trade, for the defence of the sea on that coast." "The Trade" was the English term for the Raz du Four, a patch of sea off the western tip of Brittany close to the important French port of Brest. Thirty-five-year-old Sir Edward Howard was the second son of the Duke of Norfolk. Edward must have been something of a black sheep, as in 1506 he and his elder brother, Thomas, were acquitted after being caught breaking into the manor house of John Grey, the late Viscount Lisle. Rumor had it that the incident had something to do with the viscount's daughter Elizabeth, but as her ward, the young Duke of Suffolk, intended to marry her, any such dalliance was strongly discouraged. Three years later Sir Edward led the funeral procession of Henry VII, carrying the king's banner into Westminster Abbey. He then jousted against Henry's son to celebrate his accession, and rapidly became a close confidant of the new king.

It wasn't until late June that everything was ready. Howard's fleet began operations by escorting the Marquis of Dorset's small English army to the northern Spanish port of San Sebastian. The plan was to use Spain as a base for an attack on Guyenne (the Aquitaine), in the southwestern corner of France. However, the invasion never advanced more than ten miles into France due to a lack of support from King Henry's Spanish allies, and Dorset and his men were soon recalled. For Henry this was only a diversion, aimed at placating the pope and the Emperor Maximilian. It would be the following summer before his main army was ready to take the fight to the French. In the meantime, after transporting Dorset's expedition, Sir Edward Howard was given free rein.

He had about eighteen ships at his disposal, including his flagship, the *Mary Rose*, and the *Peter Pomegranate*. The fleet achieved little at first, and acted more like pirates than men-of-war, capturing and plundering dozens of small merchantmen. According to the Venetian consul in London, the tally included twenty-six Flemish merchant "hulks" and forty small vessels from Brittany. The French warships resolutely stayed in port, even when English landing parties burned and looted Breton towns and villages within sight of the walls of Brest. In late July Howard returned to Portsmouth to drop off his prizes and to pick up supplies and the thousand-ton *Sovereign*, whose refit had been hurriedly completed. Meanwhile, the French took advantage of this temporary respite to reinforce the fleet at Brest with another contingent, which had been trapped at the mouth of the River Seine. This brought the French fleet up to twenty-two ships. A squadron of galleys based in the Mediterranean was also ordered to join the main fleet, but it would take months for them to arrive, and they played no part in the season's fighting that followed.

The French admiral René de Clermont felt he now had the men and the ships needed to give battle. He confidently positioned his fleet some twelve miles west of Brest in Berthaume Bay, where they could sail out and fight without having to negotiate the narrow Goulet Channel, which divided Brest Roads from the open sea. He flew his flag in the 790-ton *Louise*, while his deputy, Hervé de Portzmoguer (known as Primauget), commanded the 700-ton *Marie de la Cordelière*. The bay itself lay on the southern side of the main Breton peninsula, about three miles from Pointe de St. Mathieu, which marked its tip. North of this headland lay the English Channel, while twenty miles to the south lay Pointe du Raz, which marked the northern edge of the Bay of Biscay. It seems inconceivable that the French hadn't posted lookouts on the western tip of Brittany, where a fast horseman could have brought word of the English fleet's appearance several hours before it entered "the Trade," the waters off the Pointe de St. Mathieu.

August 10 was the feast of St. Lawrence, dedicated to one of the Roman deacons of the early Christian church, who was executed by order of the Emperor Valerian in A.D. 258. The French explorer Jacques Cartier named a great North American river after St. Lawrence in 1534. According to legend, the priest was laid on an iron grid, and after being "roasted" for a while, he reportedly exclaimed, "I am done on this side . . . turn me over!" This act of sangfroid was traditionally celebrated by—appropriately enough—a feast of roast meat. While the admiral entertained his own officers, as a local Breton man Primauget invited his family to dine on board his flagship, accompanied by the mayor (sénéchal) of his hometown of Morlaix.

By 11:00 A.M. the French had finished the religious part of the proceedings and were waiting for the feast to start. At that moment lookouts spotted a cluster of sails rounding the tip of Pointe de St. Mathieu. It was Sir Edward Howard and his English fleet— a threat that René de Clermont and his officers had clearly not expected to materialize for at least another week or two. The approach of the English ships must have caused pandemonium on board the French warships, and each of the twenty-two captains would have hurriedly tried to ready his ship for battle. Hervé de

Portzmoguer had no time to hustle his guests ashore, so he was left with no option but to lead them belowdecks, where he hoped they would be spared the sights and dangers of a hard-fought naval battle. Like most of his fellow captains he probably cut his anchor cables to save time, while his men raced aloft to unfurl the sails. Given the distance between the point and the French anchorage, the attackers would have been within easy gun range of the defending fleet within twenty minutes—barely enough time for the French to set their ships in order.

Sir Edward Howard's flagship, the *Mary Rose*, and her near-sister ship, the *Peter Pomegranate*, were probably two of the best-armed vessels on either side. Although many of the *Mary Rose's* guns were light swivel pieces or small stone-shotted guns, she also packed a powerful main armament of five curtows and six "murderers" (also called port pieces). The former fired sixty-pound roundshot, while the latter were wrought-iron pieces of varying size, but all could fire fairly substantial roundshot or fearsome antipersonnel charges of scrap metal. In the early sixteenth century chivalry wasn't quite dead, and so as befitted an admiral, Sir Edward ordered the *Mary Rose* to steer straight toward the *Louise*, flying the flag of René de Clermont. A duel between the two commanders was the proper way to begin a sea battle.

The two ships exchanged broadsides at close range, and a cheer must have gone up as one of the sixty-pound iron balls smashed into the *Louise's* mainmast, sending it crashing over the side. According to English reports the French flagship immediately broke off the action and headed back toward the safety of Brest. René de Clermont obviously told a different story, claiming that the rest of the fleet had already begun to steer toward Goulet Channel, and that the damage to this flagship's mainmast came when he stayed behind to cover the French withdrawal. Whatever actually happened, it seems that the bulk of the French fleet opted to flee rather than remain and fight at a disadvantage. If we accept René de Clermont's claim that he fought with the rearguard until his ship was damaged, the loss of a mainmast effectively put her out of action. Consequently she was lucky to make it back into Brest at all. However, two other French captains decided to stand their ground. One was Rigault de Berquetot from Normandy, who commanded the 336-ton

Nef de Dieppe. The other was Primauget—Hervé de Portzmoguer, commanding the *Marie de la Cordelière*.

Although the English fleet consisted of twenty-five ships, only five of them were larger than three hundred tons—*Mary Rose*, *Peter Pomegranate*, *Mary James*, *Sovereign*, and *Regent*. They were the only vessels that offered much of a threat to the two Frenchmen. While the *Mary Rose* drove off the French flagship, Sir Anthony Ughtred in the 300-ton *Mary James* steered for the *Cordelière* and fired a broadside into her at close range. Presumably the Breton ship fired back, and the two vessels may have exchanged shots for some time before the smaller English ship pulled out of range. Meanwhile, the *Nef de Dieppe* was surrounded by five English warships, but de Berquetot managed to prevent any of them from coming close enough to board him. He eventually managed to work his way slowly eastward, toward the relative safety of the Goulet. French accounts claim that de Berquetot was rescued toward dusk, which suggests that René de Clermont had managed to organize a sortie to rescue him, although one source credits the Bretons of Guérande with saving the embattled *Nef de Dieppe*. Primauget was not to be so lucky.

Before de Portzmoguer could follow de Berquetot's lead, the eight-hundred-ton *Sovereign* arrived to support the *Mary James*. The *Sovereign*, a powerful warship, was commanded by Sir Harry Gyldeford, but she also flew the flag of Sir Charles Brandon, Duke of Suffolk, who served as Sir Thomas Howard's deputy. The *Sovereign* came alongside the *Cordelière* "and lay stem to stem to the carrack; but by negligence of the master, or else by smoke of the ordnance, or otherwise, the *Sovereign* was cast at the stern of the carrack, with which advantage the Frenchmen shouted for joy." In other words, Suffolk tried to board Primauget's ship, but the Breton outmaneuvered him, leaving the English ship to trail in his wake.

Next it was the turn of the thousand-ton *Regent*, which until now had been chasing the *Nef de Dieppe*. The *Regent's* captain was Sir Thomas Knyvet, the brother-in-law of the English admiral and another member of Henry VIII's trusted inner circle. When Sir Thomas saw that the *Sovereign* had fallen astern of the Frenchman, he altered course toward the *Cordelière*. Sir Thomas proved to be a better seaman than Sir Harry or the Duke of Suffolk, as he not only managed to bring his ship alongside Primauget's carrack on her port side but also successfully grappled her. The two ships were now locked together. However, Primauget still had a trick to play. He ordered his crew to drop their anchor, and the two interlocked ships swung around to face the direction of the easterly current. A light wind was coming from the north, so the *Cordelière* was to windward of the *Regent*. This meant that the smoke of battle would blow into the faces of the English, and if the opportunity to break off came, the French ship would be in the better position to escape.

By all accounts Sir Thomas didn't bother with the niceties of firing newfangled artillery broadsides. He preferred the old method— grappling the enemy, and then sending a storm of missile fire into her before ordering his men to board. The fighting was described as cruel, and the archers, handgunners, crossbowmen, and artillerymen of both sides set to with a vengeance. The larger guns on both ships would probably have managed to fire off one shot just before the two ships came together, but after that they would have been useless. The swivel guns would have been firing their charges of scrap metal (known as diced shot) and small, solid roundshot into the enemy ranks as fast as they could be reloaded. Sir Thomas Knyvet was cut in two by a shot from one of the French guns. Still, the English seemed to be getting the better of the exchange, so his deputy, Sir John Carew, gave the order to board the *Cordelière*. Sir John was mortally wounded almost immediately, but his men pressed on and managed to gain a foothold in the waist of the French ship.

Exactly what happened next is a little unclear. When the *Regent* grappled the French ship, Sir Anthony Ughtred in the *Mary James* had worked his ship around so she lay facing the stern of the *Cordelière*. His men would have been firing into the enemy, and according to one account they "bowged [struck] her in divers places, and set her powder on fire." Another version claims that a French gunner either deliberately or accidentally set fire to the gunpowder on board the *Cordelière*. Contrary to popular belief, black powder doesn't explode if it is ignited, unless the charge is contained. Instead it creates a flash of flame, which in this case might well have ignited more powder barrels nearby. This would have created a fireball that would have ignited anything combustible, such as sails, clothing, or the timbers of the ship itself. Within seconds the *Cordelière* was blazing fiercely, the flames spreading so rapidly that her crew was unable to extinguish them. A French commentator described her as opening up like a volcano.

Later it was suggested that Primauget had started the fire deliberately, to avoid having to surrender his ship. A Breton legend that later grew up around the incident claimed that just before the fire began, Primauget had called on his men to follow the example of St. Lawrence—the roasted martyr—and to die bravely. Given that he still had his parents and grandparents on board, as well as dozens of his dinner guests, this seems highly unlikely. It is far more likely the fire was started by accident, possibly by a stray shot from the guns of the *Regent* or the *Mary James*. Unfortunately for the English, as the two ships were locked together there was no way that the *Regent* could escape the conflagration. Any of her boarding party who survived must have tried to escape back to their ship as her crew hacked through the grappling ropes with their axes. It was too late, and the flames soon spread to the rigging and then the hull of the *Regent*. The same French observer was even more graphic, describing how the English ship was consumed by torrents of flame.

By the time the smoke cleared Primauget, his guests, and most of his crew were dead. Only six badly burned Frenchmen survived, to be rescued by the English longboats that rushed to the scene. As for the *Regent*, some 420 of her 600-man crew went down with their burning ship, or died of injuries in the agony-filled days that followed. This double disaster effectively brought the Battle of St. Mathieu to a close, leaving the survivors stunned by what they had just witnessed. It was a fitting end to what was probably the first European sea battle to involve naval artillery. The engagement also demonstrated both the effectiveness of the new type of weapon and the inability of naval captains to understand how best to use it.

Sir Edward Howard didn't seem in the mood for introspection. His initial reaction was to swear an oath not to report back to his king before he had wreaked revenge for the loss of his sailors. He kept his word, his ships scouring the Breton coast for prizes. In the end his revenge was limited to the destruction of just over two dozen fishing vessels. With his men desperately short of supplies, he eventually gave the order to return home, albeit only after sailing along the Channel coast as far as Calais, capturing and burning any French ships he came across. It was an inglorious end to a disappointing and costly campaign. However, Henry VIII was far from disappointed, and considered the loss of the *Regent* a fair exchange for the "drowning" of the *Cordelière*. The king even awarded Sir Edward £66 as a reward and confirmed his position as admiral for the next year's campaign.

Henry certainly intended to renew the fight. By the following spring he managed to add several large new ships to the Navy Royal: the *Great Bark*, of 250 tons, as well as eight merchantmen, which were bought and converted for naval use. These included the *Katherine Fortune* (or *Katherine Fortizela*) of 550 tons, one of two large Mediterranean trading carracks bought from the Genoese. However, by the time Sir Edward Howard gathered his feet in Plymouth in April, she was causing no end of problems. Nobody had bothered to provision her, and in examining her hull the carpenter had riddled her with holes, not all of which had been properly patched. She leaked like a sieve and had to be put in to Portsmouth for repairs. The problems of supplying the fleet weren't limited to the *Katherine Fortune*. The admiral sent several begging letters to the king and his ministers, asking for provisions, money, and all the necessities of keeping a fleet at sea. Still, when he finally sailed for Brittany he had some fifty ships at his disposal—twenty-three of these belonged to the king's Navy Royal, while the rest were hired. This time around Sir Edward had at least a dozen ships of three hundred tons or more, and he considered his fleet more than a match for the French. He would soon be proved spectacularly wrong.

The French had been busy while the English fleet had been wintering in Portsmouth and on the Thames. The previous year King Louis had ordered the veteran galley commander Prégent de Bidoux to lead a squadron of six war galleys from the Mediterranean to Brittany. Prégent had a fearsome reputation. He was a Knight of Rhodes, and in the Mediterranean he had led his galleys to victory over the Turks, the Spaniards, and the Barbary corsairs. In Lisbon he heightened the gunwales of his galleys so they were better suited to the rougher seas of the English Channel, and by October the admiral had reached Brest. After a raid on the English coast was thwarted by bad weather, the galleys retired to St. Malo for the winter. When word reached Prégent de Bidoux that Sir Thomas Howard had sailed, he prepared his galleys for action and led them westward along the northern coast of Brittany.

On April 12 the English fleet arrived off Pointe de St. Mathieu. A screen of small, fast foists (galleys that could also be powered by sail) raced into Brest with the news, and the French fleet prepared for battle. However, an offshore wind prevented the English from making an immediate descent on Brest, so Sir Thomas had to bide his time. The contrary wind did have one advantage, though: he was able to capture a cluster of French ships that had anchored in the Trade, waiting for the wind to change. The English amused themselves by sending raiding parties ashore to burn houses and pilfer livestock. This also provided an opportunity to take a closer look at the defenses of Brest. During the winter the French had sunk a line of blockships to seal off the mouth of the Penfeld River, and the French fleet lay snugly behind this barrier, protected by several shore batteries and the stout walls of Brest Castle.

All Sir Edward could do when the wind changed was to move up to the Goulet narrows and blockade the port and its outer road-stead. Without a willing local pilot it was nearly impossible to force the narrows—in fact, the English lost the two-hundred-ton armed merchantman *Nicholas of Southampton* in an attempt to do just that. The ship was commanded by Arthur Plantagenet, an illegitimate son of the Yorkist Edward IV, whose response to striking the rocks was to kneel on his decks and pray for deliverance. Once he was rescued he immediately returned home to Norfolk, where he gave thanks for his rescue at the shrine of Our Lady of Walsingham. As for Sir Edward, he must have hoped for divine intervention, too, as he had no means of forcing the French to give battle, and his men were fast running out of supplies.

Then, on Saturday, April 23, Prégent de Bidoux appeared like an avenging angel, his four galleys taking the English completely by surprise. While a small screen of English ships lay off the Goulet, the rest of the fleet were anchored somewhat haphazardly in the lee of the Pointe de St. Mathieu. Given the disparity in numbers, the French shouldn't have had much of a chance, but unlike his English counterpart de Bidoux knew exactly how to use his artillery. Each of his galleys carried five bronze muzzle-loading guns mounted in a firing platform in the bows—one large central gun flanked by two smaller pieces on each side. All the pieces faced forward and were aimed by pointing the galley directly at a target. The main gun in each galley was a basilisk, a twelve-foot-long monster that fired a sixty-pound iron roundshot capable of smashing through anything in its path. The French admiral was about to give the English a lesson in naval gunnery.

The French launched their attack at dawn, sweeping around the Pointe de St. Mathieu and into the English fleet behind it before the defenders had a chance to react. The French oarsmen—all galley slaves—were rowing at full speed, and the galleys were among the English fleet in minutes. Then the French opened fire. The first casualty was the armed merchantman *Trinity of Bristol*, which was holed by several of the sixty-pound shots and began to sink. By this time there was complete pandemonium among the English ships, as captains gave desperate orders to prepare their own guns, or to cut their anchor cables in an attempt to escape. It was well known that the galley was designed as a ramming weapon, and it was feared that one of these iron beaks would tear into the timbers of an English ship before she could escape. However, de Bidoux had other ideas. He regrouped on the far side of the English fleet, and his galleys turned around for another pass.

Having reloaded their pieces, the French gunners sought a new target. This time it was the turn of the *Great Bark*, a brand-new royal warship of 250 tons. Like the *Trinity* she was holed several times, and she, too, began to founder. By now some of the other English ships had managed to get under way, and a few were even able to fire on the French galleys as they swept past. One of the ships— probably the *Mary Rose*—managed to score a telling hit on one of the French vessels, which was forced to run herself onto the beach to avoid sinking. By that time the French had passed safely through the English fleet and had shot around the headland and out of the battle. The beached French galley was later abandoned and set on fire by her crew.

It had been the classic galley raid—a tactic de Bidoux and his experienced galley captains would have used several times before in the Mediterranean. However, they had rarely achieved such a spectacular victory, or encountered an enemy so poorly prepared for battle. Sir Stephen Bull was lucky, and with the help of other ships nearby he was able to prevent his *Great Bark* from sinking. Captain Anthony Poyntz of the *Trinity* was less fortunate, and by noon his ship had slipped beneath the waters of Berthaume Bay, although Poyntz and most of his crew were rescued. Sir Edward Howard was furious, and sent scouting ships northward from Pointe de St. Mathieu to find out where the French had headed. It was soon revealed that Prégent de Bidoux hadn't gone far at all. Once safely past the headland, he ordered his galleys to put in to the shallow Anse de Blanc-Sablons, a wide bay overlooking the Trade just four miles farther north from Pointe de St. Mathieu. His galleys were drawn up onto the white-sanded beach in "Mediterranean style"— beached by the stern with their guns facing seaward. Defenses were thrown up on the landward side, where the sailors were reinforced by troops from Brest. It was almost as if the French admiral was tempting his English counterpart to attack him.

Sir Edward needed no second bidding. He immediately planned for a dawn attack of his own. The French defenses around their galleys were strongly manned, which ruled out the possibility of a landward attack. He would have to approach the enemy by sea, which meant attacking into the mouths of the enemy guns. As the Anse de Blanc-Sablons was too shallow to allow his larger ships to approach within gun range of the enemy, he selected the smaller vessels of his fleet for the attack, and transferred his flag from the *Mary Rose* to the eighty-ton rowing barge *Swallow*. He planned to rely on speed to cover the distance, then to overwhelm the galleys in a boarding action. The French admiral later reported that he had been attacked by twenty-five to thirty small vessels supported by as many larger ones farther out in the bay. However, it seems that Howard had fewer than a dozen vessels at his disposal that were shallow-drafted enough to reach the enemy. After hearing Mass and eating lunch the attackers set sail, and they arrived at the southern end of the bay just before 4:00 P.M.

Howard gave the order to attack. The first wave consisted of the *Swallow* and her near-sister the *Sweepstake*, and their crews strained at their oars as the small vessels raced toward the waiting French. Battle was about to be joined for the second time in two days. An eyewitness, Captain Edward Echyngham of the small armed merchantman *Germyn*, described what happened next. The French sent up a hail of fire, and as the range closed their heavier guns were augmented by swivel guns and then by small arms. Sir Edward ordered the *Swallow* to head directly toward de Bidoux's flagship, which lay to the left of two other French galleys. Somehow they made it without being smashed apart by gunfire, and grappling hooks were thrown to bind the two ships together.

Sir Edward was the first to jump aboard the French galley, followed by seventeen other volunteers. Before more men could follow, the grappling ropes parted, and the *Swallow* drifted away from the galley. Echyngham thought that the French had managed to cut the ropes, "or some of our mariners let it slip." The English commander was now stranded on the decks of the enemy ship. He called out to Captain Cooke of the *Swallow*, ordering him, "Come aboard again!" Unfortunately, Cooke was now the victim of the current, which was pulling him away, and while his men returned to their oars, the two vessels continued to separate.

According to de Bidoux's report, the English managed to put forty-five to fifty men aboard, which might well have been true if the same thing happened to the *Sweepstake*, or if he included those whose boarding attempt had been thwarted at the last minute. In any event, Sir Edward was hopelessly outnumbered. As the enemy closed in, his men formed a ring around their admiral, and the two sides hacked, stabbed, and clubbed at each other. However, the outcome was never in doubt. To prevent his symbol of office from falling into enemy hands, Howard "took his whistle from about his neck, wrapped it together, and threw it into the sea." Moments later he was submerged by a wave of French soldiers. The rest of the English assault force tried their best. The *Sweepstake* lay off her stern, her men firing arrows into the French ranks at point-blank range. Two other vessels tried to ram the French flagship, but they achieved little apart from breaking a few oars. By then it was too late, and Sir Edward Howard was dead, his body pierced with pikes and then unceremoniously flung over the side.

The English withdrew when they realized what had happened. Later that day Sir Thomas Cheyne and Sir John Wallow were landed under a flag of truce. Prégent de Bidoux met the Englishmen on the beach, and when asked what had happened to the English admiral he replied, "Sirs, I assure you I have no English prisoners in my galley save one, and he is a simple mariner. However, there was one who leapt into my galley with a gilt shield on his arm, whom I later saw thrown overboard (still stuck) with pikes. The mariner I have as a prisoner told me that this same man was your Admiral." Four days later, Sir Edward Howard's body was taken to the nearby village of Le Conquet, where de Bidoux had the body embalmed at his own expense. In his report to King Louis XII he enclosed the Englishman's gold whistle of office as a present for the queen, and asked what he was to do with the body. He also requested that he be allowed to keep the heart of Sir Edward as a memento of his epic battle. As far as we know, his grisly request was granted.

The two battles fought off Pointe de St. Mathieu on August 10, 1512, and April 23, 1513, marked turning points in naval warfare. For the first time two rival fleets had sought each other out and fought each other using naval artillery rather than just boarding weapons. Certainly guns had been used at sea before, but never by a pair of well-matched fleets, and never with any tactical deliberation. The dismasting of the French flagship *Louise* by the *Mary Rose* may well have surprised everyone who saw it happen, but the effect of that lucky shot would be felt throughout Europe. It demonstrated the potential of naval artillery to influence the outcome of a sea battle. Similarly, the sinking of the *Trinity* just over eight months later clearly showed just how effective naval artillery could be. Naval commanders, military theorists, and even monarchs would spend the next few decades trying to figure out how best to harness this great potential, by devising a whole new set of naval tactics, while shipbuilders and ordnance experts would work on providing the best possible floating platforms on which to mount these guns.

Of course, a whole different set of lessons also could be gleaned from these battles. The increased firepower of heavy naval guns was all very well, but in the end the battle fought off Pointe de St. Mathieu had still degenerated into a fighting boarding action—the same kind of hand-to-hand fighting that had been the hallmark of naval combat since man first put to sea. In fact, the ability of Prégent de Bidoux to defend his galleys against a major attack suggested that the ability to attack and defend at close quarters was probably seen as being more important than having the capability to fire at an enemy from a distance. The development of both warships and naval tactics during the following decades would lead to the advancement of both schools of thought, and while they weren't completely exclusive, some nations favored one style of fighting over the other. The naval world was still a long way off from developing the line of battle and the ship of the line, although for those willing to look for the signs, the two battles off Brest marked the first tentative steps down that road.

3

The Shipbuilding Revolution

During the fifteenth century the major ports of northern Europe would have played host to a wide variety of different kinds of ships, including the cog, the nef, the hulk, and the carrack. Things were slightly different in Spain, Portugal, and the Mediterranean, which developed their own shipbuilding traditions. The cog was an exclusively northern European design, and by the time work began on the *Grace Dieu* it had plied the sea lanes of the Baltic, the North Sea, and the English Channel for the better part of a century. Cogs were even known to have ventured into the Mediterranean, where the local shipwrights noted the differences between these bulky ships and their own. The vessel had its roots in the knorr, the trading vessel used by Scandinavian traders since the eighth century, and although the cog was a marked improvement both as cargo carrier and as seagoing vessel, the two ship types shared several features. Most notably, both were clinker-built, with pronounced stem and sternposts—features they had in common with that other famous Scandinavian ship type, the Viking longboat.

The typical cog was a squat, rather ugly-looking vessel, with a broad beam, a bluff rounded bow and stern, and high sides. The

A cog

stem and stern posts rose steeply, which gave the vessels the vague appearance of large wooden cockleshells. Like the knorr, the majority of cogs carried a single mast fitted with a large, square sail, although illustrations from the time show that by the late fourteenth century a number of cogs might also have carried a small mizzenmast. They were steered by a large stern rudder, which was an improvement over the side rudder in a knorr. By the fifteenth century the shape of the cog had changed slightly—the vessel appeared even more rounded, and the stem and sternposts became curved, giving the vessels a slightly more elegant appearance than before. However, by then these workhorses of northern Europe were fast becoming obsolete.

The other major addition to the cog during its later life was the introduction of fixed platforms in the bows and stern. While vessels were fitted with a small temporary sterncastle and sometimes a forecastle during the early fourteenth century, these could be removed when not needed. These gradually evolved into permanent structures and became larger. This made them highly suitable for conversion into warships, and during the Battle of Sluys in 1340 both the French and the English fleets consisted almost exclusively of cogs that had been hastily turned into warships. Warlike cogs featured prominently on the seals of several northern European ports during the fourteenth century, and those of the Hanseatic cities of Stralsund and Elbing show sterncastles surmounted by a crenellated bulwark—a wooden version of castle ramparts.

By the start of the fifteenth century, cogs had begun to disappear from European waters, replaced by a new kind of vessel, the hulk, which was effectively a larger and more seaworthy version of the cog. What made her so different was that she also represented a fusion between two shipbuilding traditions: the northern European and the Mediterranean. The Mediterranean method produced carvel-built ships, as opposed to the clinker-built vessels built in the North. By the middle of the fourteenth century there is evidence that the two schools had begun to borrow ideas from each other, as demonstrated by the introduction of carvel-building techniques into the non-Mediterranean shipbuilding yards of France and Spain as well as Portugal. In exchange some Mediterranean shipbuilders began producing ships with a pronounced sternpost rudder—a feature of the cog. This exchange was the first development in a series of technological developments that some historians would label a shipbuilding revolution. The hulk was the perfect love child of this marriage, combining some of the best elements from both of these shipbuilding traditions.

The hulk could be either clinker-built or carvel-built, although the latter technique doesn't seem to have been practiced outside France and the Iberian Peninsula until the end of the fifteenth century. It seems that the term was generally applied to any large ship, regardless of the way it was constructed. It is sometimes argued that the skeletal construction of a carvel-built ship raised the possibility of building larger ships than would normally have been possible using clinker-building techniques. However, the *Grace Dieu* demonstrated that size wasn't really a limiting factor. In 1418 Henry V ordered a second great clinker-built ship at Bayonne, in southwestern France, and she was only marginally smaller than the leviathan built in Southampton. This proves conclusively that neither technique nor location was a real constraint.

However, it is probably true that the average hulk—called a nao in Spain and Portugal—was generally larger than the average cog. She still kept the same rounded, walnut-shell-shaped hull, which made her an efficient cargo carrier and an excellent warship. We know that in 1410 at least one royal warship maintained by Henry IV—the *Christopher of the Tower*—was classed as a hulk, and although she had only one mast, she was much bigger than the cogs that made up the rest of the fleet. There is even some debate whether the *Grace Dieu* and the Bayonne ship were cogs or hulks. A letter written in 1419 by the Bayonne shipwright John Alcetre to Henry V proves that this smaller ship was constructed in a way similar to the *Grace Dieu*. Unfortunately, while both ships conformed to all the definitions of the ship type, we can't categorically claim that they were hulks. In fact, some historians even claim that they were prototype carracks, which was another type of ship altogether.

Like the cog, the hulk carried a large, square sail on its mainmast. However, in some contemporary illustrations it also was fitted with a topsail above the mainsail, which made the ship more efficient. While some later cogs may have carried a small mizzenmast fitted with a sail of some description, several depictions of fifteenth-century hulks show that the vessels carried a fairly substantial Mediterranean-style lateen sail on this second mast, which made it far easier to sail closer into the wind than the cog. They also carried a bowsprit, fitted with a spritsail suspended from it—used to make the ship turn more easily when under sail. All these extra masts and sails meant that the hulk could sail farther and faster than the cog and that—combined with its larger cargo capacity—meant that the cog rapidly became a thing of the past.

Like the cog before it, the hulk turned out to be an evolutionary dead end—an improvement that went no farther down the evolutionary road. Although it enjoyed a heyday during the latter decades of the fifteenth century, the hulk produced only one significant development: the nef. Even then, some maritime historians question whether it was a ship type at all, rather than just a French name for a large hulk. The French described the nef as an improved version of the cog, built in French ports. The most likely solution is that while the English came to describe a hulk as any large northern European merchant vessel built overseas, the French used the term "nef" when they spoke about large homegrown carvel-built versions of the hulk. The other identifying feature of the nef was that it had three masts rather than two. In other words, all nefs might well be hulks, but not all hulks were nefs. Unlike modern maritime historians, the chroniclers of the time don't seem to have been particularly worried about which term they used, so perhaps we should follow their lead.

While the hulk or the nef would have made a useful warship, the later fifteenth century saw the emergence of a new type of ship that would allow the proper marriage of ship and gun. While the nao still prospered as a merchant ship in Iberia and the Mediterranean (where it was known as the Mediterranean round ship), the carrack would replace it everywhere else in Europe. For a century the fully rigged carrack would be the warship par excellence, the mainstay of the emerging national fleets of Europe's maritime powers. The advances in shipbuilding technology that helped produce her meant that for the first time a ship type had been created that could support the weight of heavy ordnance, and that could bear the strain when these big guns were fired.

The Genoese were responsible for this shipbuilding breakthrough. As early as 1304 the Florentine chronicler Giovanni Villani claimed that Genoese shipwrights were adapting the design of the cog to produce a ship type known as a cocha. Only a few tantalizing pictures of these cochas exist, but the written records tell us that by 1340 the largest of these were known as cocha baronesche. This was a larger, deeper-hulled version of the earlier ship. Within two decades these larger ships were known as carracks. The early illustrations of them show vessels with two masts, carrying a square-rigged mainsail and a lateen sail on the mizzen. This makes them similar to the last of the cogs and the first of the hulks. The towering superstructures that set the later carracks apart from other ships still hadn't appeared. Therefore it is probably fair to say that before the mid-fifteenth century the carrack, the nef, the nao, and the hulk were all pretty much the same kind of ship.

The first mention of one of these new Mediterranean carracks in northern European waters comes in 1410, when a two-masted Genoese carrack was captured by English pirates. Seven years later Henry V bought eight two-masted Genoese carracks for his fleet.

The English king evidently was impressed by this new type of vessel and realized its naval potential. The word "carrack" appears more frequently in northern European records from 1430 onward, and in 1468 we have our first pictorial evidence for the new ship—a Flemish engraving of a ship labeled "kraeck" by an artist who signed himself "WA." The illustration shows a large carvel-built merchantman with three masts, a large forecastle and sterncastle, and even a row of small guns protruding from the superstructure near her stern. Both the two masts carrying square sails and the mizzenmast carrying a large lateen sail were surmounted by large fighting tops. She may have been a merchantman, but she also was equipped to defend herself. The forecastle juts out over the bow, and with her high hull sides the whole ship has a lofty, imposing appearance. This was the shape of things to come.

These towering forecastle and sterncastle structures would become the most instantly recognizable features of the carrack, while the

Shipbuilding in the sixteenth century

hull itself also was notably different from that of the hulk. Unlike its predecessor, the carrack had a far less rounded hull shape, and her forecastle and sterncastle formed part of her hull rather than being an afterthought. Another prominent feature of the late-fifteenth-century carrack was the way the planking of her lower hull bent around and upward toward the stern, creating a rounded end. This also was a feature of contemporary hulks, but by 1488, at the latest, this practice had died out. The new form was much simpler, where the planks were attached to the stern transom, the last frame in the ship's hull. This led to a flat rather than a rounded stern, which produced a far stronger hull. The "WA" carrack actually represented a halfway stage between the two styles. This simplification of her design was important in building vessels designed to absorb the fire of heavy guns.

The *Warwick Roll* also includes a depiction of a large carrack flying the standard of Richard Neville, Earl of Warwick (1428–1471), armed with a broadside of five or six guns and fitted with four masts. Then we have Henry VII's *Sovereign* and *Regent*, both of which represented the latest word in carrack design. They were both four-masted vessels—equipped with mainsails and topsails, and with lateen sails on the mizzen and bonaventure masts. This was what ship historians called a fully rigged sailing ship, although three-masted carracks were still widely used. The advantage of all these sails was that the ships were far more maneuverable than the ship types that had come before, and for the first time they could be relied on to make fairly lengthy voyages. While this would have a profound impact on the Age of Exploration, it also played a major part in the development of the warship.

The advent of the fully rigged ship would transform the maritime world by giving ships the ability to sail closer into the direction of the wind than before. Thus merchant ships were less likely to be stuck in ports waiting for a favorable breeze, ships of exploration could sail more or less where they wanted, and warship captains could take advantage of the wind to give their ships a tactical edge. While improvements in hull shape made carracks much more efficient at traveling through the water, and integrated superstructures meant the ships were far more robust than before, the greatest single technological improvement of the period was the way the ship could take full advantage of the wind.

This was the shipbuilding revolution of the Renaissance. For the first time a type of ship existed that was not only strongly enough built to take the stresses and strains of naval combat in its stride but that also possessed the room to carry substantial numbers of soldiers, sailors, and ordnance. Just as importantly, naval commanders could now maneuver these ships under sail so they could make the best possible use of the armament they carried. While the *Grace Dieu* was an impressive floating leviathan, it was almost certainly difficult to maneuver, and she was probably an extremely slow sailer. Now, with fully rigged purpose-built vessels such as the *Sovereign*, the *Marie de la Cordelière*, and the *Mary Rose*, the sailing warship had finally come of age.

The *Mary Rose*

Shipwrecks rarely look like they do in films. The image many people might have is of a slightly battered wooden hull resting on her keel with her masts still standing and a colorful school of fish flitting into and out of her open gunports. The truth is disappointingly different. The *toredo* worm eats at wooden hulls when a ship is still afloat, and once it sinks, the process continues. Just like a wooden building on dry land, a wooden shipwreck gradually rots, its deck timbers collapse, and soon it becomes little more than an unrecognizable jumble of rotten wood. In most cases the process doesn't stop there, and the decay continues until there is nothing left apart from the remains of the iron fasteners that held the hull together, and other metal fittings. Even these are prone to decay, and they attract particles of sand or stone to form a layer of concretion that looks more like a lump of weed-encrusted concrete than anything else.

That was why in 1966 the British journalist and diver Alexander McKee didn't have any high expectations when he began searching the seabed of the Solent for lost shipwrecks. The Solent is the stretch of water between Portsmouth and the Isle of Wight that for centuries has served as an anchorage for the British fleet. The section directly in front of Portsmouth Harbor is also known as Spithead. McKee knew of several historic ships that had foundered in the area, so the previous year he encouraged the local scuba diving club to work with him in trying to find them. Conditions in the Solent were brutal: underwater visibility was measured in inches rather than feet, and a combination of tides and shipping conspired to hamper the search. Fortunately, the local archaeologist Margaret Rule volunteered her services, although neither she nor McKee really knew much about conducting archaeology underwater. The plan was to write the book as they went along.

Their big hope was that the seabed of the Solent consisted of thick, cloying mud. The team knew that if a wooden ship settled in the mud quickly enough—and if the process was helped by the tides that scoured out a hole for her to slip into—then the timbers of the ship might be preserved. The local mud was anaerobic—proof against the teredo worm. Once the mud closed over the timbers, they would be protected. Of course, the problem with this theory was that archaeologists didn't really know what to expect, as nobody had ever examined the way shipwrecks decay on the seabed. It also meant that if the theory was correct, there would be little left to see on the seabed. Everything would be hidden by a thick layer of mud.

The team spent a year looking for the wrecks of the British flagship *Royal George*, which sank off Spithead in 1782, and the *Boyne*, which caught fire and sank at the entrance to Portsmouth Harbor thirteen years later. They found the remains of both, and surveyed what they could. Then McKee and his team turned their attention to the *Mary Rose*. Henry VIII's favorite warship was lost in battle with the French somewhere off the entrance of Portsmouth Harbor in 1545, and the site had been partially salvaged by the diving brothers John and Francis Deane in 1836. These nineteenth-century salvors described seeing ship timbers protruding from the seabed, and when they dug a little deeper, they came across better-preserved timbers surrounded by all the detritus of a maritime disaster—pieces of wreckage, ship fittings, personal possessions, and even human bones. It sounded as if the mud of the Solent had been doing its job. Better still, in early 1966 the team unearthed a copy of an Admiralty chart dated 1841 that marked the site of the Deanes' excavation with a neat red cross. They had what every shipwreck explorer ever dreamed of: a chart where "X" marks the spot.

The story of the sinking of the *Mary Rose* has all the hallmarks of a Shakespearean tragedy. In 1545 England and France were once again at war, and the Tudor kingdom was threatened with invasion. In mid-July a French fleet under the command of Admiral Claude d'Annebault appeared in the Solent and began preparations to land troops. The English fleet under Viscount Lisle was in Portsmouth Harbor, and Henry VIII arrived to muster an army and watch the ensuing naval battle. On July 19 the Tudor fleet of about a hundred ships sailed out to give battle. They were outnumbered, but the fleet had confidence in their ships and their firepower. As befitted their rank as flagships, the first warships out of the narrow harbor entrance were the *Mary Rose* and the *Henri Grace à Dieu*. Early that morning the French admiral had sent a squadron of French galleys forward to probe the harbor entrance, and they began bombarding the fleet at long range. It has been suggested this had goaded Viscount Lisle into making a sortie, but in truth the move had been planned the night before. However, nobody anticipated what happened next.

Without warning, the *Mary Rose* began to heel over and sink. The French gunners probably imagined they had scored some lucky hit, but the reason was far more prosaic. The great warship had heeled over in the wind as she emerged from the harbor entrance. This could easily have been corrected, but instead the heel to starboard increased, probably due to some small error in seamanship by her helmsman as he concentrated on steering toward the enemy rather than compensating for the wind. There is archaeological evidence that the ballast in her hold shifted, which would have aggravated the problem. The whole process might well have gone on for several minutes, as the crew fought to bring the ship under control. The largely inexperienced crew might well have panicked. The commander of a passing ship hailed Sir George Carew of the *Mary Rose* and asked him what the problem was. Carew shouted back that he "had the sort of knaves whome he could not rule." The ship continued to list, and eventually this brought her lower gunports in line with the water. Naturally, the gunports were open because the ship was about to engage the French in battle. The sea began to pour in.

The crew didn't have a chance. Antiboarding netting had been stretched over her waist to prevent the French from clambering on board. It now prevented the crew from escaping. The cold waters of the Solent flooded into her hull, and she sank in minutes, taking almost all of her crew of seven hundred men and boys with her. Henry VIII had watched the disaster from the safety of Portsmouth Castle, and together with the thousands of other onlookers he could do nothing but watch in horror as his great warship slipped beneath the waves. Soon only her masts remained, surrounded by a cluster of floating debris and a few lucky survivors. Although there were a few halfhearted attempts to salvage her in the months that followed, after her masts and sails were removed she was left in peace for the best part of three centuries.

When McKee and his scuba partner, John Towse, dived on the site on May 14, 1966, they saw no clear sign that a shipwreck lay under the mud—nothing like the clear mounds they'd viewed on their previous two shipwreck sites. However, they noticed that the needles of their compasses began swinging wildly, which suggested there might be a lot of metal beneath all that mud. It was time to call in the experts. In 1967 an American-based company was persuaded to try out its sonar equipment over the wreck site, and the results were analyzed by the company's scientific adviser, Professor Harold Edgerton of MIT. They used two different types of sonar—a subbottom profiler, which bounced a signal directly off the seabed and revealed anything under its surface, and a sidescan sonar system, which sent signals at an angle from a ship. When they were bounced back, any features on the seabed would show up on a paper trace on the search ship. This equipment had been pioneered during World War II, and while it was primitive compared to modern sonar equipment, the survey still managed to produce some startling results.

Professor Edgerton revealed that an anomaly some two hundred feet long and seventy-five feet wide lay about twenty feet below the mud, its site marked by a mound just four feet high. It was little wonder the team hadn't seen anything in the poor visibility when they searched the site. If this was the Mary Rose, then not only was she protected by the mud, but she also was going to take a lot of effort to reach. On the basis of this, Alexander McKee and Margaret Rule joined forces with a naval diving expert, Commander Alan Bax, and a nautical researcher, Bill Majer, to form the Mary Rose Committee. The following year they obtained the rights to salvage that patch of the seabed, then set about clearing a pathway through the mud using pumps, fire hoses, and water jets. Conditions were appalling, but the work continued off and on for two years, until in late 1970 they finally stumbled across a gun. When it was recovered and examined, they found it was a wrought-iron breech-loading piece, just like some of the guns recovered by the Deane brothers 134 years before. Morale immediately soared. They were looking in the right place.

The breakthrough came on May 1, 1971—the first dive of a new season. Divers were sent down to locate the site of the previous season's digging, but after a few minutes diver Percy Ackland broke the surface beside the dive boat, pulled the mouthpiece from his lips, and yelled, "There's wreckage—including planking—sticking out of the mud!" The team had finally found the Mary Rose. Winter storms had done their job for them. Over the next few hours the divers surveyed the entire site and discovered that the ends of ship timbers could be seen sticking out of the mud in a long row—clearly the tips of the wooden frames that once held the hull together. The survey work continued throughout that summer and the next, until the team were finally able to work out which way the ship was lying on the seabed. Although the 1973 season was a washout due to bad weather and lack of funds, public interest in the project was growing. Just as importantly, the site was now fully protected by new national legislation that protected it from interference by sailors. The team could finally begin excavating their ship.

The work progressed slowly and cautiously over the next few years, and more of the hull was uncovered. Many people knew the story of the sinking of the Mary Rose—how water had poured in through her lower gunports when she heeled over in the wind. The divers were amazed to find archaeological evidence of this— gunport lids were recovered where the inner face had been eroded, but the inner face was in good condition, as it had been pressed against the side of the hull when the ship sank. Here was proof that the stories were true, and her gunports had been left open. By 1978 most of the outer surface of the hull had been uncovered, although much of the internal part of the ship was still covered in thick, black mud. The ship was lying on her starboard side, and while most of her stern superstructure and her bows had rotted

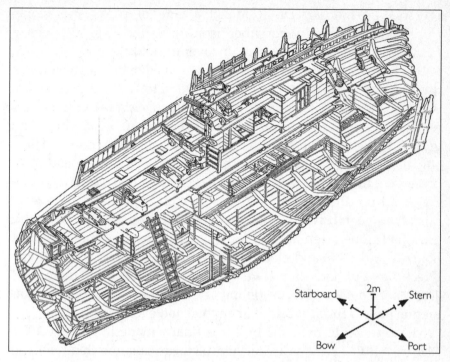

Mary Rose *cutaway drawing*

away, and all of her port side, the rest of the hull looked surprisingly intact. A trench cut across the hull near the bow revealed that the interior of the ship was a treasure trove of information, and most of her internal decks were still intact. If ever a shipwreck deserved being called a time capsule, it was the wreck of the *Mary Rose*.

The year 1979 was something of a watershed, for that was when the *Mary Rose* Trust was formed—a not-for-profit body charged with excavating and preserving the shipwreck. It was headed by Margaret Rule, who by now had become one of Britain's leading experts in underwater excavation. Funds began coming in from public bodies and private donors, which allowed the team to consider what had previously been unthinkable: raising the shipwreck. A new diving barge, the *Sleipner,* a purpose-built salvage vessel that had already been used in Sweden during the excavation of the early-seventeenth-century warship *Vasa*, was bought for the trust by the Portsmouth City Council. She allowed operations to be scaled up considerably, and the excavation could be put on a thoroughly professional footing. Dr. Rule led a core of paid professional archaeologists and diving supervisors, who then used a pool of trained volunteers to help them uncover the shipwreck.

By 1980 a metal grid had been laid over the wreck site, which was used as a reference point to survey finds and to keep the divers from damaging the fragile timbers beneath them. Several airlifts were used to carefully suck the mud and sediment out of the hull, and gradually the true extent of the find was revealed. By now a steady stream of artifacts was being recovered, and all of these had to be preserved, then conserved. It was later claimed that a month of diving could produce enough artifacts to keep the conservation team busy for a year. It was probably no exaggeration, as that anaerobic mud had done a remarkable job of preserving the finds. Leather, bone, wood, rope, and clothing were things you rarely found at a wreck site, but here they were being recovered in large quantities. The *Mary Rose* was fast becoming one of the best sources of information on the Tudor world that anyone had ever found.

The decision to raise the hull was finally made in January 1982. Margaret Rule saw it as a vital step, as the excavation that removed the protective coating of mud from the ship had also exposed her to further decay. If the *Mary Rose* was to be saved, she had to be raised from the seabed and towed ashore. This sort of thing had been done only once before, when the *Vasa* was raised from the bottom of Stockholm Harbor in 1959. A steel cradle was positioned over the hull by the summer of 1982; then a series of holes was drilled in the hull and steel bolts were attached to her timbers. Wire cables connected these to the cradle, supporting the hull. The next stage was to tunnel through the mud beneath the shipwreck so cables could be slid under her; these supported her hull. Simultaneously another, larger cradle had been built, and was sunk onto the seabed beside the shipwreck. The idea was to lift the hull, then place her gently down onto this new cradle.

This complex process took place smoothly, although the archaeological team also had to make sure they protected the exposed timbers and any of the thousands of pieces of timber inside her hull that might be damaged. Once this underwater lift had been completed, the final stage involved lifting the whole cradle to the surface. On October 11, 1982, at just after 9:00 A.M., the timbers of the *Mary Rose* finally broke the surface after 437 years. The Royal Navy had allocated an old dock in the Portsmouth Naval Base, right next to HMS *Victory*, Admiral Nelson's flagship at the Battle of Trafalgar in 1805. The move to her new berth took the best part of an entire day, but at last the *Mary Rose* was safely laid to rest in her new home. Henry VIII's great Tudor warship had finally arrived back in port.

The Carrack Revealed

The *Mary Rose* is now on display in a purpose-built museum in Portsmouth. After two decades of conservation her hull has now been fully preserved, her decks have been slotted back into place, and she can be seen in all her wooden glory. The fact that half of her hull rotted away on the seabed even works to her advantage—she looks like a full-scale cutaway model, and visitors can easily see what she looked like inside. Maritime historians also have been able to examine her and have managed to figure out exactly how she was built. As the only surviving early-sixteenth-century warship to have been raised from the seabed, she offers us a unique chance to understand Renaissance ship construction and imagine what it must have been like to sail in her. She was built shortly after Henry VII's *Sovereign* and Louis XII's *Marie de la Cordelière*, and before the Tudor king's huge *Henri Grace à Dieu*. The *Mary Rose* will therefore have shared many of the construction techniques of all these ships.

The shipwrights would have started by laying her keel, made from three sections of elm joined together using diagonal scarf joints for a long, square-shaped strip of timber 104 feet long. Then the dozen frames would have been erected, starting with the stern transom frame. These V-shaped structures were bolted to the keel and formed the ribs of the ship, like a large wooden skeleton. These frames curved out slightly, particularly in the midpoint between the bow and the stern, and gave the hull its shape. In those days shipwrights had no plans to follow or complicated shipbuilding formulas to adhere to. Instead they built what they thought was the best hull shape they could, drawing on their own shipbuilding experience. The ship then tapered off slightly toward the stern. The line of the hull was rounded a little more abruptly in the bows, where a stempost rose from the keel to form the bow of the ship.

Next came the deck beams. These were secured to the frames using thick oak "knees," turning the V of the frames into a D, with the flat side uppermost. Longitudinal stringers were then put in place to link the frames together and to give the whole structure a little more rigidity. Then the keelson—a smaller version of the keel—was bolted into place where the frames joined the keel. Effectively this created a wooden sandwich that helped strengthen the joint between the base of the frames and the keel. The transom frame at the stern was supported by extra oak knees and braces; then the structure was curved outward above where the rudder would be fitted by adding two horn-shaped extensions to the rear side of the transom frame. This provided a framework for the stern superstructure, which was already given its shape by the frames, which curved inward as they rose, until the shape resembled the profile of a wineglass.

The next stage was to add the hull planking. Unlike the *Sovereign* and the *Regent*, the *Mary Rose* was designed from the outset as a carvel-built ship, with an outer skin of planking that fitted edge to edge instead of overlapping in the clinker-built fashion. The outer planking of the hull and transom stern was secured directly to the frames and the stringers using wooden "treenails"—wooden dowels. Most hull planks were cut from oak and were about four inches thick. Once these were pegged in place, they were reinforced by additional iron nails or fasteners. The joints between the planks were then caulked with a mixture of animal hair or some other fiber, mixed with hot pitch. Once the hull planks were in place, a series of extra reinforcing timber bands known as ribbands were laid around the lower part of the outer hull. They were designed to take the strain if the ship grounded or was beached, although they also gave her a little extra strength. Finally, another skin of planking was laid on the inner side of the hull below the waterline. In effect this was a second skin, which was designed to protect the ship slightly if she struck a rock or had her lower hull pierced by a roundshot.

The internal decks and the upper deck were built using thick oak planks. These were laid on top of the deck beams, just like laying a wooden floor in a modern house. The *Mary Rose* was built with four deck levels—a hold, an orlop deck just below the waterline, a gun deck just above it, and the upper deck. Of course, the only part of the upper deck exposed to the elements was in the waist—a forecastle and a sterncastle covered the rest of it. These were built by creating a fifth deck, which formed the upper deck of the forecastle and sterncastle areas. The only difference between this and the way the *Henri Grace à Dieu* was built was in scale, and in all likelihood the Henrician flagship had another, sixth deck level—a poop deck built toward the back of the sterncastle.

The upper deck and the gun deck below it were designed to hold large pieces of ordnance, so therefore these decks had thicker knees and deck beams than elsewhere in the ship. Finally, a wale ran around the outer hull of the ship at the level of each of the three

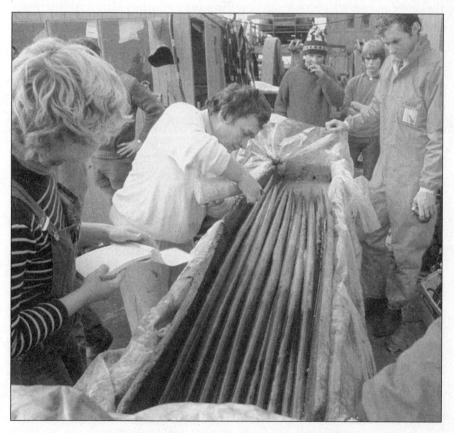

A chest of longbows recovered from the Mary Rose

lower decks, providing a little extra reinforcement to the whole structure. Like the hull planking itself, these three wales followed the sheer of the vessel, rising toward the bow and the stern. The wales also prevented weakening of the hull when it was pierced with gunports—the Mary Rose had seven ports cut into either side of the vessel. The upper wale, at the level of the upper deck, also acted as an anchor for external ship fittings, such as the chainplates that supported the rigging for the masts.

The Mary Rose was first built in 1509, and in the decades that followed even greater emphasis was placed on the mounting of heavy guns. Therefore she went through two refits in Portsmouth during her life—a small one in 1526, and then a major rebuilding program in 1536. In both cases her hull was strengthened, allowing her to carry more or heavier guns. The work the shipwrights did during these refits can still be seen today. She was given additional horizontal and diagonal braces, while extra knees and riders were added to reinforce the stringers that bound her frames together. We know just how much extra weaponry she was meant to carry. When she sailed into action against the French in 1512, she carried sixteen heavy guns of various types, as well as sixty-eight smaller pieces. In 1545 she carried no fewer than twenty-six heavy guns:

- two bronze muzzle-loading cannons
- two bronze muzzle-loading demicannons
- two bronze muzzle-loading culverins
- six bronze muzzle-loading demiculverins
- two bronze muzzle-loading sakers
- twelve wrought-iron muzzle-loading portpieces

plus sixty-two smaller pieces, mainly wrought-iron swivel guns and hackbuts (large hand-held guns). It is little wonder that they needed to strengthen her hull.

Like most other large carracks of this period, the Mary Rose was fitted with four masts, the traces of which can be seen in the mast steps cut into her keelson. The incredible preservation of her remains meant that a lot of her running and standing rigging survived when the ship was excavated, along with some of the ropes, blocks, sheaves, and deadeyes. When she was first built, observers remarked how well she performed under sail, and in 1513 Sir Edward Howard praised her as "the flower of all ships that ever sailed." Although other ships entered service, she remained Henry VIII's favorite ship, with the possible exception of the *Henri Grace à Dieu*. That day in 1545 when she sailed out to do battle with the French, she may have been more than three decades old, but the *Mary Rose* would have made a brave spectacle, with flags flying from her mastheads and her guns run out. Then, before the horrified gaze of the king and his courtiers, the great ship was gone, taking her captain and nearly all of her seven hundred crewmen with her. It would have been little consolation to Henry VIII had he known that more than four and a half centuries later the *Mary Rose* would become a lasting reminder of his reign, a ghostly remnant of a fleet that had long since sailed into history.

4

The Great Rivals

Scotland's Renaissance King

In the early sixteenth century Scotland might have been one of the proudest and most fiercely independent nations in Europe, but it was hardly the richest. It was therefore an extremely unlikely participant in the great race, but that didn't seem to deter the Scots or their young king, James IV. The story began late in the evening of November 30, 1512, which, appropriately enough, was the day dedicated to St. Andrew, patron saint of Scotland. It was a grim, blustery night, and a full gale was howling its way into the Firth of Forth. An armed merchant ship was trying to anchor off the port of Leith, her French flag flapping wildly at her masthead. She was carrying Charles de Tocque, the seigneur de la Mothe, French ambassador to the court of James IV. The ambassador ordered ten guns fired to announce his arrival, a standard diplomatic gesture of the time. Unfortunately, nobody told the citizens of Edinburgh, two miles to the south, who thought they were being attacked, and a brief flurry of panic swept through the Scottish capital. The gesture was also a little premature, as the ship then began to drag her anchors.

It was clear that nobody was going to disembark. The French captain had no choice but to recover his anchor and make sail again, heading deeper up the great estuary in search of a more sheltered anchorage. The ship passed the narrows of Queensferry, where today great road and rail bridges span the Forth. Finally they put in to the far more sheltered small roadstead of Blackness, some ten miles west of Leith, on the southern shore of the estuary. The ambassador recognized the Scottish warship *Margaret* in the lee of the small promontory where Blackness Castle stood sentinel over the anchorage. Beyond the *Margaret* was another ship, which towered over both the consort and the castle. He must have asked the Scottish pilot what this mighty new ship was called. The answer would have come back that she was the *Great Michael*, "the greatest scheip that ewer saillit in Ingland or France." Clearly the Scots were mightily proud of their new warship.

This pride was never more evident than on the following day, when King James IV and his court appeared to welcome the new ambassador, and the whole court rowed out to the *Great Michael*. The French ambassador was invited to present his credentials on board the great ship. James IV was out to impress his visitor, even before the man was allowed to step ashore. It worked. He later wrote to Louis XII that the ship "was the mightiest to be found in Christendom." James had a reason for this unexpected display of maritime power. The ambassador wasn't just arriving in Scotland to fulfill his diplomatic duties; he also was carrying a secret treaty, a Franco-Scottish alliance that had already been signed by King Louis. All it needed was the signature of James IV. France was at war with England, and the alliance would guarantee that a Scottish army would march south, pinning down troops who might otherwise be sent to the main theater of war, in Flanders. In return the Scots would receive a valuable war subsidy. One look at the *Great Michael* and the seigneur de la Mothe realized that the Scots would want a lot more from the deal.

The great ship that had so impressed the French ambassador was the perfect symbol to characterize James IV and his reign. It was powerful, impressive, and thoroughly modern, and it completely failed to live up to the high expectations everyone had of it. Like the warship he commissioned, James was a monarch who broke the mold

Model of the Michael

in Scotland, a true Renaissance prince who pointed the way toward a golden future for his small country. In the end he died in a muddy, blood-soaked field just two years after the meeting with la Mothe, a victim of his own political ambition. Given his childhood, it was amazing that James achieved anything at all. He was born in 1473, a time of trouble in Scotland, where the king and his nobles were at each other's throats. He was only fifteen when his father was killed in battle on the field of Sauchieburn in 1488. Worse, Prince James had been fighting on the side of the rebels. As penance for his fratricide he wore a heavy iron cilice around his waist every Lent until the day he died, adding extra weight to it as the years went on.

Surprisingly, he turned out to be exactly the kind of king Scotland needed. He secured his hold on the throne by crushing another

James IV of Scotland and his Tudor wife, Margaret

rebellion, and then subdued the wily Highland chieftain John Macdonald, Earl of Ross, known as the Lord of the Isles. However, James's real achievements were measured in his ability to drag Scotland into the modern age. James had a fascination for science, invention, military technologies, and anything that smacked of progress. He established a gun foundry in Edinburgh Castle, created a college of surgeons, founded two universities, and even encouraged the establishment of Scotland's first printing press. He was an extremely intelligent, cultured man, and it was claimed that he was fluent in several languages; yet he also promoted the publication of literature in the old Scots tongue.

If James had contented himself with improving the lot of Scotland, he would have been seen as one of the greatest monarchs of his day. However, his foreign policies were every bit as aggressive as his domestic ones. Scotland didn't have many decisions to make in this sphere. Everything was dominated by England, its big, hectoring neighbor to the south. A Scottish monarch could either try to live in peace with England or pursue a more aggressive stance, seeking ways to undermine England's position. For a century the Scottish kings had vacillated between the two policies, although their long-running struggle against the Scottish nobility meant that military action against England was a rarity. Having subdued the nobles, James was free to meddle.

The English had just emerged from a bruising civil war—the Wars of the Roses, an intermittent struggle for the crown that had dragged on for more than thirty years. The defeat and death of the maligned hunchback Richard III, at the Battle of Bosworth (1485) left Henry Tudor as the last man standing—the sole remaining claimant to the English throne. As Henry VIII he set about rebuilding his shattered kingdom and protecting himself against any attempt to reignite the old conflict. The only real threat came from Perkin Warbeck, who claimed to be Richard, Duke of York, the sole surviving son of Henry IV of England. The real Richard had almost certainly been killed—one of the two young princes murdered in the Tower of London in 1483. However, Warbeck attracted supporters, including Edward IV's sister Margaret of Burgundy. Another backer was James IV. By offering support to Warbeck, the Scottish king was effectively declaring war against Henry Tudor. This didn't seem to worry the young Scottish king.

In fact, in September 1496 James decided to invade Tudor England on Warbeck's behalf. Workmen were sent ahead to prepare the roads for James's artillery, and as their guns trundled southward, the rest of the Scottish host gathered a few miles inside the border. Finally, on September 20, James's army crossed the River Tweed into England, where according to the English propagandist Polydore Vergil his men "laid waste the fields, pillaged and then burnt the houses and villages." While this might have been lucrative, it hardly constituted an invasion. He was really biding his time, playing havoc in the English border county of Northumberland while Perkin Warbeck and his followers tried to drum up enthusiasm for a rebellion. The Northumbrians were too canny for that, and eventually Warbeck gave up the attempt and returned to Scotland.

As for James, he spent his time playing with his new artillery train, besieging and destroying an English castle a day for five days. Then, when news reached him that an English army was marching north to meet him, he slipped back over the border. It was one of the shortest invasions in history—more of a lucrative plundering raid than anything else. However, the Spanish ambassador, Don Pedro del Ayla, was impressed by James's performance, writing: "I have seen him often undertake most dangerous things in the last war. I sometimes clung to his skirts, and succeeded in keeping him back. On such occasions he does not take the least care of himself." This rashness might have been noble and chivalric, but it also was extremely foolhardy, and betrayed a sort of romantic attitude toward warfare that would cost Scotland dearly.

Henry VII's response to the invasion was to declare war on the Scots, and Parliament duly set aside £120,000 as a war kitty. The imbalance between Scotland and England at the time becomes a little clearer when we note that this was twenty times the entire annual revenue available to James IV. It included money set aside to equip the Tudor fleet: Henry's flagship, the *Regent*, together with two newly built warships, the *Sweepstake* and the *Mary Fortune*. These warships were to be supported by twenty armed merchantmen, and another twenty-six merchant ships would be used as transports. This armada would transport an English army to Edinburgh, where Henry planned to besiege and destroy the Scottish capital. James had badly underestimated Henry's resolve and was well aware that he lacked the ships and the men to do little more than to delay this English juggernaut. He was left with only one option.

He withdrew his support of Perkin Warbeck and kept him under what amounted to house arrest. James then convinced the Spanish ambassador to act as a peace envoy, and soon secret diplomatic letters began to fly between Edinburgh and London. Don Pedro's counterpart in London was convinced that James's abandonment of Warbeck had removed the sole reason for war. However, he reckoned without James's rashness. While these delicate negotiations were taking place, James laid plans for a preemptive invasion of northern England. Once again his great guns were trundled south toward the border, and in August they began bombarding the powerful English castle of Norham, on the southern bank of the River Tweed.

As a diversion James sent Perkin Warbeck to Waterford in Ireland, where once again the claimant to the English throne tried to raise an army. He was just as unsuccessful as he had been in Northumberland, but at least this time he was no longer James's responsibility. As soon as Warbeck landed on Irish soil, James's ship the *Cuckoo* returned to Scotland, leaving their passenger to fend for himself. Warbeck then tried his hand in Cornwall, but once again nobody wanted to join his cause. Finally, on October 5 he was captured by Henry's soldiers, and he was dragged back to the Tower of London in chains. The unfortunate Perkin Warbeck would remain there until he was hanged two years later.

Back in Scotland the siege of Norham was broken off when James ran out of money to pay his laborers, and he had to send his guns back to Edinburgh. After some border skirmishing the rest of the army followed in their wake, and the war petered out. Meanwhile, a summer of nearly constant contrary winds had kept Henry's armada in port, while the threat posed by Warbeck encouraged him to keep his troops close to home. As the eminent Scottish historian Ian Arthurson put it, "the war that Henry VII planned collapsed under its own weight." With his treasury drained, Henry decided to reopen the abandoned peace talks.

First a seven-month truce was arranged, and James sent Don Pedro south again to broker a new peace deal. The result was the optimistically titled Treaty of Perpetual Peace, signed in 1502. To seal the agreement Henry VII sent his daughter Margaret Tudor north to Scotland, and in August 1503 she married King James in a lavish ceremony in Edinburgh's Holyrood Abbey. James must have been delighted that his extremely risky strategy had paid off so handsomely. Unfortunately, this "perpetual peace" would only last a decade. From the moment the French ambassador set foot on board the deck of the *Great Michael*, James IV and his people would be committed to a new war with England. This time James wouldn't be so lucky.

The "Great Shippe"

During the decade of perpetual peace, King James IV of Scotland was able to indulge in his new obsession—the creation of a Scottish navy.

The ease with which Henry VII had so cavalierly planned a landing near Edinburgh obviously rankled, and in August 1506 James wrote to Louis XII of France, telling him that building a fleet was a project he was set on realizing. If he was prepared to boast of his plans to the French king, then he certainly meant what he said. The Scots had a small merchant fleet, but given Scotland's geographical position, its merchants relied heavily on their ships to compete in the marketplaces of Europe. There was no royal fleet. In time of war the king was forced to hire well-armed merchantmen to patrol his home waters and to hunt down privateers or pirates. James planned to change all that.

Part of the impetus might have been the way his rival Henry VII had embraced the same project. When Henry Tudor seized power in 1485 he inherited a small royal fleet of ten warships, and although several of these were considered unfit for service and were sold, those that remained formed the basis of the Tudor Navy Royal. As we shall see later, Henry, his son, and his granddaughter would build on this to create a powerful fleet. Although James lacked the resources available to Henry, he at least had a group of experienced sea captains—men such as Sir Andrew Wood of Largo, William Merrymouth of Leith, and the Barton family of Fife, father John and sons Andrew, Robert, and John. James had already used a small flotilla of ships to crush the power of the Lord of the Isles during the early 1490s. Most of these were hired vessels, but at least one vessel, the *Christopher*, was bought by James and operated as a royal warship. She would be the first of several.

By 1502 he had the beginnings of a small fleet. Workmen were fitting out the hired ships *Eagle*, *Douglas*, and *Towaich* in Leith that summer, ready for a voyage to Denmark, where James hoped to support his ally King Hans I of Denmark against Swedish and Norwegian rebels. Another small royal warship, the *Trinity*, was already operating in Danish waters. Particularly noticeable was that James's ships were operating on Scotland's eastern coast, rather than in the west. Evidently he thought the Lords of the Isles was no longer a threat, allowing him to pool all his maritime resources on the other side of the country. Leith was the port of Edinburgh, and his small fleet gathered there that summer, ready for the voyage across the North Sea. It was ludicrous to think that the Scots could send an expeditionary force to participate in a European conflict, but James was determined to punch above his weight.

In the end the expedition proved a fiasco. About two thousand rather reluctant Scottish troops were mustered on Leith Sands, then transported to Norway, where they helped the Danes storm a rebel-held castle, an action the Norwegians claimed cost the lives of hundreds of the poorly trained Scottish foot soldiers. The small army was reembarked and shipped home within two months of leaving Scotland. Even James was forced to admit that his expeditionary force "achieved less than it should have done and returned sooner than was expected." Not only had the Danish fiasco cost the Scottish treasury a small fortune, but also, as one chronicler put it, it didn't return home "with greit honour."

James blamed his merchant captains, many of whom were understandably reluctant to risk their ships in a foreign war. It was clear that he couldn't rely exclusively on hired ships. He needed his own navy, with ships crewed by his own men. The trouble was, Scottish shipbuilders might have the experience to build armed merchant ships, but they knew little or nothing about constructing purpose-built warships. James got around this by hiring shipbuilders from outside his kingdom. Clearly Henry VII wasn't going to help him, so James's agents approached the French. On November 20, 1502, the French royal shipwright Jean Lorans arrived in Leith and was given his own offices, along with an advance on his first monthly wage of ten French crowns. That cold November day in Leith marked the birth of James IV's Scottish navy.

The next few months saw a frenzy of activity. The Scottish ship captain John Barton escorted Jean Lorans to Cambuskeneth Woods near Stirling, where timber was selected and cut under the Frenchman's supervision. In May he was joined by a second French shipwright, Jenne Diew, who led an expedition into the remote Scottish Highlands in search of good ship timber, this time escorted by John Barton's son Robert. Despite all this, the shipwrights couldn't find enough of the good hard timber—primarily oak—that they needed to build the keels and frames of these new warships. Consequently James was forced to import timber from France—keel timbers that Jenne Diew selected. When the timber-laden ship arrived, it brought a third French shipwright, Jacques Terrell, who had already procured keel timbers from a forest near Dieppe, along with hundreds of oak planks. More timber was shipped in from Scandinavia. Scotland's first proper warship was a real international venture.

On May 26, 1503, a bonus was paid to the sailors "that brocht hame the keill of the Kingis schip," and work began immediately on the construction of the *Margaret*, the first ship of James's new fleet. She was built at Leith, in a dock James had specially built for the task. Work progressed smoothly, and she was taken off the stocks in the dry dock in January 1505. The occasion was marked by celebrations presided over by James, who wore the ceremonial gold whistle and chain of an admiral around his neck. Although he had no intention of venturing farther afield than the entrance to the Firth of Forth, he wanted to demonstrate his commitment to all things nautical. As the new warship was named after the king's young English wife, Queen Margaret would almost certainly have been given the honor of naming her.

However, this was only part of the job. It took the best part of another year to fit her out—the masts were fitted that winter, and it wasn't until June 1506 that she was finally floated out of the dock into Leith Roads and commissioned into service. The momentous event was celebrated by yet more fanfare and feasting. This was just two months before James wrote his letter to Louis of France. When James wrote, it was in the full throes of his naval obsession. The *Margaret* was a four-masted carrack—the latest word in warship design—and would have displaced about six hundred tons. This made her pretty similar in size and design to the English warship *Mary Rose*, which was built three years later. The *Margaret* would have been armed with a mixture of French guns and weapons produced in James's own foundry in Edinburgh Castle. Although there is no record of her armament, we know from other contemporary French and English warships of similar size that she would have carried a mixture of powerful large guns and a host of smaller close-range antipersonnel weapons.

Although at about £30,000 the *Margaret* had cost James almost a third of his annual national income, James was prepared to build another, much grander ship. While the *Margaret* was the equivalent of the best modern warships afloat, James wanted to go one stage farther. He wanted a warship that would intimidate his

English rivals and impress his potential allies in the rest of Europe. However, not only would this stretch the royal budget to its limits, but there also were significant logistical hurdles to overcome. For a start, the *Margaret* could only just clear the sandbanks off the small river mouth that constituted Leith Harbor. A larger ship would be unable to reach the open sea. Consequently James began casting around for another harbor, one where he could build his new ship and float her without difficulty. He also needed a safe haven to moor his ships in winter.

In May 1504 James and his shipwrights were rowed up the Forth, scouting out potential sites for a deepwater shipbuilding site. They settled on a small natural inlet a mile or so up the coast, and appropriately enough the site was christened the New Haven of Leith. Work began immediately on construction of a new dockyard, even larger than the one at Leith. While the Scots provided the labor, the project was supervised by specialists from France, Flanders, and Spain. A small village sprang up to service the new dockyard, and in 1507 a chapel was built to serve the village. By the time the *Margaret* was floated in Leith, the Newhaven dockyard was nearing completion, and so the men and supplies from Leith were sent up the coast to help finish the job.

Meanwhile, James was thinking ahead. Both Leith and Newhaven were vulnerable to attack, but just a few miles up the Forth, at Queensferry, the estuary was less than a mile wide. Even more important, the small island of Inch Garvie sat in the middle of the narrows, and the fort and gun battery James had built there protected the upper waters of the Firth of Forth from attack. He needed a safe anchorage for his growing fleet, somewhere west of Inch Garvie. After another reconnaissance the king and his advisers settled on the Pool of Airth, another deepwater anchorage where the Firth of Forth narrows to less than a mile and becomes the River Forth. Today the Kincardine Bridge spans the river near the spot where James's great ships once lay at anchor. Work must have begun immediately, because the royal accounts of October 1506 describe the dockyard there as having been completed, and ready for the repair or fitting out of the king's ships.

In August 1506—just two months after the *Margaret* took to the water—the Franco-Scottish trader James Wilson of Dieppe arrived at Newhaven with "plankis and treis to the gret schip." For the next five years Newhaven would be a bustling hive of activity as more ships arrived carrying timber imported from France, Norway, and Denmark, while barges ferried locally cut wood culled from forests in Fife, Perthshire, and even the Highlands. The shipbuilders certainly needed all the stout timber they could get. The vessel they were building would be the largest and most powerful sailing ship of war ever seen in the British Isles—a floating fortress that made the *Margaret* look tiny by comparison. King James named her the *Michael*, although inevitably she was soon referred to as the *Great Michael*.

We don't know exactly how big the *Michael* was, as our only two sources are a late-sixteenth-century historian of dubious accuracy and a long-lost garden. The first was the Scottish chronicler Robert Lindsay of Pitscottie, whose *Historie of Scotland* was written in the 1570s. Norman MacDougall, who wrote the definitive biography of James IV, said of Pitscottie's chronicle that it "is as quotable as it is generally unreliable." He went on to say that "one is at first tempted to dismiss Pitscottie's lengthy description of what he sees as one of the glories of the reign." However, the sixteenth-century historian was the only man to cover a crucial fact missed in the contemporary accounts—the size of the "great scheip callit the greit Michell." He's all we have to go on. According to his *Historie* the Michael was 12 score feet long, and 35 feet broad between her walls, which were each 10 feet thick. That gives her an overall length of 240 feet and a 35-foot beam.

These dimensions seem excessive. The *Mary Rose*, which was roughly the same size as James IV's earlier ship the *Margaret*, had a keel length of 105 feet and a 38-foot beam. Even if we add the extra feet to make up her length from stem to stern, that takes her to only 134 feet, or 147 feet if we add the overhang of her forecastle. As she is a surviving ship of the period, we can pretty much accept that her proportions were similar to other "new" warships of her time, such as the larger *Michael*. As the *Mary Rose* had a length-to-breadth ratio at her waterline of $3^1/_3:1$, this makes the dimensions given by Pitscottie more than a little suspect. If we take his length to represent the overall size of the *Great Michael*, that would give her a waterline length of about 200 feet and a length-to-bream ratio of about $5^2/_3$:1. As the *Mary Rose* dimensions tie in nicely with other historic shipwrecks of the period, and with archival and pictorial evidence, we can see that Pitscottie was almost certainly wide of the mark.

That's where the lost garden comes in. Almost as if he expected his readers to be somewhat incredulous, he added a statement as corroborative evidence. "If any man believes that this description of the ship be not accurate as we have written, let him pass to the gate of Tullibardine, and there remains the same, for he will see the length and breadth of her planted with hawthorn again, by the wrights that helped to make her." Amazingly enough, this extraordinary statement may bear up under scrutiny. Tullibardine is a tiny hamlet in Perthshire, about fifteen miles due north of James IV's anchorage at the Pool of Airth. There was a small castle there, but by the start of the nineteenth century it had been demolished, its stones used to construct farm buildings in the area. However, the *Statistical Account for Scotland* written in 1837 claimed that the ship-shaped sunken garden of the castle remained, although it had become an overgrown pond. Only three of the hawthorn trees survived. Unfortunately, no trace of the garden remains today, although the feature possibly showed up on an aerial photograph taken by staff of the University of St. Andrews. Problems interpreting this kind of evidence are manifest.

As nobody has gone to the time and expense of excavating or running a geophysics survey of this lost garden, or because trying to guess the size of a patch of discolored soil from the air is virtually impossible, we have no real way of substantiating Pitscottie's claim. For all we know, the feature could well be the "12 score feet" he claimed as being the length of King James's warship. We also don't know if the garden was meant to be an accurate full-scale representation of the ship or merely a ship-shaped horticultural curiosity. Even more worrying, because Pitscottie makes such a point of mentioning the Tullibardine garden, we're left with the uneasy suspicion that his detailed measurements for the *Michael* were derived solely from a collection of hawthorn trees planted some fifteen miles from the nearest saltwater.

Whatever the real size of the *Michael*, she was big enough to impress the French ambassador. This favorable impression wasn't just because she was so big. He also would have noted her modern armament. As we've already seen, this was an age when the new science of gunfounding was really coming into its own, and for the first time ship designers were building warships with artillery in mind. The *Michael*, produced by one of Europe's secondary powers, was a truly groundbreaking ship—one of the first gun-armed warships, and certainly the largest custom-built gun-armed warship when she first entered service in 1512. Unlike earlier warships that were converted to accommodate a handful of artillery pieces, the inclusion of her main armament of heavy guns was an essential design feature. She represented the first step on that long road toward the floating gun battery that was the ship of the line, the ultimate sailing ship of war.

Pitscottie was a little more accurate when he spoke about the guns. He claimed that the *Michael* carried twelve large bronze muzzle-loading pieces on each side, as well as three large basilisks—one forward and two aft. These basilisks—just about the largest guns of their day—were almost certainly the "iii great gunnys" cast by James's master gunfounder, Robert Borthwick. They were transported from Edinburgh Castle to Newhaven in August 1512, to be mounted in the "great schip." The size of the *Michael*'s armament—twenty-seven large guns—ties in with that of another large ship built in England the following year, so Pitscottie's figures are entirely reasonable. While some have dismissed his figure of three hundred guns in total as ridiculously far-fetched, it is probably quite accurate. The records of the Tudor navy show that most contemporary lists included all kinds of missile weapons in the armament total, including crossbows, longbows, handguns, close-range swivel guns, and hailshot pieces—gunpowder weapons that were about the size of a World War II bazooka and packed with scrap metal and sharp stones.

Pitscottie was also right when he said that the *Michael* had a crew of 300 men. Surviving accounts list them by name and verify Pitscottie's claim. Even Pitscottie's figure of 120 gunners is probably right, as this total would include all those trained to fire the big guns and swivel pieces, rather than all those who fired the smaller weapons. The only crew members who weren't listed by name in the Scottish naval accounts for the summer of 1513 were the cooks.

It would be nice to think that as the ship was bound for France the Scots expected to replace these anonymous souls with exotic French chefs when they arrived, but the truth was probably far less exciting. They were probably anonymous because they were considered supernumeraries—the staff of the admiral and his staff, rather than full members of the ship's company.

The *Michael* took the best part of five years to build, from August 1506, when her timbers arrived, until October 12, 1511, when she was floated clear of her dry dock in Newhaven. James IV was there to watch the great event, while three trumpeters sounded a fanfare. It took nearly a year to fit her out. On February 18, 1512, she was towed to an anchorage off Leith, and three days later James IV arrived to dine aboard her. A few weeks later he went aboard her again, this time for a test of her sailing capabilities—a short voyage up the Firth of Forth to Queensferry. She was then taken up the estuary to the Pool of Airth, where her fitting out was completed, and by August she was back down in Newhaven to collect her armament of light guns. Once again James dined aboard her, her cabin being decorated by tapestries borrowed from his hunting lodge of Falkland Palace for the occasion. Her great guns arrived in early August, and they must have taken the best part of a month to mount and provision.

Finally, in September 1512, after eleven months of fitting out, the workmen clambered ashore. The *Michael* was now ready for service, and she was sailed up the Firth of Forth to join the *Margaret*, which lay at anchor off Blackness. The whole business had taken six years and had been almost prohibitively expensive for such a relatively poor country. Pitscottie claimed that the *Michael* had cost £30,000 in Scottish money to build, and that didn't take into account the building of shipyards and repair dockyards, or the day-to-day running costs of the vessel. As the royal income for 1512–13 was estimated at about £30,000 to £40,000 pounds Scots, this represented Scotland's entire national income for a year. The modern-day equivalent would be if Mexico had decided to build a fully equipped nuclear-powered supercarrier, boasting the latest stealth technology. It was little wonder that the French ambassador was impressed.

However, the political situation changed very subtly during the six years the *Michael* grew from a pile of timbers into a leviathan.

Henry VIII

On April 21, 1509, Henry VII of England was at his palace at Richmond when he suddenly fell ill. The court physicians were called to the royal bedside, but they were unable to help, and within twenty-four hours the English king was dead. Popular legend suggests that he died of a broken heart after his wife, Elizabeth, died in childbirth, just a year after his eldest son, Arthur, died of tuberculosis. Of course, sending his daughter north to marry James IV that same year would have done little to improve the king's constitution. While his body was prepared for its last journey to Westminster Abbey, the king's crown was presented to his surviving son, Henry Tudor, Prince of Wales. Within two months this robust seventeen-year-old would be crowned Henry VIII, King of England, "by the Grace of God." As the man charged with healing England after half a century of bloody civil war, his father had always put the economic good of his kingdom above military glory. His son would have no such qualms, and James IV could hardly have chosen a more dangerous rival for his games of international brinkmanship.

The Tudor Response

In July 1511 a northeasterly gale battered the coast of Kent, and the wind would have howled in the rigging of the little gaggle of ships sheltering in the lee of the treacherous Goodwin Sands. This anchorage off the little towns of Deal and Ramsgate in the southeastern corner of England provided a relatively safe haven. However, for mariners farther out to sea the Goodwins were a shallow, wave-lashed menace, a ten-mile strip of hidden sandbars that had long held the unenviable reputation of being a sailors' graveyard. Even today, in this age of satellite navigation and electronic light beacons, the weathered bones of wrecked ships still poke above the sands at low tide, bearing testimony to the dangers lurking beneath the surface of the gray sea.

Among the ships riding uneasily in the stormy swells of Deal were two Tudor warships: the 140-ton *Barbara* and her smaller consort, the *Mary of Barking*. Both were armed merchantmen from London, temporarily hired and crewed by order of the young English king. They were commanded by Sir Edward Howard, the same man who would go on to lead his fleet into action against the French the following year. In the early summer of 1511 Henry VIII appointed Sir Edward as his admiral and ordered him to hire two wafters (convoy escorts) to protect a group of ships belonging to the English Merchant Adventurers bound for Zeeland (now the southern Netherlands). The convoy was created as a response to the threat posed by a pirate who was known to have been operating in the waters where the North Sea turns into the English Channel. The pirate was none other than James IV's own admiral, Sir Andrew Barton.

Of course, Sir Andrew would never think of himself as a pirate, only as a privateer, operating under a letter of reprisal issued by the Scottish king. It all stemmed from an incident off the Flemish port of Sluys in the 1470s, when a Scottish merchant ship belonging to Andrew's father, John Barton, was captured and plundered by Portuguese pirates. Consequently, King James III issued John a letter of reprisal that allowed him to seek out and attack Portuguese ships for reparations. This was a form of letter of marque, the privateering contract between a government and a captain that allowed him to legally prey on enemy shipping in wartime. In return, the issuing government earned a percentage of the plunder. In July 1507 James IV reissued this letter of reprisal to John's three sons—Robert, John (the younger), and Andrew. The fact that the Portuguese attack happened thirty years earlier didn't seem to matter.

In 1508 Robert Barton captured a Portuguese ship off the Flemish coast but was arrested on a charge of piracy when he took his prize into the port of Veere in Zeeland. Only the intervention of James IV's diplomats saved the Scottish privateer from the gallows. The following year his brother John seized another Portuguese ship, whose cargo included goods being transported for an English merchant. This caused an outcry in London, and a hearing was held in Edinburgh that December, when it was decided to defer any decision pending a fuller investigation. It seemed that the Bartons weren't too particular about where their plunder came from. In June 1510 James IV suspended the letters of reprisal, and while the other Bartons knuckled down and followed the letter of the law, Sir Andrew charted his own course.

James IV's expedition in support of King Hans I brought Sir Andrew into contact with the Danish king, and in late 1509, when the Bartons' lawyers were representing them to the Scottish Lords of Council in Edinburgh, Andrew was signing a fresh privateering agreement. In return for a Danish privateering license, the Bartons would use their own ships to attack the shipping of the Hanseatic League. In its heyday this German trading league was the superpower of the Baltic, but by the early sixteenth century its power was declining rapidly, and King Hans wanted to scoop up what he could of its territories. Sir Andrew pursued the ships operating from the Hanseatic port of Lübeck with such zeal that in late 1510 the Emperor Maximilian wrote to James IV to complain that the economy of the port was being jeopardized by Barton's depredations.

Andrew Barton returned to Scotland, but in early 1511 King Hans asked for his help again, as his war with the Hanseatic League was reaching a climax. The timing was perfect. In March 1511 the Lords of Council had reconvened, and this time they had even more evidence against the Bartons. They had proof that a French ship bound for Antwerp had been captured by Sir Andrew off the coast of Zeeland. As a favorite of the king, he would have been forewarned that he might be arrested, so he immediately set sail for Copenhagen in the family privateering ship *Lion*. Once there he did little to help the Danish cause, but set off on his own cruise. Worse still, he took one of Hans's ships with him—the small sixty-ton Scottish ship *Jennet of Purwyn*, which King James had recently presented to his Danish ally. As Sir Andrew wasn't carrying a valid letter of reprisal or a letter of marque, he was technically a pirate. By late July he was cruising off the mouth of the Thames estuary, unaware that Sir Edward Howard was lying in wait for him.

When the storm passed, Sir Edward ordered his two ships to put to sea. He was probably returning form his "waysting" mission when he was forced to put in to the shelter of Deal. He now planned to take advantage of the second part of his commission: to protect his charges from "the rovers of the see." Given the circumstances, it seems likely that the English admiral had some knowledge of his Scottish rival's plans. The sea battle that followed was later described in Edward Hall's *Chronicle*, published in 1542, and by the Scottish chronicler Bishop John Lesley, whose account was published in 1578. This means that like Pitscottie, neither historian really knew what happened, but rather based their accounts on versions that had been passed down to them. There also was a fair bit of national bias involved. Bishop Lesley claimed that Barton was attacked illegally while sailing peaceably home to Scotland. By contrast, Edward Hall claims that the attack on Barton was justified, as he was a pirate.

As even the Scottish Lords of Council had deemed that Sir Andrew Barton had been acting illegally, Sir Edward's actions were probably justified. In any case, Hall's account is generally more believable. In his version of events the two English ships became separated amid the dirty weather soon after leaving the anchorage, and the *Barbara* was on its own when her crew spotted the *Lion* and the *Jennet of Purwyn*. The *Barbara* gave chase and eventually overhauled the *Lion*. In Hall's words, "There was a sore battle—the Englishmen were fierce, and the Scots defended them[selves] manfully, and Andrew ever blew his whistle to encourage his men." He continued, "Yet, for all that, the Lord Howard and his men by clean strength entered the main deck. Then the Englishmen entered on all sides, and the Scots fought sore on the hatches, but in conclusion Andrew was taken, and was so sore wounded that he died there."

This account is interesting as it places Sir Edward's brother Lord Thomas Howard in charge of the *Barbara*. The handful of Scots who survived the fight were taken prisoner, and a prize crew took control of the *Lion*. By that stage Sir Edward had appeared on the scene in the *Mary of Barking*, and he quickly overhauled the second Scottish ship. According to Hall, Sir Edward "fiercely assailed him, and the Scots as hardy and well-stomached men them[selves] defended." The Scots were heavily outnumbered, and the result was never in doubt, "the Lord Admiral so encouraged his men that they entered the bark and slew many and took all the other." The English victory was complete.

Although the Scottish version didn't argue about the outcome, they blamed English duplicity and numbers for their defeat. Sir Walter Scott took this line one stage farther when he claimed, "the noble brothers showed no ensign of war but put up a willow wand on their mast, as being the emblem of a trading vessel, but when the Scotsmen attempted to bring them to, the English then cut their flags and pennants and fired a broadside from their ordinance." This smacks a little of sour grapes, as judging by his reputation Sir Andrew Barton was no stranger to trickery. Sir Walter even put words into Barton's mouth: "Fight on my brave hearts. . . . I am a little wounded but not slain . . . meantime stand fast by St Andrews Cross" (the Scottish flag). Scott continued, "He encouraged his men with his whistle, while the breath of life remained. At length the whistle was heard no longer, and the Howards boarding the Scottish vessel, found her daring captain was dead." This was all good romantic stuff, but the truth was probably a lot less noble, and a lot bloodier.

A few days later, on August 2, the two Scottish prizes were towed into Blackwall on the River Thames, just below London. The news must have reached Henry VIII that evening, while the Scottish ambassador must have learned of Sir Andrew Barton's fate soon afterward. Of course, the sea battle immediately erupted into a full-scale diplomatic incident. James IV was furious that his favorite sea captain had been slain and that Scottish ships had been attacked in peacetime. He immediately sent a herald south to demand an apology, and financial recompense for the Bartons. Hall went as far as to claim that James even threatened to revoke the Treaty of Perpetual Peace, and demanded that the Howard brothers be brought north to stand trial. This was nonsense, as James knew perfectly well that Barton had been operating outside the law. For his part Henry stood by his own captains and sent the Scottish herald home with nothing to show for his efforts except the release of the Scottish prisoners. The surviving Barton brothers must have taken consolation the following year when news reached them that Sir Edward Howard had not only been killed, but also his French rival had kept his heart as a souvenir.

The affair was over, but the resentment it caused in Scotland might well have contributed to James's willingness to consider a military alliance with England's greatest enemy, an alliance that was proposed by the French ambassador to Scotland within a year of Barton's death. Another result of the battle was that it deprived James of his closest naval adviser. While all the Bartons helped James build up his navy, it is almost certain that Sir Andrew helped advise the Scottish king on the design of the *Michael*. His fighting experience made sure she was purpose-built for the new kind of naval warfare that involved artillery rather than swords and pikes. Without Sir Andrew at his side James would struggle to find a fitting way to use his new warships to best advantage. The battle between Howard and Barton also demonstrated that Henry VIII was taking a tougher maritime stance than his father. He decided that he needed to create his own powerful fleet, and above all he needed to counter the threat posed by the *Michael* with a great ship of his own.

The *Great Harry*

Exactly when Henry VIII decided to build a warship even bigger and better than James IV's *Michael* was never recorded. However, the decision was made sometime during the year following the death of Sir Andrew Barton. Very possibly Henry made up his mind soon after the English ambassador in Scotland reported that James IV's great warship had been launched and was being fitted out. The timing suggests that Henry's main motive for commissioning his own great warship was jealousy—he wanted to prove that anything Scotland could do, England could do better. He also planned to use English shipwrights rather than rely on foreign experts. Certainly by the summer of 1512 the great project was already well under way.

We don't know who Henry's master shipwright was, although William Crane became what today would be called the project manager, while his colleague William Bond balanced the books. Their first problem was gathering the materials together. In all, some 1,752 tons of timber would be needed, and all this had to be brought to the shipyard in Woolwich, a few miles down the River Thames from London and just past Blackwall, where Sir Thomas Howard brought his Scottish prizes the year before. Woolwich had been chosen because it was sheltered from the predominant northeasterly winds by the woods of Barking and Beckton on the northern bank of the river and by Bostal Hill to the west. It also lay above a six-mile loop in the river where Barking Creek flowed into the Thames and offered some protection against the tidal surges that plagued Erith and Dartford farther downriver.

If we assume that the keel of the new ship was laid in June or July 1512—a keel built from sixteen tons of English oak—then work must have progressed at an unusually rapid pace. Evidently part of the reason for building her on the Thames rather than in Portsmouth was that the king was better placed to chart her day-to-day progress. Hundreds of shipwrights, carpenters, caulkers, and ironworkers were hired and brought to the new dockyard site, where they were housed and fed at the king's expense. Similarly, a long storehouse was built, along with an iron foundry and a blacksmith's workshop. Workmen also were needed to unload the ships that brought timber and other supplies to the site, along with cooks, stable hands, farriers, errand boys, and night watchmen. In effect Henry VIII created a shipbuilding village on the banks of the Thames, much as James IV had done in Newhaven. Both existed for the sole purpose of build-ing the largest warship in Europe.

Several accounts survive that suggest the effort put into her construction. A total of 3,739 tons of timber were used, of which just over half didn't cost the Tudor exchequer a penny, as it was donated to the king by benefactors as part of various semifeudal dues, or as gifts designed to curry favor with Henry VIII. Still, the 56 tons of iron, almost 8,000 pounds of oakum (used for caulking the hull), and 1,711 pounds of flax all cost money, and the total bill for build-ing the *Henri Grace à Dieu* came to some £8,708—the equivalent of £40,000 Scots, or 25 percent more than the cost of building the *Michael*. Even more impressively, this total also included the cost of building three small galleys, which had been ordered at the same time. Given that the Tudor ship was significantly larger than her Scottish counterpart, and that the work was completed in a third of the time, we can see that William Bond and William Crane earned their pay. Part of this good value stemmed from Henry's emphasis on getting value for money. For instance, several Tudor contracts of the period included strict penalty clauses, which severely penalized contractors who didn't supply the goods on time.

We really don't know much about the appearance of the *Henri Grace à Dieu* before she was refitted in the 1530s. We have no mea-surements for her and have to work out her dimensions based on her tonnage. But the weight of a ship was rarely calculated in a methodical way in the early sixteenth century, so even this involves a certain amount of blind faith and guesswork. In the Tudor navy lists, all ships were recorded in tons burden—the theo-retical amount of cargo a ship could carry if it was turned from a warship into a merchantman. This is completely different from the way we measure tonnage today and therefore can only serve as a rough guide to exactly how big the ship was. The practice stemmed from the days when royal warships were hired out as merchantmen, and their capacity was measured in the amount of wine they could carry. A "tun" (cask) of French wine consist-ed of about 252 gallons, which took up 60 cubic feet of space on board the ship. That means that as the *Henri Grace à Dieu* was recorded as being 1,500 tons, she could carry the equivalent of 190,000 bottles of the best claret. It is hardly surprising that in 1720 the Royal Navy adopted a more reliable system, although they still hung on to the term "tonnage."

Maritime historians have come up with a formula to figure out tonnage based on ship size:

$$\text{tonnage} = \text{length} \times \text{breadth} \times \text{depth}/100$$

Even this is open to misinterpretation, because it depends on whether you measure the length of the keel, the ship at the waterline, or the overall length of the ship. Is her depth measured when she's fully loaded with guns, men, and stores, or when she's completely empty? Of course, it gets even harder if you try to work backward—trying to calculate her size from her tonnage. Clearly the whole calculation is little more than a rough guide. Still, we know the dimensions of the *Mary Rose*, and if we accept that the *Henri Grace à Dieu* was built in roughly the same proportions, we can come up with some figures. Based on this calculation, she would have had a waterline length of about 160 feet, a beam of 48 feet, and a depth (from the waterline to her keel) of about 19 feet.

To confuse things a little more, when Henry VIII's flagship was rebuilt in 1539, her tonnage was given as 1,000—a full third less than before. Clearly the hull hadn't shrunk, although her superstructure might have been lowered a little and her hull pierced to carry more guns. However, these modifications wouldn't have influenced the way modern maritime historians calculated her size, which highlights the big flaw in the calculation. Clearly the Tudor navy used its own method, which was far more closely related to internal capacity than to external measurements. Incidentally, if we apply this formula to James IV's 1,000-ton *Michael*, we come up with a waterline length of about 140 feet, a beam of 42 feet, and a draft of 16 feet. Although this doesn't sound like much, that extra 20 feet of deck space would have allowed the English ship to carry significantly more heavy guns.

Just how many more guns is revealed by a detailed storekeeper's record from 1514, the year the *Henri Grace à Dieu* first entered

The Henri Grace à Dieu

service. While the *Michael* was pierced with eight gunports a side, this larger English warship was probably fitted with twelve, giving her an extremely potent broadside. Her main armament consisted of sixteen port pieces of iron; four large bronze guns; and two other "great guns," designed to fire stone rather than iron shot. The bronze guns—two culverins, a bombard, and a curtow—were more than a match for the three basilisks carried on board the *Michael*. Just as impressive was her midsize armament of six bronze falcons and twenty-two breech-loading guns firing stone shot, all of which would have been mounted in her forecastle and sterncastle.

Finally, there were the swivel guns—short-range antipersonnel weapons designed to cut down an enemy boarding party, and which worked like big shotguns. She carried no fewer than 126 of these, the majority being classed as serpentines made from wrought iron, but the total also included three bronze serpentines and a slightly larger iron sling. As if all this weren't enough, the inventory went on to list her smaller weapons—carried by soldiers and designed to be used in a boarding action. A total of 193 hackbuts (a primitive form of handheld firearm) were augmented by 124 bows, complete with boxes filled with arrows, more than 100 javelins, and more than 600 darts, which were hurled onto the enemy decks from fighting platforms high in the masts. If all this didn't stop a determined French or Scottish attack, then the *Henri Grace à Dieu*'s complement of soldiers was also issued pole arms—144 bills and 80 spears. The great Tudor warship was as well armed as the greatest castle in the kingdom.

The same detailed records help us build a better picture of the great ship. She carried four masts—a foremast, a mainmast, a main "mezon" (mizzen), and a bonaventure mast. The inventory listed all the spars, sails, ropes, and rigging that turned these bare poles into the powerhouse of the ship. She also was fitted with a bowsprit, which carried its own small sail. Other details included her four great bower anchors, her main longboat—known as the "grete bote"— and another "cockle bote," which was the Tudor equivalent of the captain's launch. Other letters from the period tell us she was "built loftie," with a large forecastle that resembled a citadel, and a towering sterncastle structure, which might have made her look extremely imposing but would have made her difficult to handle in anything stronger than a light breeze.

Although a German visitor claimed she had "seven tiers, one above the other," it is more likely that she boasted two decks in the forecastle, two or three in the sterncastle, and two more below the upper deck, for a total of six or seven. However, the German might have included a small mezzanine deck built toward the rear of the main gun deck. That was a feature introduced on the *Mary Rose* during her midlife refit in 1536 and may well have been included in the *Henri Grace à Dieu* from the start. It was designed to counter the way the decks loped upward toward the stern—a feature common in all ships of the period, as the deck lines followed the curving lines of her hull. The mezzanine created a lower chamber, which broke the level of the main deck at the stern, creating a small lower chamber, which soon became known as the gun room. This was a sensible way of lowering the position of the guns mounted in the stern so they sat on roughly the same level as the rest of her broadside armament. That helped ensure that the ship's center of gravity was kept as low as possible and may have accounted for the German's seventh deck.

The other striking thing about her was that she was carvel-built, just like the *Mary Rose*. That more than anything proved that she was designed first and foremost to carry heavy guns. After all, you couldn't easily cut gunports in clinker-built hulls. The last substantial clinker-built warship built for Henry VIII's Navy Royal was the *Great Galley*, completed in 1515, a year after the *Henri Grace à Dieu*. However, as she was built as a copy of a largest French galley (or "lanterna"), there was no need to pierce her hull with gunports. However, even she was rebuilt with a smooth carvel hull some eight years later. Like the *Mary Rose* and other near-contemporary warships, Henry's namesake flagship also had a squared-off stern, which not only simplified construction but also allowed the sterncastle structure to form an integral part of the ship. This marked the end of a long shipbuilding tradition where the sterncastle was a separate structure from the hull—a fighting platform that set warships apart from mere merchantmen. In fact, some merchant ships had fighting platforms bolted onto them when they were hired by the navy. Like the *Mary Rose* before her, the *Henri Grace à Dieu* would be a thoroughbred warship.

If we compare contemporary engravings of ships with the remains of the *Mary Rose*, we can see just how far developed this process of specialization had become. The sterncastle of the *Mary Rose* sloped gradually upward from the waist and tapered slightly as it ran aft, in an effort to reduce the top hamper of the ship. This fits in with the depiction of the *Henri Grace à Dieu* in the *Anthony Roll*, a pictorial register of Henry VIII's Navy Royal produced in 1545. It shows the great warship with a sterncastle that slopes gracefully upward toward the stern, where it ends in an elegant but narrow poop deck. The *Anthony Roll* also shows that like its depiction of the other "great ships" or carracks in the Tudor fleet, the forecastle of the *Henri Grace à Dieu* appeared to be higher and more imposing than the sterncastle. In this it seemed to more closely resemble the design of earlier warships such as Henry V's *Grace Dieu*. Somehow the elegant tapering sterncastle looked less important. However, evidence from the *Mary Rose* suggests that this feature was exaggerated in the

Anthony Roll illustrations and that the sterncastle was the dominant feature of the warship's profile.

The name of Henry's new warship was decided on quite late in her construction. At first she was called the *Henry Imperial*, although some records simply called her the *Great Carrack*. Another document, a report sent to the doge of Venice by his ambassador, "describes the carrack which the King is building, of 4,000 butts, the largest ship afloat. Its name is the *Regent*, the same as the other which was burnt." By early 1514 the new name was established as the *Henri Grace à Dieu*, the fourth English warship to be commissioned "By the Grace of God," although this new ship was the first to prefix this standard royal appellation with the name of a living sovereign. Similarly, several men were proposed as the captain of this prestigious new vessel, including Sir William Trevenyan, Edmund Howard, and Sir Robert Morton, but in the end Henry opted for one of his veteran sea captains, a man who would remain in command of the Tudor flagship for a decade.

The *Henri Grace à Dieu* finally entered service on June 13, 1514, less than two years after work on her first began. It is a testimony to the organization of the Tudor state and to the dedication of the king's shipwrights that this second British leviathan was built in a third of the time it took James IV's team to build the *Michael*. The commissioning ceremony in Woolwich was a magnificent affair, and the king, accompanied by his queen, his ministers, and several foreign dignitaries, toured the new ship. The ambassador of the Hapsburg emperor Maximilian I reported back to his master, "We were most honourably received, and conducted by the King through the ship, which has no equal in bulk, and has an incredible array of guns." It is hardly surprising he was impressed, as Henry had lavished his money on the occasion, dressing the ship up with streamers and banners, while more than a hundred little bunting flags were draped between the masts. With a true theatrical flourish Henry finished the proceedings by ordering all her guns fired at once—a convincing demonstration that the *Henri Grace à Dieu* was as deadly as she was impressive.

Her first captain was Master Thomas Spert, an experienced mercantile and naval sea captain from Devon. Before taking up his new appointment he commanded Henry's other new warship, the

Mary Rose, which served as Sir Edward Howard's flagship during his naval campaign against the French off Brittany. Spert had recently bought a fourteenth-century manor house overlooking the Thames at Blackwall, and from its windows his family could see his new command grow from a skeleton into a mighty warship. Spert was also involved in naval administration, and while he commanded the *Henri Grace à Dieu* he also supervised the establishment of Trinity House, a body dedicated to the safety of English mariners and the collection of navigational information. When he retired his command a decade later, he went on to become the clerk controller of the Royal Navy, which meant he was effectively the navy's administrative chief. He held the post until ill health forced him to retire in 1540, and he died the following year.

The ship was crewed by 700 men—260 sailors, 40 gunners, and no fewer than 400 soldiers. The small number of gunners suggests that this was enough to crew the large guns with experienced men, while the myriad of smaller swivel guns probably were crewed by soldiers. Thomas Spert was assisted by his clerk, John Hopton, and by his purser, William Bonython (or Borythan). The *Henri Grace à Dieu* must have made a magnificent sight as it worked its way down the River Thames toward the open sea. However, she had narrowly missed her baptism of fire in a war that had already involved a major sea battle, the blooding of the Scottish *Michael*, and the death of a king. Spert still hoped to take part in the war with France, but by that stage the fighting was slowly coming to an end. Despite plans to include the *Henri Grace à Dieu* in an invasion fleet later that summer, the diplomats managed to broker a peace before Henry's new flagship could fire her guns in anger. The peace also came before the great ships of Scotland and England could face each other in what would have been the ultimate naval duel of the age.

The Flowers of the Forest

By the time Charles de Tocque, the seigneur de la Mothe, met James IV on board the *Michael* in November 1512, three countries were on the brink of war. The French ambassador to the court of James IV had come to talk of a secret alliance rather than to observe the niceties of international protocol. Obviously a lot had happened in the decade since James IV and Henry VII had signed their Treaty of Perpetual Peace. For the first five years the peace worked smoothly enough, with cross-border cooperation in hunting down the bandits known as Border Reivers, and neither king risking upsetting the other through military or diplomatic posturing. However, James still maintained close diplomatic relations with the French, whom the English saw as their natural enemy. The Scots saw this French connection as vital for trade, and as a useful gambit on the international stage. The English simply saw it as a threat.

The first setback came in late 1507, when James IV sent James Hamilton, the Earl of Arran, to France on a diplomatic mission. He sailed on the *Treasurer*, a small warship the Scottish king used as a diplomatic shuttle between Edinburgh and Paris. Arran was being sent to politely reject King Louis's request for Scottish troops to help him in the campaigns he was fighting in Italy, but he also was there to stress James's commitment to the French king and to emphasize the Scottish monarch's great friendship. On the return voyage in early 1508 bad weather forced the *Treasurer* to put in to an English port, and the Earl of Arran was arrested on the grounds that he lacked proper paperwork. Of course, it was a trumped-up charge, but the arrest provoked a war scare that ended only when Henry VII ordered Arran released.

His release had been negotiated by the young Thomas Wolsey, who was sent to Scotland to assuage King James and to dissuade the Scottish king from forming any alliance with the French. However, Wolsey also reported that although James himself was anxious to support the Anglo-Scottish treaty, his advisers were all pro-French. King Henry's response was to offer a carrot and show a stick. While he released Arran, he also gave orders to strengthen the defenses of Berwick-upon-Tweed. Although the town sat on the Scottish side of the River Tweed, for the past quarter century it had been occupied by an English garrison—both as a defensive bastion and as a base from which to invade Scotland. Meanwhile, James entertained a visit from a new French ambassador, and sent the *Treasurer* to France with his own ambassador. This time the unlucky vessel was shipwrecked on its return journey, and its survivors were arrested and interrogated by the English authorities. Although they were released before the end of 1508, diplomatic relations between the two countries had now reached a new low.

Things improved a little following the death of Henry VII in April 1509. On June 29 King James and the new King Henry renewed the Treaty of Perpetual Peace, and once again everything appeared peaceful. However, the young Henry VIII had his own political agenda. As a youth he was something of a hothead. One historian even described him as "an egocentric teenager whose tantrums and petulance bespoke an inferiority complex." While this was probably a little harsh, the eighteen-year-old king certainly lacked his father's diplomatic skills. Within months of his accession he publicly vowed to wage war against the French, and he began building up his navy as a strategic tool that allowed him to threaten the French with invasion. To the Scots, Henry VIII seemed a hotheaded warmonger.

The one thing that prevented Henry from declaring war against Louis XII was his lack of political support in Europe. However, Pope Julius II (known as the "warrior pope") changed all that when he formed a political and military alliance whose aim was to humble the French king. By the time Henry VIII joined it, Pope Julius's Holy League already included the Emperor Maximilian and the doge of Venice. Henry's role in the alliance was to distract the French at home while the rest of his allies drove Louis's troops out of Italy. By the time Sir Andrew Barton was killed in July 1511, an Anglo-French war was all but inevitable. James would have to choose sides, and the Barton incident did little to endear him to the English. Henry's reply to a personal letter from James seeking redress can hardly have helped. It said, "Kings did not concern themselves with the affairs of pirates." Consequently, while Henry prepared to fight the French, James began preparations for his own war against the English.

In December 1511 King James wrote to Pope Julius, asking the pontiff to free him of the sacred oath that bound him to peace with his English neighbor, as he felt that Henry had begun to wage open and secret war against him. Given the pope's political allegiances, the reply was inevitable—and the letter only served to warn Henry of James's intentions. For good measure, the pope excommunicated James "for threatening the peace of Christendom." The uneasy peace continued for another year, and while the *Michael* was being fitted out in Newhaven, the rest of the country prepared for war. The visit of the French ambassador in November 1512 marked a turning point. The French and Scottish monarchs were now committed to a joint war against England; the war would be launched the following summer. When an English embassy visited Edinburgh in April 1513, the ambassador quickly realized that James was about to openly declare himself as Louis's ally.

The final deal was struck the following month. Louis promised to send weapons and military advisers and to equip and victual the Scottish fleet when it arrived in French waters to support his own fleet. He also promised a subsidy of 64,000 francs—the equivalent of £29,000 Scottish (or £5,850 in English sterling)—as well as a squadron of French galleys, commanded by an experienced admiral, Gaston de Bidoux. In effect the offer covered the cost of building the *Michael*. In exchange, James would invade England if Henry invaded France, and James's fleet would set sail for France. Equally importantly, the French queen sent James a ring and asked him to be her champion. The French clearly knew their man—James was just the sort of monarch to rise to the chivalric challenge. When Henry led his troops across the English Channel, James finally committed himself to war. Therefore, on August 11 the Lyon herald of Scotland arrived in Henry VIII's siege camp outside Thérouanne, some thirty miles southeast of Calais, and calmly handed over James's declaration of war.

By that time the Scottish fleet had already sailed. Just over two weeks earlier, on July 25, the *Michael*, the *Margaret*, and at least ten other hired warships left the Firth of Forth and headed into the North Sea. The expedition was commanded by the king's cousin James Hamilton, the Earl of Arran, who flew his flag in the *Michael*. The king himself sailed on board his flagship as far as the Isle of May in the mouth of the estuary, and then returned home to prepare for his land campaign. Because the English fleet was blocking the Strait of Dover, it was decided to sail northward around Scotland, then down through the Irish Sea to rendezvous with the French off either Cherbourg or Brest. The voyage took the best part of six weeks, partly because the Earl of Arran decided to linger off the coast of Ulster and to participate in what could only be described as a military sideshow.

The castle of Carrickfergus in County Antrim was the principal English stronghold in Ireland, and home to an English army of occupation. While it is unclear whether Arran was following orders, King James had recently signed a treaty with a local Irish warlord, Hugh O'Donnell, and consequently the dalliance at Carrickfergus might well have taken place at the behest of the Scottish king. The fleet arrived off Belfast Lough in early August, and Arran sent his ships in to bombard the castle in what was probably one of the first naval artillery bombardments in history. Dramatic though this was, there is no account that the guns of the *Michael* made any impression on the walls of the castle. A near-contemporary engraving of the place shows a stout stone-built keep overlooking a sheltered harbor, protected on the seaward side by a small battery of guns pointing out into Belfast Lough.

At least one historian has suggested that the fleet ignored its stone-built defenses completely and concentrated on leveling the town beneath its walls. The contemporary Scottish chronicler Sir David Lindsay suggested as much in this contemporary verse:

> As they sailed past Ireland's coast,
> The Admiral dared land his host,
> And set Carrickfergus into fire,
> And saved neither barn nor byre.

After the attack the fleet put in to Ayr, in the southwestern corner of Scotland, either to stock up with stores and ammunition or to justify Arran's actions to the king. After all, the first time the *Michael* fired her guns in anger it couldn't even destroy a small castle— hardly the denouement James would have wished for.

By late August the fleet was under way again, and it arrived off Brest in early September. After taking on French pilots as well as water and supplies, the Scottish fleet continued up the English Channel to the French port of Honfleur, at the mouth of the River Seine, where it finally linked up with the French fleet. Either shortly before its arrival or soon after, the fleet was battered by a severe storm, which temporarily scattered it. The *Michael* even ran aground, and it took nearly a month to prize her off the sandbanks and refloat her. It was now late October. In the midst of the business of setting the leviathan to rights, the news of a cataclysmic tragedy reached the allied mariners—reports of what would be the greatest military disaster ever to befall the Scottish people.

On August 22 James IV led a Scottish army of about thirty thousand men across the River Tweed into England. In what seemed like a repeat of his invasion of 1496, he spent five days besieging and capturing Norham Castle, as well as several other smaller English strongholds. He had now done all he needed to honor the terms of his agreement with Louis of France. However, this time James lingered in the English country of Northumberland for another week, by which time an English army had been gathered to oppose him. When Henry VIII left for France he ordered Thomas Howard, the Earl of Surrey, to defend his northern border against the Scots. Surrey was a veteran field commander, and he wasted little time gathering his men—the levies of the northern English counties. They were joined by a small caucus of experienced soldiers rushed over from France under the command of Surrey's son Lord Thomas Howard, the admiral of England and the brother of the man who slew Sir Andrew Barton. Henry VIII evidently placed a lot of faith in the martial prowess of the Howards.

By the end of the first week in September an English army of about twenty-six thousand were within a few miles of James's encampment on Braxton Hill. Desertions had whittled down the Scottish numbers a little, so the two armies were probably evenly matched in numbers, and the English advantage in cavalry was offset by the Scottish preponderance of artillery pieces. The Scottish military track record was hardly promising. With a few notable exceptions, the majority of pitched battles between the two nations had ended in victory for the English. The Scots seemed to specialize in glorious defeats. However, James IV thought he had a battle-winning advantage. Shortly before the campaign began, the shipment of French weapons and military advisers had docked in Leith, and James's infantry was now armed with French weapons—eighteen-foot-long pikes, which were considered far superior to the shorter spears the Scots normally carried. Unfortunately, his troops had barely enough time to learn how to carry the new weapons, let alone learn to fight with them.

The Earl of Surrey relied on the combination of weapons that had dominated English warfare for a century—the longbow and the bill, a staff weapon that resembled a can opener mounted on a short pole. In the military version of the scissors, rock, or paper game, he couldn't have come up with a more effective counter to the pike. On Friday, September 9, the English host advanced through the rain to give battle, but stopped short of the strong Scottish hilltop position. The battle began with an exchange of artillery fire, but this soon petered out. Surrey must have wondered what to do next, when he saw the Scottish army begin to move down the hill toward him. Tired of waiting, or more likely unable to control his raw army, James had given the order to advance.

The two armies clashed along the length of Braxton Stream, and the hard-fought struggle began. At first the Scots seemed to have the edge, but once the momentum of the advance was halted, the long pikes were at a disadvantage. The English billmen found it much easier to wield their weapons than their Scottish opponents did, and although the grim slogging match continued, the tide began to turn in England's favor. Although one of the four Scottish "divisions" succeeded in defeating its English counterpart, the rest were pinned in place by the English bills and then gradually chopped to pieces. The majority of Scotland's nobility fought in the front ranks of the pike blocks that day and probably were the first to die. The small stream was soon choked with bodies, but still the carnage continued. King James was in the thick of it, locked in battle within yards of the Earl of Surrey.

It was there that they found James's body, within a spear length of his enemy, his jaw pierced by an arrow and his throat slashed by a bill. Beside him lay the bodies of his illegitimate son Alexander, Archbishop of St. Andrews, and a cluster of Scottish earls. By evening it was all over. Those Scots who could escape were in full flight toward the border, while their king and as many as ten thousand of their countrymen lay on the blood-soaked battlefield. English losses were estimated at about fifteen hundred. The Battle of Flodden was an unmitigated disaster for Scotland. The majority of Scotland's nobility had died on the battlefield, and it was said that barely a family in Scotland had escaped the loss of a son, father, or brother. The king's crown would be passed to his infant son, while his few surviving advisers would immediately sue for peace. James IV's great dream of a resurgent Scotland had died with him. A popular Scottish song commemorating that "Black Saturday" lamented, "The Flowers of the Forest have all withered away."

When news of the disaster at Flodden reached Honfleur, the Scottish sailors realized it was all over. The Earl of Arran abandoned the fleet and sailed home in a small, fast ship, as he realized that the surviving nobles would be scrambling for power and vying for regency over the eighteen-month-old King James V. For a while his mother, Queen Margaret, kept the nobles at bay, and she successfully signed a peace treaty with her brother Henry in July 1514. In Honfleur the abandoned Scottish mariners were increasingly sidelined by the French, who began to question the value of keeping their allies supplied while their country was trying to make peace with the enemy. Deprived of its French war subsidies, the Scottish government found itself desperately short of funds, and the most obvious area of cost-cutting was the fleet. Consequently, on April 2, 1514, the *Michael* was sold to the French crown for 40,000 francs, or £18,000 Scots. That was just under a third less than what James had paid for her when she was completed less than two years before.

The *Michael* was renamed *La Grande Nef d'Écosse* (The Great Ship of Scotland), and despite claims to the contrary, there is some evidence to suggest that she remained a potent member of the French fleet for another three decades. If so, then she may have witnessed only one more battle, in July 1545, when a French fleet appeared off Portsmouth, the main base of the Tudor fleet. One of the largest of the French ships in the French fleet fitted her description. The *Henri Grace à Dieu* was there, too, and although she sailed out to give battle, the two ships never got the chance to fire at each other. Instead, the captains of both great ships watched as the *Mary Rose* heeled over and sank, a victim of her own overheavy armament.

As for Henry VIII's own great flagship, she had a far less illustrious career than her sovereign had hoped. For a start, she was just too expensive to operate, so unless there was a war or at least the chance of one, the ship was kept in mothballs. In the early sixteenth century the process of mothballing a ship involved towing her into a dock, then removing most of her sails, rigging, and even her masts. The *Henri Grace à Dieu* was sometimes kept in Portsmouth, but more often she was berthed beside the River Thames in Woolwich; in the "pond" at Deptford; or close by, in the larger dock at Erith. Just how extensive this mothballing was is revealed in a survey of the fleet in early 1539, when it was reported that while a few of the docked ships could be readied for sea within a month, others, including the *Mary Rose*, would take up to three months to prepare for active service. In most cases warships were laid up in October, then readied for sea again the following April. However, simple economics meant that while it cost £40 a month to keep the *Great Harry* in mothballs, it cost more than ten times that to maintain her on active service.

This meant that the great Tudor flagship was readied for sea only about once every four or five years, or sometimes longer. When she first entered service she was used as the flagship of Sir Thomas Howard, who returned to sea after winning his laurels on the battlefield of Flodden. In 1518 she returned to the Thames for a refit, but she was ready for sea again in June 1520, when Henry VIII traveled to France to meet the new French king, Francis I. This young monarch succeeded his uncle Louis XII in 1515, and he wanted Henry as an ally in his struggle against the new Hapsburg ruler, the Emperor Charles V. When Henry sailed from Dover the *Great Harry* was forced to lie off the entrance to the harbor, as her draft was too deep to allow her into the port. The same thing happened at Calais, and Henry's flagship rode at anchor in Calais Roads, while the English king was taken into the port by a smaller ship. While the presence of the *Henri Grace à Dieu* lent a certain grandeur to the occasion, she wasn't of much practical use.

The meeting did little to change Henry's dislike of the French, and in early 1521 he formed an anti-French alliance with Charles V. Four years of war soon followed, although the naval campaign was lackluster at best, and the *Great Harry* spent most of the conflict anchored off Northfleet in Kent, at the mouth of the River Thames. Although she was held in readiness for service, there is little evidence that she actually sailed out against the enemy. Another period of mothballing followed, although another war scare in 1535 saw her prepared for service. She was certainly looking presentable and ready for action that summer, when Henry VIII visited Portsmouth with the French ambassador in tow, and they dined together on board the Tudor flagship. The following year she was one of four ships sent to escort Henry's new bride, Anne of Cleves, across the English Channel from Calais to London. Despite having been married three times before, Henry was determined to welcome his new bride with as much pageantry as he could, and for three months before her arrival a team of sailmakers produced enough flags, pennants, and streamers to decorate the *Henri Grace à Dieu* from stem to stern.

In 1539 she underwent a major refit—in fact, it was more akin to a complete rebuild. By the time she emerged, the *Great Harry* had been reclassified as a vessel of just a thousand tons and rearmed with a far more comprehensive battery of heavy guns. These were subsequently listed in the *Anthony Roll* of 1545, a record that also provides us with a picture of the great but aging warship. She was readied for service but not used during a brief war with Scotland in 1542, although she did set sail with the fleet during the subsequent "Rough Wooing" of 1544–1545, when Henry used his fleet to land an army at Leith and burn Edinburgh—a retaliation against the Scots, who preferred that the granddaughter of James IV and Margaret Tudor should marry a French prince rather than Henry's own son Edward. Then by 1545 she was back in Portsmouth, facing off against the French during the Battle of Portsmouth. At least she briefly got to fire her guns in anger, probably for the first time, but the skirmish never developed into a full-scale battle.

When Henry VIII finally died on January 28, 1547, his only surviving legitimate son, Edward, succeeded him, and three weeks later he was crowned Edward VI. This sickly boy was just nine years old, so his affairs were managed by a council of regency until he reached maturity. He never survived that long, and died of tuberculosis in early July 1553, when he was just fifteen years old. The *Henri Grace à Dieu* had been renamed the *Edward* within weeks of his coronation, but she still spent most of her time in mothballs at Woolwich. Still, she remained a useful member of the Tudor fleet, and a survey of 1552 reported that she was "in good case to serve," as long as she "may be grounded, and caulked once a year" to keep her watertight.

However, the *Edward* didn't long survive its namesake. Within weeks of the teenage king's death she was destroyed by fire as she lay at anchor in the Thames off Woolwich, having recently been brought out of mothballs and prepared for a spell of active service. A report into the accident claimed that her destruction was an accident caused "by negligence, and for a lack of oversight." Her blackened timbers probably still lie in the mud of the Thames, a few yards from where she was first built. It was a sad end to a once proud ship. The *Michael* had probably been lost, too, although chances are that she suffered a far more lingering fate, abandoned at her moorings off Brest and left to rot.

With hindsight, the *Great Michael* and the *Great Harry* were failures. Both were extremely expensive to build and represented a waste of resources, particularly for the Scots. One could have built two or three warships the size of the *Margaret* or the *Mary Rose* for the same money, and although these would have been less prestigious, they probably would have been a lot more useful, and certainly much cheaper to operate. However, to be completely fair, these were experimental times, and the ships were groundbreaking. When the *Michael* was first laid down there was no clear idea of how large guns should be employed on ships, or how they would be mounted.

If we accept the French legend that gunports were first invented during the first decade of the sixteenth century by a French shipwright called Descharges of Brest, then chances are that the *Michael* was one of the first ships to take advantage of this new invention. Evidence from the remains of the *Mary Rose* suggests that she was designed to carry her main armament on a gun deck pierced with gunports. Therefore, when work began on the *Henri Grace à Dieu* some two years later, she was designed the same way. This means that both ships were at the forefront of warship design, and it is little wonder that the monarchs who ordered these flagships wanted to push shipbuilding and ship design to its limits. Both James IV and Henry VIII were fascinated by warship design and artillery, and it was inevitable that their flagships would reflect these interests. While nobody really knew how big gun-armed warships of this kind would operate, both monarchs were eager to find out.

Just as important, the *Michael* and the *Henri Grace à Dieu* were built for prestige. This is reflected in the eagerness with which both monarchs showed off their flagships to ambassadors and visiting dignitaries. For James his great ship also offered a chance to place himself among the major players in the game of European war and politics. That this participation on the world stage led to disaster is less important to our story than the fact that the Scottish king saw building a powerful warship as a means of expressing his country's importance. It shows that warships were being built as much for their latent potential and international prestige as for their practical worth. Similarly, Henry VIII may not have used the *Henri Grace à Dieu* much after she was built, but it was always there to bring out, a tool with which he could impress rival monarchs, visiting ambassadors, or blushing young wives.

By the middle of the century the two royal rivals and their nautical leviathans had passed into history. James IV and Henry VIII had both strived to create prestigious and powerful "battleships," the ultimate floating forms of political statement. The way the two monarchs also embraced the new technologies of shipbuilding and gunfounding in such an impressive way also demonstrated their own legacy as enlightened Renaissance monarchs. However, ultimately both monarchs had been unsuccessful, as their magnificent flagships failed to live up to all those high expectations. Soon, a new breed of monarchs and shipwrights would take up the challenge, and the search for the Renaissance "battleship" would continue.

5

The Black Art of Gunfounding

The First of the Big Guns

The Chinese are generally credited with the discovery of gunpowder, which probably took place in the ninth century. According to Chinese tradition the find was made when scientists in the imperial court were looking for the elixir of immortality. Instead they came up with a weapon of sudden death. The first recipe for gunpowder was written by a Chinese scholar in 1044, and in the centuries that followed his countrymen used the discovery to produce exploding shells, which were fired using conventional siege engines. They also specialized in rockets and fireworks. At some stage in the thirteenth century the secret of gunpowder production was passed on to Arab merchants, who regarded it as a novelty.

By the mid-thirteenth century the invention came to the attention of Roger Bacon, a monk with a penchant for science. His *Opus Majus*, produced in about 1260, included a pretty alarming description of the newly discovered black powder: "With saltpeter and other substances we can compose an artificial fire that can be launched over long distances . . . by only using a very small quantity of this material much light can be created, accompanied by a terrible blast, and it is possible to destroy a town or an army with it." Like the Chinese before him, he described the substance as a carefully concocted mixture of saltpeter, charcoal, and sulfur blended in the ratios of about nine parts, three parts, and one part, respectively. Those ratios remained fairly constant ever since, although today the proportions for black powder usually are given as 75 percent, 15 percent, and 10 percent.

Unfortunately this concoction wasn't used just to make fireworks. By the time Roger Bacon was writing his book, the Chinese had been using artillery for more than a century. In 1341 Zhang Xian even wrote a poem about it, "The Affair of the Iron Cannon," whose fire could "pierce the heart or belly when it strikes a man or horse, and can even skewer several people at once." The apparent obsession with the killing potential of a weapon was not the invention of the modern arms industry. By then artillery had come to Europe, its first known advocates being the Moors, who used some form of gun during their siege of Seville in 1246. From there the use of artillery spread to the Spanish and then the Italians, who by 1280 at the latest were using primitive handguns on the battlefield. An English illustration of the late 1320s shows a gunner firing an arrow from a strange vase-shaped gun cast from bronze, using the same technology available to medieval bell founders. For a while large arrows seemed to be considered a viable form of projectile.

The big breakthrough came during the Hundred Years' War between England and France. In the mid-fourteenth century, English royal accounts mention the presence of "ribaldis" (ribaudekins), a gunpowder weapon on a wheeled carriage that could fire solid shot or large, arrow-shaped projectiles. After the Battle of Crécy in 1346 the Florentine chronicler Giovanni Villani—the same man who first described the carrack—wrote, "The English guns cast iron balls by means of fire. . . . They made a noise like thunder and caused much loss in men and horses." He also claimed that after the battle "the whole field was covered by men struck down by arrows or roundshot." While archers did most of the killing that day, it seems that a handful of gunners also played their part in the carnage. In the same year, the English used their guns to besiege Calais. It was now only a matter of time before someone tried to use guns at sea.

Henry VIII's departure from Dover

The first sailor to have the dubious honor of being killed by one of these contraptions was probably a Danish ship commander, a relative of King Valdemar IV. He died during a sea fight off the Danish fortress of Helsingfors (Hamlet's Elsinore) between the king's Danish fleet and ships from the Hanseatic city of Lübeck in 1362. According to an account of the battle, he was slain by a ball fired from one of six *donnerbuschsen* (thunderboxes) carried on board the German cogs. These guns were still novelties, firing a strange assortment of projectiles that probably were incapable of causing much serious damage—unless you happened to be standing in the wrong place. However, from about 1370 this early experimental period gave way to a second phase—the era of the bombard—where at least on land the idea seemed to be that size was everything.

It would be another half century or more before shipborne guns were effective enough to be taken seriously. An English naval inventory of 1410–1412 records that the royal warship *Christopher of the Tower* carried three iron guns with stocks, and five associated powder chambers, while the *Mary of the Tower* carried just one iron gun and two chambers. Then came the *Grace Dieu*, with its three guns. These wrought-iron breech-loading pieces were almost certainly quite small—probably not much bigger than the swivel guns on Tudor warships a century later. However, in the Mediterranean, guns were playing a much more prominent role in naval warfare. As early as the 1380s, Venetian galleys carried large bombards— wrought-iron, muzzle-loading guns that fired substantial iron or stone shot. This demonstrated the big advantage of galleys over an army on land. It was relatively easy to move a gun around on a galley, while the same piece would need a whole team of horses, oxen, or men to drag it where it would be needed.

The fifteenth century therefore saw the development of two basic types of artillery pieces—large, muzzle-loading bombards and smaller, breech-loading antipersonnel weapons. While both types of guns could be made from bronze, the majority seem to have been made using easily forged wrought iron. While the smaller guns were little more than a complicated alternative to archery fire, the largest guns could do considerable damage—either to the wall of a castle or the side of a ship. The first time these larger weapons were used at sea was in 1380, during the Genoese naval blockade of Venice. The Genoese naval commander was killed by artillery fire from Venetian galleys, and these gun-armed warships were used as floating batteries during the subsequent siege of Chioggia. Other Mediterranean nations took heed of this demonstration of naval firepower, and by the last half of the fifteenth century most of the region's maritime powers were using artillery pieces as the main offensive weapons of their galley fleets.

The largest wrought-iron or cast-bronze bombards of this period were truly enormous. Mons Meg, a wrought-iron bombard produced in Flanders in 1449 for King James II of Scotland, weighed 6 tons, had a bore just short of 2 feet in diameter, and could fire a 400-pound roundshot. She still stands sentinel over Edinburgh Castle. Just four years after Mons Meg was built, the Turkish sultan Mehmed II— "the Conqueror"—used several huge bombards to besiege and capture Constantinople in 1453. One of these weighed seventeen tons and was so large that it was cast in two pieces, which could be screwed together. She fired a stone shot weighing 660 pounds and reputedly had a range of about a mile. This monster gun was last fired in anger in 1807, when a British squadron tried to force its way through the Dardanelles, south of Constantinople. Two of its shots actually struck a British warship and reportedly caused 60 casualties. The "Dardanelles Gun" is now a museum exhibit, displayed at Fort Nelson outside Portsmouth.

Of course, these guns were the exceptions, and by the late fifteenth century they were rarely if ever used at sea. Instead, Mediterranean war galleys relied on the new technology of gunfounding to produce lighter and more efficient bronze pieces, or else smaller and more manageable wrought-iron, breech-loading weapons. With muzzle-loading guns the powder and shot are rammed down the barrel from the muzzle or front end of the cannon, just as in an old-fashioned black-powder musket. These guns were essentially long tubes that had one end permanently sealed. By contrast, a breech-loading gun had a removable section, at the rear of the barrel, which formed the powder chamber. The front part of the gun was just a big tube, open at both ends. Once the chamber was loaded with both powder and shot, it was placed behind the tube and locked into place. The end result was essentially the same, the only major difference being that muzzle-loading guns loaded from the front, and breech-loading guns from the back.

There were a few other differences. The weakness of the whole breech-loading system was that it was often difficult to form a tight seal between the breech chamber and the barrel. This meant that when the gun fired, some of the explosive gases leaked out, and therefore the force with which the ball was blasted out of the barrel was reduced. At close range this probably didn't matter, but at more than a few hundred yards this loss of hitting power meant that the shot couldn't penetrate the hull of an enemy ship. Their advantage over muzzle-loading guns was speed: they could be loaded far more quickly than guns loaded from the front of the barrel. This meant that while breech-loading guns were excellent as close-range antipersonnel weapons, they weren't really suited for pounding an enemy ship at long range.

By the time these giant bombards appeared in the mid-fifteenth century, it seemed that their obvious limitations had become apparent to everyone but the rulers, who seemed to revel in their firepower. They were simply too large to transport easily, and fired too slowly to make them practical weapons of war. The solution was to produce smaller guns, which meant that these pieces—smaller than bombards but heavier than small swivel guns—could be used at sea as well as on land. This was when things really began to change. This development coincided with the introduction of the carrack—both ship designers and gunfounders were working on technological improvements in their own spheres, and together they would change the world. From 1470 on, evidence for use of naval guns becomes far less fragmentary. There was a definite change in emphasis. Before this, guns were seen as novelties or auxiliary weapons. By the last few decades of the fifteenth century they had become part of an integrated system of naval weaponry, and their importance was growing fast.

These smaller heavy guns were known by a whole variety of names throughout Europe—"bombardettas," "fowlers," "port pieces," "murderers," and "bombardellas" being the most common. However, they all were roughly the same sort of weapon—large, wrought-iron tubes and powder chambers set into a wooden bed or gun carriage. While these pieces were larger and more effective than the swivel guns, which remained the most common form of naval gun, they soon would be outclassed by a new breed of cast-bronze guns. An English gun list from 1455 mentions "cannon bombards," "veuglers" (fowlers), "ribaudekins," and "serpentines." In this context serpentines were guns about eight feet long, firing lead shot weighing about three pounds. Serpentines used at sea were much smaller—swivel guns rather than large pieces. Another list of naval guns, from about 1495, mentions the first cast-bronze guns—curtows and demicurtows.

This means that before the sixteenth century began, English warships were carrying bronze muzzle-loading guns. This development meant

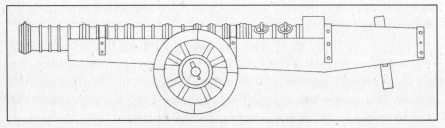

Wrought-iron gun from the Mary Rose

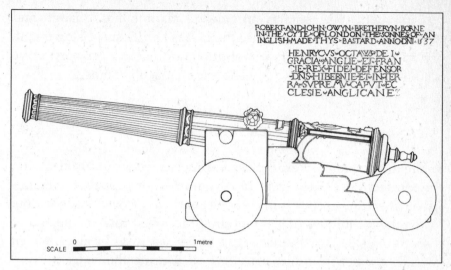

ROBERT·AND·IOHN·OWYN·BRETHERYN·BORNE
IN·THE·CYTE·OF·LONDON·THE·SONNES·OF·AN
INGLISH·MADE·THYS·BASTARD·ANNO·DNI·1537

HENRYCVS·OCTAVVS·DE·I
GRACIA·ANGLIE·ET·FRAN
CIE·REX·FIDEI·DEFENSOR
·DNS·HIBERNIE·ET·INTER
RA·SVPREMV·CAPVT·EC
CLESIE·ANGLICANE

SCALE 0 1metre

Bronze gun from the Mary Rose *cast by the Owen Brothers of London, 1537*

that for the first time, warships could destroy other ships at long range. The only problem was that their captains didn't realize it. Within a decade a whole range of gun types and sizes would be cast in bronze and deployed onto warships, from the monster basilisks carried on the Scottish *Michael* to the small falcons mounted in the *Henri Grace á Dieu*. As the century progressed, the tendency would be toward greater uniformity of these gun types, and also the deployment of an increasing number of the heavier pieces. Although the older wrought-iron, breech-loading guns were considered largely obsolete by the mid-sixteenth century, they could still be found on some European warships and armed merchantmen until the end of the sixteenth century.

The smaller wrought-iron or cast-bronze swivel guns would never go out of fashion, as however well they were armed, warships still needed to back up their heavy guns with weapons designed for close-range defense. Ships still carried all the paraphernalia of hand-to-hand combat, but by the later sixteenth century the emphasis had changed. While guns were still part of an integrated system of naval weaponry, in the navies of most maritime powers they had become the dominant type of weapon rather than just one of many. It seemed that only the Spanish still clung to the old ways, an emphasis that had more to do with their own experience of sixteenth-century naval warfare than with any deep-rooted rejection of firepower. This was a century when sea captains struggled to adapt to these changes and to work out how they could use them. It is hardly surprising that in the adoption of the black arts of gunfounding and gunnery, some nations would prove more amenable to change than others.

The Black Art Explained

While the first known examples of artillery pieces produced during the fourteenth century were cast from brass or bronze, the majority of fifteenth-century guns were constructed from wrought iron. When the techniques of gunfounding improved toward the end of the century, the finest guns began to be cast from bronze—which is really brass with a bit more tin in it. During the sixteenth century wrought-iron and cast-bronze guns were both used, although bronze pieces became more popular as the century progressed. Finally, from the 1540s on, gunfounders began to produce cast-iron guns, although their production was fraught with technological problems until the end of the century, so cast-iron pieces were relatively rare before the seventeenth century.

Making a gun out of wrought iron was a fairly straightforward process, and in theory it could be done by any blacksmith using the tools and materials at hand. After all, the barrel was nothing more than a long tube open at both ends. It was made from long iron strips hammered to form flat rods. These were curved slightly by hammering them into shape around a wooden former. The gunmakers probably used a wooden former to curve the staves around, to make sure the finished tube was the right size. The idea was that when they were all grouped together they formed a hollow circle, a bit like the staves of a wooden barrel. The length of the whole thing was whatever length the finished barrel was supposed to be—usually six to eight feet long. Swivel gun barrels were made the same way but were only a couple of feet long.

After finishing this hollow tube of wrought-iron staves, the next stage was to fit on the wrought-iron rings that held the gun together. This series of rings usually varied in size—some being thicker than others, and others slightly longer and more cylindrical. This technique is sometimes called "hoop and band" construction. Whatever the size of these rings, they were all made with their inner hole the same size as the outer diameter of the bundle of staves. The rings were heated in the forge and then slipped over the bundle, like putting a ring onto a finger. They were hammered into place next to each other, and when these cooled they shrank, forming a tight seal over the staves beneath them. In effect this created a two-layer gun—the inner staves running one way, then the outer bands running at right angles to them, forming a sort of protective jacket. The end result was a long, thin, wrought-iron tube open at both ends.

The slightly more difficult part was making the powder chamber, which held the explosive charge. This was usually built the same way, just a shorter version of the barrel, and was then plugged with an end piece that was heat-shrunk into one end of the tube to create a chamber. When the inner tube was reinforced it was often finished off with an end piece shaped like the cap of a bottle. After all, it was vital that when the gun was fired, the charge was directed out the muzzle and didn't simply blow the back off the powder chamber. A variant of the powder chamber was sometimes cast in the shape of a tankard, complete with a handle. However, the technology of cast-iron production was in its infancy, and when examples of these cast chambers are found, they tend to be associated with small swivel guns rather than with larger pieces such as bombardettas or port pieces.

Finally, a touchhole was drilled through the metal at the bottom of the side of the chamber so the gunpowder charge inside could be fired. Another feature was that these powder chambers were tapered slightly at the open end, so that when they were pressed against the end of the main wrought-iron tube, it would form a tight seal. It also was common to fit these powder chambers with carrying lugs and rings so they could be easily lifted into and out of the carriage when the gun was being reloaded. The same features are often found on surviving examples of the barrels themselves.

Once the wrought-iron construction was complete, the gun was still not ready for use. It needed some form of carriage. With swivel guns this was often less of a carriage and more of a brace, a cradle-like extension fitted to the end of the barrel that could house the powder chamber. Once the powder chamber was slotted into place it was held tight against the end of the barrel using a small iron or wooden wedge. The other special feature of a swivel gun was that it almost always came complete with the swivel mount that gave the weapon its name. This looked like the rowlock used on a rowing boat, the open arms of which ended in little circles. At the point of balance of the weapon one of the wrought-iron hoops or rings was fitted with two lugs, and the holes on the swivel mount fitted over these. In effect the whole thing looked like a modern machine gun—the kind fitted to the top of a tank. Another feature was a tail (sometimes called a monkey tail) that stuck out the back of this holder, allowing the gun to be aimed easily and quickly.

The swivel gun went by several different names, depending on how big it was. The English used the terms "sling," "base," and "serpentine," while the Spanish called theirs "versos," or even "verso dobles," for the larger pieces. Although most Renaissance swivel guns were made from wrought iron, bronze and eventually cast-iron versions were sometimes used. Like all other types of artillery from this period, they came in a wide range of shapes and sizes, and their form of construction varied almost as widely as everything else about them. For instance, one common variant involved using very small outer bands to form the outer tube, then sealing the whole thing in molten metal designed to fill any gaps. Another type involved encasing the outside of the piece in a single sheet of metal rather than a series of hoops and bands, which produced a sleeker finish to the gun.

Making the carriage for a larger wrought-iron gun was a little more complicated. The gun was effective only if the chamber could be held up against the end of the barrel when the piece was fired. The seal had to be as tight as possible. The gunmakers came up with the idea of sinking the barrel into the carriage itself, creating a kind of wooden cradle that became an integral part of the gun itself. A large tree trunk or slab of wood was used, and this would be cut into the final shape needed for the carriage. Then the carpenter would carve out a trough to take the gun, and would usually mirror the shape of the cylinders and rings of the outer barrel. Once it was finished, the wrought-iron barrel would be lowered into the carriage, which made it look as if the barrel were half sunk into the carriage itself. This trough also included a space at the back for the powder chamber. The barrel was then strapped into place using iron bands or even rope. The finished carriage could then be mounted on a pair of wheels, like ones found on the *Mary Rose*—two of which had two small, solid "truck" wheels, while others had two wheels similar to those used on the gun carriages on land.

When the whole contraption was ready to be fired, a wooden or iron wedge was hammered into place between the back of the powder chamber and the end of the trough in the carriage, which effectively closed the seal between the chamber and the barrel. It was crude, but it worked. These guns were relatively easy to make, and they were cheap. Their big limitation was that however hard the gunners tried, they could never get a tight enough seal between the chamber and the barrel, which meant that these guns always lacked the hitting power of their muzzle-loading counterparts.

The business of casting guns from bronze was a lot more complicated. Man had been casting bronze for centuries—the Greeks and Romans used simple casting techniques to produce statues, and the same techniques were used throughout the Middle Ages. However, the difference between casting a statue and an artillery piece was one of scale, and it was not until the Renaissance that founders managed to cope with production on the industrial scale needed to successfully cast large guns without impurity or blemish. In theory the way cast-iron guns were manufactured was similar—only the type of molten metal used was different. However, it took far longer to find the right composition of metal—the gun had to be as strong as possible, without the metal being so brittle that it would shatter into pieces when the gun was fired. It was only in the 1550s that cast-iron production became a viable alternative to cast-bronze production, and even then, mariners preferred to rely on bronze pieces until well into the seventeenth century, despite the far higher production costs.

Whatever material was used, the casting methods were virtually identical. The whole procedure started with a long wooden rod whose diameter was a little smaller than the intended bore size of the gun when it was finished. Rope was tightly wrapped around this wooden core, and then clay was daubed over the whole thing and packed into the bumps in the rope until it formed a smooth tube. A template known as a stickle board was used to gauge when the clay had been built up enough for the size of the gun the gunfounder

Gunfounding in the sixteenth century

planned to make. Then the sculptor added all the important extra features of the finished gun barrel, such as the reinforcing bands that girded the barrel itself, the flare around the muzzle, or any extra piece of decoration designed to make the buyer happy with the finished product. In effect the sculptor was creating a full-size model of the gun, only in clay rather than metal. The clay was then carefully dried over a fire to create a relatively tough model, which could take several days.

Next the clay model was brushed with a thick layer of molten wax, which also was sculpted to conform to the chosen shape of the gun. At this stage any last extra decoration was added, such as the "dolphins" that were often used as lifting handles, or any inscription or coat of arms that would embellish the finished piece. Usually these extras were sculpted in wax and were attached. Finally, wooden versions of the trunnions were pinned in place. These were usually where the founder thought the balance point of the finished gun would be. On the finished gun they would rest on the gun carriage and would be the pivot points that allowed the gun to be elevated.

The finished model was then coated with another very thin wax layer; then an outer mold was built up around it, like a cocoon. For this the gunfounders used loam, a mixture of clay, sand, and water. The first few coats would have the consistency of paint and would conform to the shape of the gun model underneath. Each subsequent layer was allowed to dry before the next one was applied. After a few coats the loam mixture became thicker, until it formed a thick claylike crust that could be as many as three inches thick. The end result was a huge gun mold. To protect it from clumsy apprentices the whole fragile mold was then banded with iron strips and bands. It was now almost ready for the next stage.

First the whole mold had to be lifted from the turning frame where it had been built, then lowered onto a specially built wooden cradle. Now came the delicate bit. The wooden spindle around which the whole thing had been built up was tapered, so it narrowed toward one end. With a few gentle taps with a hammer it could be dislodged, then carefully pulled free from the mold. The rope also was pulled out, as by that stage it probably had come loose. Next the clay was picked away from the inside of the mold until the founders reached the wax layer beyond it. If this was done properly, the wax and loam that made up the rest of the mold would remain undisturbed. A slightly harder business was the removal of the wooden trunnion formers and any pins that had held the coat of arms or any other inscriptions in place. Before anything else happened, the apprentices would fill these holes or damaged bits with clay and smooth the inner surface of the mold. The mold was then heated again, which melted the wax but baked the loam a little more and left it intact.

The inside of the loam mold was now brushed with a grease solution called lye, which prevented the molten bronze or cast iron from sticking to the clay mold. Finally, one end of the mold was closed using another premade mold, modeled into the shape of the cascabel, or rear face of the gun. The mold of the cascabel was much thicker than the main mold, because when the whole thing was ready to be filled with molten metal it would be placed on its end, with the muzzle uppermost. This meant that all the weight of the mold would rest on the cascabel. Once the molds were fitted together, another series of iron straps was wrapped around the two parts to hold them together.

By this stage the inside of the mold was a mirror image of what the exterior surface of the finished gun would look like. However, if the metal were poured in now, it would simply create a gun-shaped lump of metal, without a barrel. Therefore another mold was needed, which would form the approximate shape of the inside of the barrel. This mold, the core, was made similar to the way the original mold was made. An iron bar was wrapped in rope, then daubed in clay to create a tube. Once this was fire-dried it had to be inserted into the barrel and held in place. It was vital that the barrel walls were the same thickness all the way around. If not, the weaker part of the gun wall could burst if the piece were fired.

In most gun foundries the core was held in place using a wooden support near the base of the outer mold. This core piece, or chap-let, supported the core in the mold when the whole assemblage was placed on end, ready for the molten metal to be poured into it. A clay disk held the core in place at the muzzle end of the mold, although some other foundries opted for the simpler but less accu-rate method of suspending the core over the main mold using a winch and chains.

The bronze was made from a mixture of about 90 percent copper and 10 percent tin, although the exact proportions varied a little from foundry to foundry. All master founders felt that their recipe was the best, and some even added traces of other metals, such as lead or zinc. Before the pouring began, this mixture would have been created by throwing metal scraps or bars into the melting pot, then heating until it was white hot—a process that could take several days. Whatever the mixture, the casting process was the same. The gun mold was stood upright in a casting pit directly in front of a tapping hole, from where the molten metal would gush out. A funnel-shaped feeding head ensured that the molten metal would run smoothly from the tapping hole into the mold. Once everything was ready, the inside of the casting pit was packed with earth to hold the mold in place. Usually several guns would be cast at the same time, and the mouths of the molds would be connected to the tapping hole by a network of brick channels. Everything was now ready for the molten metal.

Often spectators would be invited to watch the process— Henry VIII was a frequent visitor to the site of his royal foundry at Houndsditch, just north of the Tower of London. When the big moment arrived the master founder would knock open the tapping hole with a hammer, and the molten metal would flow out. Foundry workers would be on hand to divert the flow using metal plates, or to shut the tapping hole when the job was done. This was a spectacular moment, as the white-hot molten brass or iron flowed through the conduits and into the waiting molds. Any excess was diverted into a reservoir, where it would be used for the next batch of guns.

Once the molds were filled, they would be left to set for at least a day. Then the inner cores would be pulled out, and a nervous founder probably would peer inside, hoping that everything looked just as it should. Laborers were called in to dig away the earth—a thoroughly unpleasant job, as it would have retained the heat of the metal, making it baking hot. This revealed the reinforced clay molds standing in a line. They were lifted out of the casting pit; then workmen would take off the metal banding and break the clay mold, using hammers and chisels. If everything had gone according to plan, a perfect new gun barrel would be revealed, complete with all its dolphins, trunnions, coats of arms, and fancy decorations.

It still wasn't ready to leave the foundry. First the feeding head had to be cut off; it would have looked a little like the sprue on a child's plastic model. This sawing could take as long as three days for big guns. Then the gun was ready for the finishing process. The bore had to be cleaned out, making sure it was free of imperfections. One of the most common methods of checking the bore was to mount a candle and a mirror on a long pole, then slowly push these down the barrel while the founder looked for flaws. This was the most important bit of the gun, and nothing was allowed to get in the way of that perfect shot. Any holes, such as those left by the core piece, would then be sealed with metal plugs. Finally the master founder would check the whole gun for problems, while his staff would remove any unsightly blemishes. Once he was happy, the final task was to drill the touchhole or vent, using a specially constructed drill. The gun would then be ready for delivery to the fleet or the royal arsenal.

Bronze guns came in a range of shapes and sizes. As each gun was cast individually, in theory no two guns were identical. Every size of gun had its own name, based on the length and shape of the barrel, and the size of the shot it fired. Unlike the guns of the eighteenth and nineteenth centuries, which were classified by the weight of their shot, bronze guns cast during the Renaissance were given far more exotic names, some based on mythological creatures and others on real birds or animals. For example, gun types included the basilisk, the saker, and the falcon. However, in general bronze guns could be divided into two general classes, linked by general rules of proportion. The culverin group consisted exclusively of culverins, named after a type of snake. The curtow was an early hybrid between the two main gun classes, and it should really be seen as a prototype for the cannon.

The cannon class pretty much consisted of all of the rest, including basilisks and smaller guns such as sakers, minions, and falcons. Culverins were proportionately thinner and lighter than cannons, which made culverins a little more suitable for use on ships. Although these days people tend to class all ship guns of this period as cannons, to be pedantic this is quite wrong: a cannon is only one of a whole range of gun types. Several sixteenth-century lists try to classify these guns, but because each barrel was a little different from the others, these probably represented ideals rather than exact proportions. The table below, which comes from a list by a general rather than a naval commander, sets forth a few of the major gun types of the time.

The pot gun fired stone shot. These were also called pedreros, perriers, or simply stone-shotted guns. Compared to other pieces they were characterized by being short and stubby, with a large bore and thin walls. Once the gun was fired, the stone would shatter,

Artillery Required by Army, 1513

Gun Type	Weight of Shot (pounds)	Weight of Powder (pounds)
Bombard	260	80
Curtow	60	40
Culverin	20	22
Minion	8	8
Pot gun	4 (stone)	40

List of Ordnance, from William Harrison's An Historical Description of the Iland of Britaine, which Introduced Holinshed's Chronicles (1587)

Gun Type	Caliber (inches)	Gun Weight (pounds)	Shot Weight (pounds)	Powder Charge (pounds)	Point-Blank Range (paces)
Old cannon	7	8,000	42	60	400
Cannon	8	7,000	60	20	400
Demicannon	6½	6,000	30	28	760
Culverin	5½	4,000	18	18	500
Demiculverin	4½	3,000	9	9	400
Saker	3½	1,500	5	5	360
Minion	3¼	1,100	4½	4½	340
Falcon	2½	800	2½	2½	320

creating a hail of stone fragments that would have been useful as a close-range weapon fired into the faces of an enemy boarding party. Another, more detailed English table, from the end of the sixteenth century, provides a more comprehensive catalog of bronze weapons (see above).

This table doesn't mention any wrought-iron breech-loading guns. By the time of the Spanish Armada the English regarded these cruder pieces as being completely obsolete, with little or no role to play in naval combat. The result is that although we know how these guns looked, how they were built, and how they operated, we know little or nothing about how effective they really were, or what exactly someone meant when they called a gun a murderer rather than a port piece. However, these guns had a large part to play in the earlier Tudor navy. The table of the top of the page 140 shows the importance of the guns on some of Henry VIII's major warships during the early years of his reign.

Unfortunately, we can't tell if the stone guns on this list were made from wrought iron or bronze, but the suspicion is that they were iron, as were the slings. The two cast guns on the *Mary Rose* were probably experimental cast-iron pieces, as they seem to have been quietly

Armament of Henry VIII's Major Warships, 1512

Gun Type	Henri Grace à Dieu (1,500 tons)	Great Elizabeth (900 tons)	Gabriel Royal (700 tons)	Katherine Fortileza (700 tons)	Mary Rose (500 tons)	Peter Pomegranate (450 tons)
Culverins	2	—	2	—	—	—
Curtows	1	—	1	1	5	—
Murderers	18	8	3	14	6	11
Stone guns	24	29	9	13	26	6
Falcons	6	—	14	2	5	2
Slings	1	6	2	6	2	3
Cast guns	—	—	—	—	2	—
Others	5	—	—	—	—	—

Armament of Henry VIII's Major Warships, 1545

Gun Type	Mary Rose (500 tons)	Peter Pomegranate (450 tons)	Great Galley (500 tons)	Small Galley (400 tons)	Sweepstake (300 tons)	Jennet (200 tons)
Cannons	—	2	5	2	—	—
Demicannons	4	2	—	6	—	—
Culverins	2	1	—	—	—	—
Demiculverins	2	—	2	6	—	—
Sakers	5	5	4	2	2	1
Falcons	2	—	2	—	3	1
Port pieces	9	10	12	10	9	6
Fowlers	6	15	—	—	2	4
Bases	—	—	50	30	8	6
Slings	6	4	2	7	4	7
Quarter slings	60	52	10	10	16	21

dropped by the time the inventory was drawn up again. By comparing this gunlist with one from the end of Henry's reign (see page 140 bottom) we can immediately see that there was a marked increase in firepower during the intervening years.

The last four groups were all types of swivel gun, which shows that Henry VIII still placed a lot of emphasis on the close-range defense of his ships. However, between the time the first and second lists were compiled the *Mary Rose* had almost doubled its complement of heavy guns, and the majority of them were modern bronze pieces. It is also striking that these varied in size and were not grouped into homogeneous batteries, which probably would have been a lot more efficient. That was a development for a later century, one that would lead directly to the creation of the ship of the line. However, it is clear that by the middle of the sixteenth century warships were armed with enough powerful bronze muzzle-loading guns to make a real difference in a sea battle. It is surprising that it took another four decades to make the most of all this firepower.

6

The Baltic Connection

The Hanse

According to German legend, the decline of the great Hanseatic League was largely due to the activities of one man: Klaus Störtebecker, a surname that roughly translates as "emptying the beer mug with one gulp." While his beer-guzzling prowess was impressive enough, his abilities as a pirate were unmatched. Apparently he was born in the German Baltic port of Wismar in about 1360, and he originally went by the name of Nikolaus Storzenbecher. Wismar was a member of the Hanseatic League, the alliance of guilds that established a trading monopoly throughout the Baltic Sea and much of the North Sea during the later Middle Ages. However, Störtebecker was not cut out to be a merchant. Instead he joined a pirate brotherhood known as the Vitalienbrüder (Victual Brothers), who hired out their services to the highest bidder. Their unusual name came from one of their exploits: in 1392 they ran supplies through a Danish blockade and into a beleaguered, rebellious Stockholm. At first the Hanseatic League supported these mercenaries, as they concentrated on fighting the Danes, who were the league's greatest economic rivals. The pirates were even given free access to Wismar, which is probably when Störtebecker signed on as one of their crew.

This uneasy alliance between merchant league and pirate brotherhood ended when the Victual Brothers sacked the Norwegian port of Bergen, a city run by the Hanse. The pirates were barred from all Hanseatic ports, so they seized the Baltic island of Gotland from the Danes and used it as a pirate lair. Queen Margaret of Denmark neatly sidestepped the problem by ceding the island to the fearsome Teutonic Knights, who were based in Poland. These white-coated German crusaders launched an amphibious invasion of the island in 1398 that caught the pirates unawares. The brotherhood was crushed, and Störtebecker was one of the few survivors, as he had been ravaging the Finnish coast when the crusaders arrived. He became the leader of the last of these pirates—the Likedeelers, who established a new base on the island of Helgoland, off Germany's North Sea coast.

Naval battle—detail from the Carta Olaus Magnus

Over the next few years Störtebecker and his captains, Gödeke Michels, Hennig Wichmann, and Magister Wigbold, played havoc with the Danish and Hanseatic shipping sailing into and out of Hamburg. Finally the Hanse had enough, and in 1401 they sent a squadron led by Simon of Utrecht to deal with the pirates. Legend has it that Störtebecker tried to escape from the Hanseatic ships in his flagship *Seetiger* (Sea Tiger), but a prisoner on board managed to sabotage her rudder, allowing Simon's flagship, *Die Bunte Kuh* (The Colorful Cow), to overhaul her. After an epic battle Störtebecker and seventy-one of his men were captured, then shipped back to Hamburg to face trial and execution. According to Hamburg legend, Störtebecker struck a deal with the magistrates: all of his crewmen whom he could walk past after his head was cut off would be pardoned. As the story goes, he managed to stagger past eleven of his shipmates before he fell—tripped by the executioner. While much of this story is too colorful to be believed, it demonstrates that by the start of the fifteenth century the once-mighty Hanseatic League was barely able to deal with a threat by a band of Baltic pirates.

The word *hansa* means "guild," a mercantile alliance, and this is exactly what the Hanseatic League was—a loose confederation of semi-independent German ports that banded together for mutual protection and economic advancement. By the late thirteenth century the Hanseatic League had expanded to include the ports of Lübeck, Hamburg, Danzig (Gdansk), Stettin, Rostock, Stralsund, Wismar, and Bremen. Farther inland the league also controlled the important trading centers of Cologne, Dortmund, and Brunswick, while smaller *kontors* (trading posts) were established in what is now the Netherlands, Scandinavia, and the Baltic states. By the time Störtebecker began his activities the Hanseatic League was at the height of its powers, an economic empire that dominated northern Europe. However, a series of clashes with the Russians, the Danes, and the Teutonic Knights affected trade, while the growing economic powerhouse of Italy began to undercut Hanseatic domination of European marketplaces.

The pirate attacks had damaged the ability of the league to export Baltic grain through Hamburg and the Netherlands, so Burgundian (Dutch) merchants tried to establish their own Baltic trading links with eastern Europe. This led to a hard-fought war in 1438,

A cog on a Hanseatic seal

culminating in a series of sea battles that the Dutch won. The result was a breaking of the Hansa monopoly. Although the Hanseatic League survived into the early sixteenth century, and it could still gather a reasonably impressive fleet if it needed to, it was no longer a political force to be reckoned with. Instead, cities such as Lübeck hired out their naval forces to the highest bidder—rather like the Victual Brothers before them. They still controlled some of the most important and busiest ports in the Baltic, and most of the largest ships. These could easily be converted into warships when required, while the cities themselves became regular employers of veteran German mercenaries.

Because the Hanseatic cities relied on maritime trade, their city seals almost always depicted a ship. As the ships changed, so too did the seals, which leaves us with a fantastic record of the development of Hanseatic ships throughout the fourteenth, fifteenth, and early sixteenth centuries. The vessels of the mid-fourteenth century are most definitely cogs, clinker-built, and equipped with a single large, square sail. However, a seal dated 1400 showing a ship from the Hanseatic port of Danzig demonstrates that in the Baltic, the cog had been replaced by a version of the hulk. The ship still has a single mast, but the sterncastle is most definitely part of the hull, while the ship also has a noticeable forecastle. It makes sense that the Hanseatic cities would keep abreast of the latest trends in ship-building design, even if they no longer led the way.

The next change appeared in the mid-fifteenth century, at about the time the Hanseatic League lost its Baltic monopoly. Then the ships looked virtually identical to the early carrack depicted by the Flemish artist who signed himself "WA." A seal from Lübeck shows a three-masted ship with a large, sloping sterncastle and a high and very pronounced forecastle. The side of the gunwale appears to have been pierced with two or three circular ports, clearly designed to be used by heavy guns. While this ship was not a carrack of the type seen in English and French ports, it nevertheless represented a major step forward in ship design. This would have been the type of Hanseatic ship that took part in the war against the Burgundians in about 1440 and that was hired out to Baltic or Scandinavian rulers later in the century.

A Hanseatic ship seal from Lübeck dated about 1470 shows that toward the end of that century these Baltic shipbuilders had gone one stage farther. The ship is almost identifiable as a carrack, although one with a far less pronounced superstructure than the carracks found outside the Baltic. It looks more like the Iberian nao—a ship like Christopher Columbus's *Santa Maria*—than like a northern European warship. The big difference is that the Baltic ship appears to have been clinker-built. It has three masts, all carrying a single sail, and its gunwale is pierced to carry three heavy guns a side. Additional apertures in the forecastle and the sterncastle are clearly designed to house swivel guns. The overall impression is that by the end of the fifteenth century the ships of the Hanseatic League were similar to those outside Baltic waters, but their shipbuilders preferred to retain certain elements of the hulk design rather than wholeheartedly adopt the carrack. It was almost as if the southern

European traditions of shipbuilding had never managed to make much of an impact that far north.

The Hanseatic League certainly needed warships, as in 1509 Lübeck and several allied towns found themselves at war with Denmark, and with the Dutch, whose merchant ships threatened to dominate trade within the Baltic. Naturally, the Swedes joined in the fun, grasping the opportunity to rebel against Danish authority. Matters came to a head in the early summer of 1511, when a powerful Danish fleet escorted some two hundred Dutch merchant ships into the Baltic and then attacked and sacked the Hanseatic town of Wismar. The Lübeckers put to sea seeking revenge, and on August 9 a fleet of eighteen Hanseatic warships caught up with the twenty ships of the Danish fleet off the island of Bornholm. Both sides relied on missile fire and artillery to overcome their enemies, but as dusk fell, the battle remained a draw. The fleets drew apart in the night, and three days later the Lübeckers bumped into the Dutch convoy, escorted by just four warships. The Lübeckers fell on the merchantmen with a vengeance, capturing, burning, or driving ashore the Dutch ships before the Danes could sail to their rescue. This spirited action demonstrated that while the Hanseatic League might be in decline, the Lübeckers at least were still dangerous foes.

By the first decades of the sixteenth century the shipbuilding revolution was in full flood—or at least it was everywhere except the Baltic. The magnificent *Carta Olaus Magnus*, drawn in 1535, is a fanciful map of Scandinavia. The map is decorated with a splendid array of sea monsters, rumbling volcanoes, battles among Laplanders, Finns, and Russians—and a collection of ships. Among them are several that can be identified as Hanseatic League vessels. One, from Hamburg, is shown battling a Scottish armed merchantman. The high superstructure suggests a carrack, while the poor sailing rig indicates a hulk. Whatever it might be, by this stage the vessel is equipped with a powerful battery of heavy guns, as the cartographer showed it pounding the Scottish ship to pieces.

Close by are ships from Lübeck and Bremen, suggesting that the Hamburger might be escorting the other vessels. Farther to the south, in the North Sea, the artist has shown a ship from Danzig, with heavy guns mounted on two-wheeled carriages in her waist. Strangely enough, yet more guns on carriages are shown mounted on top of her sterncastle and forecastle, while her hull is pierced with three gunports, with two more guns mounted in her stern as chase pieces. It isn't clear whether the ship is clinker-built or carvel-built, but the presence of gunports suggests the latter. While the map itself might be too outlandish and inaccurate to be used as hard evidence, at least it shows that the artist thought that the Hanseatic League was still a force to be reckoned with. However, by that time a new star was rising in the Baltic, and the artist was unable to resist including this new naval player in his map.

Dominum Maris Baltica

One of the fascinating pieces of information you can glean from the *Carta Olaus Magnus* is the nationality of the ships shown by the artist, and their location. The poor Scottish ship encountered her Hanseatic nemesis off the southern coast of Iceland—a popular destination for both Scottish and Baltic fishing boats and whaling ships during this period. In the Denmark Strait between Iceland and Greenland lies an English whaling ship, her crew having tied a whale to their vessel while the crew worked on its carcass. They were lucky to have encountered such a tame sea creature—just to the right a German and a Danish ship are being attacked by sea monsters off Norway. A Dutch ship is shown sailing out of the mouth of the Baltic, no doubt heading home with her cargo of grain. However, inside the Baltic Sea itself the cartographer has shown only one ship of any size. This powerfully armed three-masted vessel is marked "Navis Svetica" (Swedish Navy).

This represented the new status quo in the Baltic basin. The decline of the Hanseatic League led to a power vacuum, and the German princes of central Europe missed the opportunity to take advantage of this. In effect Germany had ceased to be a naval power of any significance by the middle of the sixteenth century, and it would only rediscover its interest in sea power during the late nineteenth century. This allowed the Nordic kingdoms of Scandinavia to assume the role of regional superpowers. The Danes had always maintained a reasonably strong navy, and although a series of minor wars, territorial campaigns of expansion, and internal conflict all tended

Polish warship fighting the Swedes, 1627

to place heavy demands on Danish resources, the state managed to
retain this naval muscle throughout the Renaissance.

Of course, they were helped by geography. Denmark effectively acted as a cork that sealed off the Baltic Sea from the rest
of the maritime world. Any ships wanting to enter this Dominum
Maris Baltica (dominion of the Baltic Sea) had to pass through The
Sound—a strait between the Danish and Swedish shores. Until
1658 the Danes controlled both sides of this strait, and the guns
of the fortress of Helsingfors (Hamlet's Elsinore) dominated the
narrow channel. Passing ships like that Dutch ship in the *Carta
Olaus Magnus* had to pay a Sound Toll, which was used to fund the
Danish navy. This toll would continue to be charged for more than
four centuries. King Hans (reigned 1482–1513) first began building
purpose-built Danish warships; before then the state had relied on

requisitioning armed merchantmen or hiring mercenary warships in wartime.

During the first decades of the sixteenth century the navy's chief role was to keep the Swedish rebels in check—a task it was singularly ill-equipped to do. It was a strategic situation similar to that encountered by Britain 250 years later—attempting to maintain military control of an overseas colony using overstretched maritime lines of communication and secure bases centered on major ports. Farther into the wooded hinterland the rebel force grew stronger every year. However, like the British during the American War of Independence, the Danes had the naval strength to ensure control of the seas. A contemporary engraving of King Christian II of Denmark's fleet at anchor off Stockholm in 1521—the year after the "Stockholm bloodbath"—shows two well-armed carracks, each fitted with three masts and topsails as well as mainsails, and armed with a potent mixture of heavy and light guns. Their only limitation appears to be that their hulls were clinker-built and lacked gunports, which meant they could carry only a very limited number of heavy pieces.

Within ten years many of these impressive warships had been lost—either abandoned following a coup and the subsequent exile of the king in 1523, or captured after Christian II's abortive attempt to recapture his kingdom in 1531. The king was captured and incarcerated by his uncle, who in 1523 had already proclaimed himself King Frederick I. Unfortunately, the new king lacked his nephew's enthusiasm for things maritime, and the Swedish rebels took advantage of this respite to create their own navy.

The first of these new ships were armed merchantmen, purchased by the Swedish Parliament in 1522 from the city of Lübeck. Part of the deal included significant trading concessions for the Hanseatic merchants, but it was a cheap enough price to pay for naval security. In 1990 the wreck of a wooden sixteenth-century warship armed with heavy guns was found in the deep water of Nämdö Fjord, a little south of Stockholm. At first it was hoped she was the *Lybska Svan* (Swan of Lübeck), the largest of these Hanseatic ships, which wrecked in the area in 1524. However, after excavation it was found that she was too small. A far more likely candidate is the unnamed ship described as one of the king's best kravels (carvels). She had just finished salvaging guns from the *Svan* when she was wrecked. Not only was the vessel carvel-built, but also her timbers have been dated to about 1515 and identified as coming from near Lübeck. Almost certainly she was one of Sweden's newly bought fleet.

One of the most impressive features of the shipwreck is the large number of wrought-iron breech-loading guns recovered from her—eleven have been located so far, and more probably lie in deeper water, lost as the ship tumbled down the steep underwater sides of the fjord. This represents the largest number of wrought-iron guns ever found on a single Renaissance shipwreck. Many were larger than those recovered from the wreck of the *Mary Rose*, and all were still attached to their sledlike wooden carriages. It was little wonder that the Swedes wanted to recover the guns from the *Svan* so badly. They represented a potent military force and suggested that when the Lübeckers supplied their Swedish allies with ships, they also provided enough guns to turn these merchant vessels into powerful warships.

The Lübeckers also had a hand in the Danish revolt against Christian II, so they evidently still considered themselves a major player in the game of Baltic politics. A decade later they would again intervene in Danish affairs, but this time the results would be a lot less favorable. Following the death of Frederick I in 1533, Denmark was plunged into civil war, and the Lübeckers took advantage of this to seize control of Copenhagen and the remains of the Danish royal fleet. Using the city as a base, they then closed The Sound to Dutch ships in an attempt to regain their monopoly of trade.

The elected Swedish king Gustav Vasa (reigned 1523–1560) didn't like this development and decided to intervene on behalf of Prince Christian, the son of the late king. Christian raised his own small fleet of armed merchantmen and joined forces with the Swedes. Gustav Vasa had added to his fleet since his accession, and it now included three purpose-built warships of 500 to 1,000 tons, and one leviathan, which appropriately enough was called the *Elefant* (Elephant). She was built in Stockholm in 1534, and her nickname of *Stora Krafvel* (Great Carvel) suggests that she was carvel-built—one of the first Baltic warships we can associate with this imported style of shipbuilding.

When the *Elefant* was launched she became the largest ship ever seen in Baltic waters. She had a keel length of 130 feet, a beam amidships of 40 feet, and a draft of 22 feet. Her towering sterncastle rose 54 feet above the water of Stockholm Harbor, climbing up from her waist in two steps—a forecastle and a poop deck. Her mainmast added another 122 feet to her height. Her overall length was estimated at an impressive 180 feet, not counting her beak and bowsprit. According to the formula used to work out the size of the *Henri Grace à Dieu*, she would have been rated as a vessel of 1,200 tons burden, which made her even bigger than her English counterpart, although some estimates have suggested she could have been as large as 1,700 tons. We also have no real idea of her armament, although she was considered to be an extremely well-armed and powerful ship of war.

On June 9, 1535, the allied fleet encountered the Lübeckers near the island of Bornholm, off the southern tip of the Swedish peninsula. Many of these Hanseatic ships were actually Danish royal warships—the fleet of Frederick I that had been captured when the Lübeckers seized Copenhagen. For the most part the attackers relied on gunnery to defeat the enemy, which eventually broke and ran for the safety of The Sound, where another Hanseatic squadron maintained its economic blockade of the waterway. Led by the *Elefant*, the Allies scattered this force, too, then blockaded any surviving Lübeck ships in Copenhagen. Having lost control of the sea, the Lübeckers had little option but to sue for peace, and in early 1536 Copenhagen was handed over to the Danish prince, who duly became King Christian III. This small war demonstrated that while the Lübeckers might still have a role in Baltic affairs, they were no longer a power on the same level as Denmark and Sweden. After some three centuries the Hansa had finally become a bit player on the Baltic stage.

Christian III would use his small fleet to regain control of Norway, and as an early supporter of the Protestant Reformation he was also anxious to flex his naval muscles against the Catholic powers of Europe by attacking the Spanish Netherlands. However, in 1543 a planned amphibious attack on the island of Walcheren was thwarted by bad weather, and peace was concluded with the Hapsburg emperor, Charles V, the following year. Despite this, Christian was not primarily a naval enthusiast, and he spent most of his time and energy improving his political position on the mainland of central

Europe, not worrying about control of the Dominum Maris Baltica. It was not until the accession of Frederick II (reigned 1559–1588) that the Danish navy would undergo a major expansion. By that time they had lost their naval supremacy and would spend the best part of a century battling the Swedes in an attempt to regain it. The new Danish king built an extensive naval dockyard at Bremerholm outside Copenhagen, and while the Sound Toll paid for the new ships, the Danish towns and cities were expected to supply their quota of guns, men, and supplies.

The Sound Toll was more than just a levy on passing foreign ships. In exchange the Danes agreed to mark their channels with navigation aids and to keep the Baltic free of pirates. However, with two powerful navies in the region, pirates had become a thing of the past. Frederick's real concern was the Swedish navy. The Danish king was eager for a war—he even incorporated the Swedish royal symbol of three crowns in his own coat of arms as an indication that he still regarded Sweden as part of his own king- dom. The showdown finally came in August 1563—a conflict that became known as the First Nordic War. Another name for it was the Nordic Seven Years' War, which is how long the fighting lasted before the protagonists ran out of men, money, and martial enthusi- asm. Although the two sides fought it out on land—mainly in what is now southern Sweden—the real fighting took place at sea, where seven sea battles would be fought in four years.

Technically Denmark and Sweden were still at peace when on May 30, 1563, the Danish fleet appeared off the island of Bornholm. They demanded the respect due a foreign warship—the firing of a gun and the dipping of a flag—and when the Swedes ignored them the Danes opened fire. It was all a charade—a fumbled Danish attempt at a preemptive strike. It also went disastrously wrong. In the four-hour battle that followed, the Danish sailors realized that they were seriously outclassed. While their own ships were primar- ily armed with old-fashioned wrought-iron breech-loading guns, the Swedes had equipped their ships with modern bronze muzzle- loading guns cast in the royal foundries. By the time the smoke cleared, the Danish fleet was in full retreat, leaving its flagship and two other ships in Swedish hands. The battle had been a contest between two different naval doctrines. While the Danes relied on a single broadside at point-blank range followed by a boarding attempt, the Swedes opted to keep their distance and pour fire into the enemy ships at close range. As the war progressed, the Danes would dramatically rethink their tactics, and as a result the two sides would become more evenly matched.

All this would take time, and while Frederick II's ambassadors tried to buy bronze guns in Germany, the royal gunfounders did their best to increase their meager output. As the Swedes had the monopoly on Baltic copper production, this would naturally be an expensive business. Meanwhile, a new Danish admiral—Peder Skram—was appointed, the fleet was repaired, and it returned to sea. This time the Danish fleet of twenty ships was accompanied by five warships supplied by their Lübecker allies, and the allied fleet cruised as far north as Stockholm without encountering the main Swedish fleet, which had returned to port. Skram blockaded the entrance to the Stockholm archipelago, almost as if he was daring the Swedes to come out and fight. On September 11 they obliged, but in those confined coastal waters the Swedes lacked the maneuverability they needed to keep their distance from the Danes. They returned into port, and this second naval battle was declared a draw. By October the onset of winter weather had forced Skram to call off his blockade and return home.

By 1564 the Danish strategy was clear. Frederick II hoped to blockade The Sound, thereby denying the Swedes sea access to Western European markets. All he needed to do to protect the narrow waters between Denmark and Sweden was to fight a defensive naval campaign. The aggressive new Danish admiral Herulf Trolle didn't approve of this plan; he felt that the best way to defeat the Swedes was to sink their fleet. His ships had now been rearmed, tactics had been rethought, and morale had improved immensely. He clearly thought he had a chance. On May 30 his fleet of fifteen Danish and ten Lübeck ships encountered the Swedish fleet off the island of Öland. His counterpart, Jakob Bragge, commanded sixteen large warships and armed merchantmen, and his flagship, *Mars*, of fifteen hundred tons, was considered the new leviathan that could all but win the war single-handedly.

At first the Swedes had the advantage, as they kept their distance and pounded the allies at long range. They had the weather gauge, which meant the enemy were downwind of them. This meant they could dictate the course of the battle by either keeping the range long or by racing down to meet the enemy. Thinking that the Danes lacked long-range guns, they opted to stay at long range. They caused minor damage to the allied fleet, but at nightfall the guns fell silent. At dawn rose the next day the wind had changed, and this time the allies had the weather gauge. They swooped down on the outnumbered Swedes and began firing at short range. Jakob Bragge gave the signal to withdraw, and while most of his fleet managed to cut and run, his flagship was left behind. The rudder of the *Mars* had been damaged, and she was unable to escape or maneuver. The allies simply kept out of the arc of fire of her guns and pummeled her from bow and stern. By midafternoon the once-proud leviathan slipped beneath the cold waters of the Baltic. The allies lost only one Hanseatic ship, although many of the Danish warships had been battered around during the fighting.

At least one other Swedish ship was lost in the battle: the *Elefant*, a replacement for the older warship of the same name. The newer *Elefant*, built as a three-masted carrack in Stockholm in 1559, was a thousand-ton purpose-built warship. She had a keel at least 120 feet long and a beam of about 40 feet. After the battle she sank close to Kalmar on the Swedish mainland, and in the 1930s her remains were discovered and excavated by the pioneering underwater archaeologist Carl Ekman. A small part of this Swedish warship's stern is on display in Stockholm's National Maritime Museum. Although attempts have been made to locate the remains of the *Mars*, she still lies undisturbed in the cold, dark waters off Öland.

The Swedes returned to sea later that year to capture a Hanseatic convoy, homeward bound from Narva to Lübeck. Then in August the veteran land commander Claes Horn led the fleet south from Stockholm. On August 11 he encountered Trolle's fleet between Öland and Gotland, and a five-day running fight developed. Every time the allies tried to get close to the enemy the Swedish fleet sidestepped, and they kept bombarding the enemy at long range. In his report to the Danish king, Trolle described the frustration of that running battle, claiming that the Swedish ships were faster and more maneuverable than his. It seemed as if the Swedes had finally learned to make the best of their superior guns and their sleeker ships. Still, the naval campaign was far from over, and both sides would continue to learn from their mistakes.

The naval struggle reached its peak in 1565, when three major battles were fought between the Swedes and the Danes, supported by their Lübecker allies. In May a new Swedish admiral, Claes Christerson Horn, led a powerful fleet of twenty-five ships south from Stockholm. Horn flew his flag in the *Sankt Erik*, a thousand-ton carrack armed with ninety guns. That year the fighting would center on the island of Bornholm, held by a Danish garrison. The Swedes wanted this strategically placed island for themselves. The first clash took place fifty miles to the south, off the island of Rügen, close to the Hanseatic port of Stralsund. On May 21 the Swedes surprised a squadron of four Danish warships commanded by Peter Hvitfeld. The Danes were driven ashore. The Danish commander was forced to burn his own ships to prevent them from falling into Swedish hands, but at least he managed to save most of his men and their guns.

Less than two weeks later, on June 4, Horn's ships encountered the main allied force off Bornholm—eighteen Danish ships and ten Lübeckers. The allies were commanded by Herolf Trolle, who flew his flag in the eight-hundred-ton *Jaegmesteren*. The two flagships singled each other out, and in the ensuing point-blank exchange Trolle was mortally wounded by a shot from a swivel gun. With their admiral dead the allies managed to extricate themselves and beat an ignominious retreat—a humiliating rout in the face of a far more organized enemy. However, they would be back. A new allied commander was appointed, Otto Rud; the blood was washed off the decks of the *Jaegmesteren*; and four weeks later his fleet returned to the fray. This time the allies were determined to fight. The Battle of Bornholm, which followed, was probably one of the largest sea battles in the Baltic during the Renaissance, and one of the first ever where both sides relied on firepower rather than boarding to decide the battle.

Otto Rud had about twenty-seven ships under his command, including fourteen Lübeckers. He strung his ships out between Rügen and Bornholm, and at noon on July 7 they sighted their quarry: Claes Christerson Horn and twenty-seven Swedish warships. The two sides were exactly matched. Following the protocol of the period the two flagships headed straight toward each other, while the rest of the two fleets swirled around them in a wild melee. Tactical niceties were thrown aside as both sides pounded each other at close range. After four hours of this there was only one clear victim: the Swedish warship *Förgyllda Lejonet* had caught fire and drifted out of the battle, the other combatants keeping well out of her way.

However, the *Jaegmesteren* was also in trouble. Surrounded by several Swedish warships, including the *Sankt Erik*, her crew were being cut to pieces. By late afternoon fewer than a hundred of her twelve-hundred-man crew were left standing. Admiral Rud had little option but to surrender his ship. With that the rest of the allied fleet fled back toward the safety of Copenhagen. In losses the Swedes were clearly the victors, with two ships sunk or burned and one captured. The allies lost three sunk and three captured. While these losses sound minor enough, the Danes and the Lübeckers still lost 16 percent of their fleet, and these were all major warships, not the gaggle of armed merchantmen that came along to make up the numbers. With hindsight the battle was a turning point in naval history: the first time a fleet had been defeated using firepower alone.

On land the war had reached a stalemate, but at sea both sides seemed willing to have one more try. On July 26, 1566, they fought to a standstill off Öland, as they now preferred to rely on long-range gunnery rather than to risk closing the range. Given the tactics of the time, this could damage an enemy fleet, but probably not sufficiently to cause the loss of any ships. The combatants, of thirty ships a side, represented the last roll of the dice: neither the Danes, the Lübeckers, nor the Swedes had the resources to buy or to build another fleet, although new large ships were on the stocks and would enter service the following year. It is hardly surprising that both admirals appeared unduly cautious.

However, what couldn't be achieved by gunnery was managed by the weather. After the July battle the allied fleet retired to the island of Gotland to repair its ships and bury its dead. On the night of July 28 a severe summer gale swept in from the southeast, and the warships were driven onto the island's coast. Nine Danish warships and three Lübeckers were lost in the tempest, along with as many as eight thousand men. Recently divers discovered the remains of one of these ships off Visby, along with German coins, a silver dagger, and a silver whistle—the badge of rank of an admiral. According to a chart of 1680, this spot was where the Lübeck flagship *Josva von Lübeck* (Joseph of Lübeck) went down. She flew the flag of Johann Kampferbeck, who managed to survive the shipwreck, although clearly he lost his badge of office in the process. Another wreck find, a little farther to the south, has also been tentatively identified as the Danish warship *Hannibal*, which flew the flag of Vice Admiral Jens Ulfstand. Unlike his German ally, he never made it to shore.

These losses couldn't be replaced, and when the allies retired for the winter, Frederick III realized that the war was as good as lost. He ordered his envoys to begin peace negotiations. For the next two years the small allied fleet remained in port, while the Swedes roamed the Baltic as far as The Sound. This was despite the launch of three new leviathans, one by each of the navies in the conflict. The Swedish flagship *Röde Draken* (Red Dragon), the Danish flagship *Fortuna*, and the Lübeck flagship *Die Adler Non Lübeck* (The Eagle of Lübeck) were all enormous warships of more than fifteen hundred tons apiece. None of them managed to fire a shot in anger before the war ended.

At first the Swedes had resisted all overtures of peace, as they knew they had the upper hand. However, the erratic King Erik IV finally snapped under the pressure and began to purge his leading commanders. He was promptly deposed in a coup, and in 1568 his brother the Duke of Finland became King Johann III of Sweden. The Peace of Stettin was finally signed in December 1570. As wars go, the conflict resolved nothing. The Swedes renounced any claim to Norway, and in return the Danes accepted Sweden's right to rule itself. The political status quo was maintained—a small gain at the cost of the loss of thousands of Scandinavian sailors. The new Swedish king now saw the Russians and Poles as a more significant threat than the Danes, and his political and naval attentions would be focused to the east for the rest of his reign. The one achievement of the war was the lesson it provided in the way naval battles should be fought in this new age of fast, maneuverable ships and powerful bronze guns. The only question was whether the other maritime powers had learned from these battles.

The real loser was Lübeck, whose economy had been ruined by the drawn-out conflict. She rapidly slipped from being a bit player to having a nonspeaking part. The *Adler von Lübeck* was eventually converted into a large grain carrier and ended her days as a merchantman. However, one Lübeck ship rose to prominence during this period, and its actions played a major part in precipitating the largest non-Mediterranean naval campaign of the Renaissance. What is even more remarkable was that while the warships of Lübeck were licking their wounds in port after the great storm off Gotland, half a world away the crew of this other Lübecker was fighting for their lives against a completely different foe. This remarkable vessel was called the *Jesus of Lübeck*.

Hawkins and the *Jesus*

In 1544 a party of English seamen traveled to Hamburg to take charge of a ship that had just been bought by Henry VIII's agents. She was the *Jesus of Lübeck*, one of five Hanseatic ships that Henry had been interested in—the others being the *Struse of Danzig*, the *Mary of Hamburg*, the *Marianne*, and the *Christopher of Bremen*. All except the *Christopher* had been leased from their owners for a year, while Henry reserved the right to buy them when the lease ran out. Paperwork problems meant that it would be another year before the Bremen ship could join the fleet. The English king was in the market for ships because he was fighting yet another war against the French, and his own yards were unable to build ships fast enough to outpace the shipbuilding program instituted by King Francis I of France. Consequently the Lübecker would make a valuable addition to his fleet. She was described as being a stately carrack of seven hundred tons, with four masts, a prominent forecastle, and a high, sloping sterncastle. In other words, she would make an ideal warship.

The *Jesus of Lubeck*—the English quickly dropped the Germanic umlaut—was certainly an impressive ship, measuring about 135 to 140 feet in overall length, with a keel of about 118 feet, a 30-foot waist, and a relatively large draft of 18 to 20 feet. Even by the standards of her day she was notably high-sided, which made her even more

The Jesus of Lubeck

suitable as a gun platform, as it meant she had the space to carry a full run of lower-deck guns. After she was sailed to the Thames she was equipped with ordnance from Tower Wharf, then taken down to Woolwich, where she was fitted out. This is exactly how she appears in the *Anthony Roll* of 1545, the Tudor fleet record that illustrated all of the king's ships. The same document lists her armament—just nine bronze guns, compared to the fifteen on the *Mary Rose* when she sank. These pieces—a cannon, two demicannons, a culverin, two demiculverins, and three sakers—were augmented by ten wrought-iron port pieces and thirty-two swivel guns. These were manned by 24 gunners, supported by 158 sailors and 118 soldiers. While she might not have been quite so well armed as the unfortunate *Mary Rose*, she probably was considerably less top-heavy.

Before these guns were fitted she was ordered to Portsmouth, where she was used in the attempt to salvage the *Mary Rose*. When this proved impossible, she completed her fitting out and then went on active service. For almost two decades she became one of the workhorses of the fleet, often serving as the flagship of the Summer or Winter Guard that patrolled the waters of the English Channel searching for pirates, smugglers, and Frenchmen. However, by the early 1560s the *Jesus* was starting to look a little old-fashioned. During the reign of Henry VIII's daughter "Bloody Mary"—Queen Mary I (reigned 1553–1558)—the English had come into direct contact with the latest Spanish galleons, a new development in Iberian shipbuilding. The English shipwrights were impressed by what they saw, and the first three warships built along Spanish lines were commissioned into the Navy Royal during the last turbulent years of Mary's reign. By the time Queen Elizabeth succeeded her Catholic half-sister, the *Jesus* was considered a plodding liability. Therefore, when John Hawkins approached the queen with a business proposal involving a trading expedition, Elizabeth grasped this heaven-sent opportunity to modernize the old Lübecker without it costing her a penny.

Sir John Hawkins

John Hawkins is best remembered as one of Elizabeth's sea dogs, and the man responsible for building up the Elizabethan navy in time for it to take on the Spanish Armada in 1588. However, long before all that he was a slave trader and an interloper. That was the term used by the Spanish for any foreigner who ventured "beyond the line"—a boundary running from Newfoundland to Brazil, drawn on a map of the world by the Borgia pope Alexander VI in 1494. According to the terms of the Treaty of Tordesillas, every newly discovered part of the world east of the line belonged to the Portuguese, and everything to the west—which meant most of the Americas—was considered Spanish property. The Spanish took this seriously, and they actively hunted down any interlopers who crossed the line, whether they came to trade or to plunder. For interlopers such as Hawkins there would be no peace beyond the line. The pope hadn't consulted the English, the French, or the Dutch about this boundary, so they chose to ignore it.

Hawkins realized that the fledgling Spanish colonies along the Spanish Main represented a lucrative market, and the Spanish lacked the naval muscle to keep interlopers out. Officially the Spanish Main referred to the Caribbean coast of South America, but for the most part it was extended to cover all Spanish settlements and territories in the Caribbean basin. All these settlements needed slaves to work the plantations, while the territories themselves produced valuable goods that would fetch a high price in England. This realization marked the start of the shameful business venture known as the triangular trade. A cargo of trade goods, such as metal, domestic goods, or weapons, was shipped from Europe to the western coast of Africa. These goods were bartered for a cargo of African slaves.

Then came the Middle Passage, when these unfortunates were transported across the Atlantic to the Americas—crammed into the holds of the slave ships like cattle, only with less room to move. Those who survived the experience were then sold to the colonists of the New World, or traded for produce of the Americas—sugar, silver, indigo, logwood, cotton, tobacco, or fur. The final leg of the voyage involved the transport of these goods to Europe, where they were sold for considerable profit. It was an extremely lucrative business, and enormous profits could be made while the slave trade lasted. While the Spanish themselves were forbidden to trade with foreigners, face-saving deals still could be made where the guns on board the interloper ships could temporarily dominate the port, thereby forcing the local mayor to do business with them. In the 1560s the Spanish hadn't fortified many of their smaller American ports, so as long as the interlopers stayed clear of major ports such as Havana, Cartagena, and Santo Domingo, they were relatively safe from harm. For Hawkins the only real problem was keeping out of the way of the well-armed annual Spanish treasure flota.

Hawkins was born into a trading family from Plymouth in Devon, and from childhood he was groomed for a life at sea. In 1560 the twenty-eight-year-old Hawkins joined a syndicate of prosperous English merchants who wanted to profit from trade with the New World. The following year he led the syndicate's first expedition when he sailed from Plymouth with two small ships—the *Solomon* (120 tons) and the *Swallow* (100 tons). They made landfall on the West African Guinea coast near modern-day Sierra Leone, where they captured a Portuguese slave ship lying at anchor. After some difficulty Hawkins filled the holds of his ships with three hundred slaves, whom he transported to the Caribbean, making landfall east of the Spanish island of Hispaniola in early 1563. He wisely avoided the well-fortified port of Santo Domingo, landing farther up the coast. He negotiated directly with the local landowners, and when a Spanish cavalry patrol arrived, Hawkins calmly arranged that they protect the interlopers in return for a cut of the profits. When Hawkins returned to England and revealed just how much he had made, his business partners were delighted. He was now a celebrity, and the richest man in Plymouth. More importantly, Hawkins had shown that substantial profits could be made for anyone willing to venture beyond the line.

This was where the *Jesus of Lubeck* enters the story. It was inevitable that Hawkins would try his luck again, and this time he was offered royal backing. Queen Elizabeth was a canny businesswoman, and she knew that the royal seal of approval would help Hawkins attract investors. However, rather than a financial stake, the queen proposed to lease Hawkins the *Jesus of Lubeck*. The only problem was that he had to refit and refurbish her at his own expense. Obviously this was a particularly bad deal for Hawkins, but he needed royal approval, so he had little choice. He found himself lumbered with an impressive royal warship, albeit one that was old, slow, and unsuitable for his needs. He set to with a will, cutting down the towering superstructure of the *Jesus* so her forecastle and sterncastle looked much more streamlined. This wasn't an aesthetic change: by lowering her superstructure he dramatically improved her sailing qualities, making her less prone to crabbing to leeward when the wind hit her from the side, and allowing her to sail closer into the wind than she had managed before. By the time she was ready, the *Jesus* was the closest thing to a modern warship that Hawkins could create.

This second expedition began in October 1564, when Hawkins left Plymouth, bound for the Guinea coast. The *Jesus* was accompanied by the *Solomon* and two small pinnaces—the *Tiger* and the *Swallow*. This time the business of collecting a cargo of slaves proved a little harder, but eventually he gathered about four hundred Africans and transported them to the Americas. This time the Spanish were a lot less willing to cooperate—the English slavers were turned away from the island of Margarita off the Venezuelan coast and only managed to sell their cargo on the mainland when they threatened to turn their guns on the small towns they visited. By October 1565 Hawkins was back in Devon, the hold of the *Jesus* filled with valuable cargo, including gold, silver, and pearls. This time his actions earned him an official complaint from the Spanish ambassador at Elizabeth's court. However, as Elizabeth was party to this slave-trading venture, there was no risk of any official action against him. Once again Hawkins had demonstrated that a determined and well-armed interloper could break the Spanish monopoly of trade on the Spanish Main.

The third expedition was when it all went badly wrong. Once again Queen Elizabeth was anxious to back the slaving expedition, and Hawkins's lease of the *Jesus* was extended. In October 1567 Hawkins left Plymouth on his third slaving voyage. The *Jesus* was commanded by Robert Barrett of Saltash—although she also served as Hawkins's flagship—while a second royal ship, the *Minion*, of 300 tons, was commanded by John Hampton of Plymouth. This means that both of Elizabeth's ships were crewed by Hawkins's own men rather than appointees of the crown. The two ships were accompanied by the *William and John* (150 tons); the *Swallow* (100 tons); and two pinnaces, the *Judith* and the *Angel*. The *Judith* was commanded by Hawkins's young kinsman Francis Drake.

Things began to go awry even before the expedition reached the West African coast. They were hit by a storm in the Bay of Biscay, which damaged the *Jesus* so badly that Hawkins considered returning to port. Then a slaving raid on the African coast near Cape Verde ended with the ambushing of the Englishmen. Eight crewmen were killed before the slavers managed to fight their way back to the ships. Off the Guinea coast Hawkins found that his local tribal contact was at war with a neighbor, so he helped his ally capture the township of Conga, the enemy capital. His reward was five hundred Conganese prisoners, who were taken aboard the ships as slaves. Hawkins then set sail for the Spanish Main. He arrived off the Venezuelan coast in June 1568 but soon found that the settlement at Río Hatcha had been reinforced by a Spanish garrison since his last visit, and they were not so easily cowed by the *Jesus*.

After a brief exchange of fire Hawkins sailed down the coast and managed to sell about half his slaves in the nearby town of Santa Marta. Once again it took the threat of a bombardment by the *Jesus* to force the local governor to trade with the interlopers, although chances are that this demonstration of strength was staged as part of a deal. It allowed the governor to tell his superiors he had no choice but to deal with the English. Hawkins had hoped to sell the rest of his slaves near Cartagena, but when it became clear the governor was hostile, he continued to the north. Then in September the slavers were overtaken by a hurricane in the Gulf of Mexico. Although the *William and John* beat to windward and made it home, the rest of the fleet were driven into the Bay of Campeche. The venerable *Jesus* was in a bad way. One of her crew later wrote, "On either side of the stern-post the planks did open and shut with every sea, the seas being without number, and the leak so big as the thickness of a man's arm, the living fish did swim upon the ballast as in the sea." She would be lucky to make it into port, let alone back to England. Hawkins had no choice but to put into the Mexican port of Vera Cruz for repairs.

The port had been built near where Cortez first landed when he invaded Mexico and conquered the Aztec empire half a century earlier. By the time Hawkins and his men arrived on September 15 it had become a squalid but respectable port, used for the shipment of Mexican silver. A small mole stretched seaward over the mudflats from the shore, but the port's main anchorage was on the far side of the small roadstead, on the tiny island of San Juan de Ulúa—little more than a shinglebank on top of a sandbar. To the north stretched the treacherous Gallega Reefs. This bank was where the meager defenses of the port had been placed, and although called a *castillo*, the fort was really just a sand-blown five-gun battery and a small chapel. The anchorage there was deep enough for ships the size of the *Jesus*, and a quay had been built allowing vessels to berth on the western side of the island facing the town, where they would have some shelter from the prevailing easterly wind. Hawkins decided to trick the Spaniards by sailing into port under the Spanish flag. This allowed him to enter the port and seize the defenses before the Spaniards could sound the alarm. He must have wondered why the ruse had been so successful, and was horrified to learn that the garrison thought his ships were the annual Spanish treasure flota, which was due to arrive at any moment. Sure enough, just two days later the thirteen ships of the flota appeared off the harbor. A maritime emergency was about to turn into an international incident. The flota's commander, Admiral Francisco Luján, was less than happy to discover that these heretics and interlopers had seized the anchorage, but he decided to bide his time. He was also carrying Don Martín Enríquez, the governor designate of New Spain, who had no intention of making a deal with pirates. A truce was arranged, and while the English repaired their ships the Spanish set about planning a surprise attack.

Hawkins knew he was outnumbered by two to one in both ships and men, but there was little he could do but remain vigilant and hope he could extricate himself as soon as his ships were seaworthy. As extra insurance he reinforced the shore battery with six more guns and trained the pieces on the anchored Spanish ships. However, Luján and Don Martín still managed to catch the English unawares. Both the English and the Spaniards were moored in "Mediterranean fashion" to the San Juan de Ulúa quay. Mediterranean fashion meant that the ships lay with their bows or sterns facing the shore, which meant that the guns of the *Minion*, at one end of the line, faced those of the Spanish flagship a hundred yards away. In between lay a merchant hulk, which had been there when the English first arrived. During the next few nights the Spanish secretly moved two hundred soldiers on board her, creating a Trojan horse within easy grappling range of the *Jesus*. Hawkins realized that something was up and sent Robert Barrett ashore to speak to Admiral Luján on board his flagship. The Spaniards simply took him prisoner.

Finally, at 10:00 A.M. on September 23, Luján waved a white handkerchief as a signal, and the Spaniards attacked. They quickly overran the small English garrison on San Juan de Ulúa, and having captured the gun batteries, the Spaniards turned the pieces on the English ships. Although the battle that followed lasted all day, it was clear the English were in a hopeless situation. Fireships were launched against their ships, but they were repelled. The *Minion* cut her mooring ropes and slipped out into the harbor, where she began firing into the Spanish ships still ranged along the quay. The next ship in line, the *Jesus*, was closest to the Spanish, who pounded her with artillery and small-arms fire, holing her and knocking down her mainmast. After the battle five roundshot were found stuck in her mainmast. Meanwhile, the *Minion* had caused a fire on board one of the Spanish ships, and when it reached her powder store the ship blew up and the flames spread to the flagship beside her. She sank in shallow water. The battle was reaching fever pitch, and the *Jesus* was in the thick of the fight.

At this point Hawkins asked his page to bring him a beer. As the shot flew all around him he drained the silver goblet, then set it beside him. Seconds later a Spanish roundshot smashed into the goblet and hurled it overboard. This display of English sangfroid was all very well, but even Hawkins realized that the *Jesus* was doomed. He called the *Minion* to pull alongside her less exposed beam and ordered her cargo of specie and pearls carried into the smaller ship. The terrified slaves were left where they were. Hawkins was the last man to leave the *Jesus*, and 200 Englishmen were now crammed on board the *Minion* as she edged through the carnage toward the open sea. The only other English ship that remained uncaptured was Drake's tiny *Judith*, which also put to sea with 50 more survivors. More than 150 Englishmen were left behind—either dead, wounded, or prisoners, the latter including

Robert Barrett and Hawkins's eleven-year-old nephew, who had been hiding aboard the *Jesus* when the *Minion* set sail. Somehow the two ships made it to safety, leaving the shattered wreck of the *Jesus of Lubeck* behind them.

The voyage home was horrific. A hundred crewmen elected to take their chances with the Spanish and asked to be put ashore, while the rest died through wounds, starvation, or disease. By the time Hawkins steered the *Minion* back into Plymouth, fewer than 20 of her crew remained alive. Ever since, both Hawkins and Drake nursed a burning hatred of the Spanish, whom they claim attacked them under a flag of truce. They were perfectly right to be furious—most of the English sailors they left behind were either executed or sold into slavery. The *Jesus of Lubeck* was examined by her new Spanish owners, and an inventory taken of her guns, stores, and equipment. While they felt the battered carrack was next to worthless, they were impressed by her armament and by the way her guns were mounted. Unfortunately, the records fail to tell us what happened to the Lübecker after the battle. In all likelihood her battle-damaged and storm-weakened hull was never repaired and she ended her days as an abandoned hulk some forty-five hundred miles from her home waters of the Baltic. This little battle off San Juan de Ulúa was the first in a series of incidents that turned the cold war between Catholic Spain and Protestant England into a full-scale conflict. When the final showdown came, a vengeful Sir John Hawkins and Sir Francis Drake would be in the forefront of the English fleet as it sailed out to do battle with the Spanish Armada.

7

From Carrack to Galleon

The Fight of the *San Mateo*

Perched high in the Spanish mountains some twenty-eight miles northwest of Madrid is El Escorial, the monastic eyrie from which King Philip II of Spain ruled his transatlantic empire. This royal retreat is a mixture of palace and monastery, a place where the king's temporal influence and the spiritual power of the Church could find common cause. While Philip II's own quarters are remarkably austere, the builders were allowed greater rein in designing the great basilica; in the Pantheon of Kings; and in the long hall of battles, which celebrated Spain's catalog of recent military achievements. While most of Philip's military paintings celebrate victories on land, or amphibious landings that sent a veteran Spanish army onto a hostile shore, one fresco stands out from the rest. Unlike the other paintings, it depicts a naval victory—off the Azores in 1582, which saw a small and badly outnumbered Spanish armada attack and defeat the elite of the French navy.

The battle came about because of a chain of events that began in August 1580, when in a blitzkrieg campaign the Duke of Alba conquered Portugal in the name of Philip of Spain. As the Spanish flag was raised over Lisbon, Philip was able to take true stock of his victory. Not only had he conquered a neighboring country, he had also secured control over the sprawling Portuguese overseas empire in Brazil, Africa, India, and the Indies. He also gained control of the powerful Portuguese navy. Until then most of Spain's naval efforts had been directed to waging war against the Muslims in the Mediterranean, or else safeguarding its vulnerable maritime link with its colonies in the New World. He now owned eleven ocean-going Portuguese galleons of seven hundred to a thousand tons. These warships would become the nucleus of Spain's new Atlantic fleet, and within eight years they would be sent into battle against the Navy Royal of Elizabethan England.

The only part of the Portuguese empire that still defied Philip was the Azores, that cluster of nine islands in the Atlantic. They were of strategic importance to Spain, as its New World flotas made landfall there on their way back to Spain. To safeguard his flow of American gold and silver, Philip had to conquer the Azores. The Portuguese rebel leader was Don Antonio, Prior of Cato, who managed to strike a deal with the French. In June 1582 a French fleet

The Azores battle, 1582—detail from El Escorial fresco

of sixty ships sailed from Brest, bound for Don Antonio's capital on the island of Terceira. They were commanded by the Florentine nobleman Filippo Strozzi, a veteran soldier and a naval commander of some repute. In Lisbon a Spanish fleet also was being readied for sea, under the even more experienced eye of Don Alvaro de Bázan, the Marquis de Santa Cruz. Eleven years before, the marquis had turned the tide at the naval Battle of Lepanto (1571) and helped ensure that the Christian fleet won a crushing victory over the Turkish galleys. As Spain's most celebrated naval hero, the fifty-six-year-old nobleman was the king's choice as his fleet commander.

On July 10 the marquis's flagship, *San Martín*, led the Spanish fleet out of Lisbon Harbor and into the open Atlantic. Of the thirty-six ships under his command, the eleven Portuguese galleons were by far the largest and most powerful ships at his disposal. The 1,000-ton *San Martín* was one of them—a Lisbon-built galleon armed with forty-eight guns—while the 750-ton *San Mateo* acted as the flagship of the Portuguese squadron. Making up the numbers were a hastily assembled collection of Spanish and Portuguese armed merchant-men under the command of the veteran naval commander Don Miguel de Oquendo. Then came a small group of supply ships, dispatch boats, and even a hospital ship. Five of these vessels, including the hospital ship, were forced to turn back during a storm, but on July 22 the rest of the Spanish fleet made landfall in the Azores. The French had beaten them to it—they were already lying off the islands' main harbor of Punta Delgada.

Filippo Strozzi watched the approach of the Spanish fleet with quiet confidence. After all, he outnumbered the enemy, and the local pilots supplied by Don Antonio gave his captains the tactical advantage of knowing the waters. The two fleets shadowed each other for three days, each commander waiting for the other to make a mistake. Once Strozzi thought he saw an advantage when Oquendo's squadron fell behind the rest of the Spanish fleet. Don Alvaro sent his Portuguese galleons back to support his rear guard, and after a brief skirmish the French shied away. Then, on the nearly windless morning of July 26, the two fleets lay off the island of São Miguel. Strozzi saw that the *San Mateo* had become isolated from the rest of the Spanish fleet. He ordered his leading squadron to attack immediately. The French flagship was the first to smash into the Portuguese galleon, and soon all five French warships were clustered around her, like wolves clinging to a bear. The *San Mateo* fought them off for two hours until her decks were littered with dead, fires were burning from incendiaries, her masts were shot away, and her hull was pierced by more than five hundred roundshot. Still she held on.

By that time the rest of the Spanish fleet managed to come to the rescue. First on the scene was Oquendo, who smashed his small 350-ton flagship, *Juana*, into a French warship. One observer later claimed that "he handled his ship like a cavalryman handled his horse." He fired a broadside and boarded in the smoke, only to find that the French ship was sinking fast. Oquendo called his men back and let the French ship sink. By now the fighting had turned into a general melee, although the French rear guard—some thirty ships—was becalmed and unable to join the fight. This gave the Spanish something akin to parity in numbers, but in this kind of bitter close-quarters fighting they had one great advantage: all their ships carried a full complement of Spanish soldiers, who were then reckoned to be the best infantrymen in Europe. Once the Spanish ship captains managed to get close enough to grapple a French ship, they could rely on their superb troops to do the rest.

In keeping with the chivalric spirit of the times, Don Alvaro sought out Filippo Strozzi's flagship, which was still fighting the *San Mateo*. The *San Martín* ranged alongside and fired a broadside into her French counterpart. Then the Spanish troops swung across, and the fighting raged across the decks of the French flagship. By the time the melee ended, some four hundred Frenchmen lay dead on the decks of their ship, and a mortally wounded Strozzi was carried to Don Alvaro so he could surrender. He died before he could make this last gesture. The Spanish admiral had his counterpart's body thrown overboard along with the rest of the French dead, while his men battled to keep the French flagship from sinking beneath them. By that time it was clear that the Marquis de Santa Cruz had won a spectacular victory: without losing any ships himself, the Spanish had sunk six French warships, captured the enemy flagship, and abandoned four battered wrecks to drift ashore. It was hardly any wonder that Philip II chose to commemorate this great achievement with a fresco.

The Spanish Galleon

The ability of the doughty *San Mateo* to hold her own against overwhelming odds impressed the Spanish sea captains, who declared that she was vastly superior to the ships used by the French. It is hardly surprising that they thought her well designed, as although Portuguese, she was based on a thoroughly Spanish design. The largest warships in the French fleet were carracks—little different from the *Jesus of Lubeck*, which had battled the Spanish treasure flota at San Juan de Ulúa fourteen years before. However, as a warship type the carrack was fast becoming obsolete. Improvements in gunnery meant that these high-sided warships with their towering superstructures were vulnerable to artillery. Their size made these carracks excellent targets, while their height also made them top-heavy and prone to wallowing, which reduced the accuracy of their gunfire. This height also made them difficult to handle, as the wind tended to push them to leeward as they sailed, making it hard to steer a straight course. However, the *San Mateo* was a galleon, one of a new breed of ships that represented the future of warship design.

The Spanish galleon must be one of the most romantic types of ships ever invented—forever associated with sunken treasure, pirates, and the long-lost days of the Spanish Main. Our image of them is heavily influenced by Hollywood—we can immediately visualize large, lumbering, stately warships with towering sides, richly decorated, and with holds brimming with the treasures of the New World. The reality was a little different, and while Spanish galleons were indeed the treasure carriers of the Spanish Americas, they were known more for their maneuverability than their grandeur. The origin of the galleon is a little obscure, but the term first appeared during the first two decades of the sixteenth century.

The first Spanish galleon probably was built in 1517 to fight the Barbary pirates of the Mediterranean and almost certainly was a copy of the Venetian *galleoni* of the late fifteenth century—vessels that combined oar and sail power. The Portuguese used a similar type of vessel—a *galleone*—in the Indian Ocean during the early sixteenth century, where they served as patrol craft around Portuguese trading posts. By the 1530s the Spanish galleon had become something altogether larger and more powerful—contemporary pictures of them show that the galleon was no longer a small oared warship, but a sailing ship with its own distinctive appearance. However, as late as the 1560s some small Spanish galleons were still built with covered oar ports, which allowed them to be powered by oars when there was no wind to fill the sails. The galleon had become a ship type in its own right—immediately identifiable as something completely different from a carrack or a hulk.

It has been argued that the galleon was a development of the carvel, the kind of small, light, lanteen-rigged trading vessels used by the first Portuguese and Spanish explorers on their voyages of discovery. We know even less about the origin of the carvel (or caravel) than we do about the first galleons, although in the mid-thirteenth century the word *caravela* was used to describe Portuguese fishing boats. Images of late-fifteenth- and early-sixteenth-century carvels seem to support this idea that the group could include large coastal boats as well as ships big enough to make long ocean voyages. Columbus used two carvels—the *Nina* and the *Pinta*—during his first transatlantic voyage of exploration in 1492, when they accompanied his flagship, the *Santa Maria*, which was a nao. The main feature of these small ships was that they were normally furnished with two or occasionally three masts, each fitted with a lateen-riggged sail. As their name suggests, they were also carvel-built, which, like the lateen sails, betrayed their Mediterranean or Iberian origins.

Certainly the early galleons and the carvel had certain features in common, such as a low forecastle—at least when you compared it with a nao or a carrack—or their carvel-built form of construction. However, they also had things in common with these large ship types, such as sturdiness of construction; their sailing rig, which included square as well as lateen-rigged sails; and, of course, their size. While the first galleons might have been fairly small, by the mid-sixteenth century they were generally accepted as being ships of the same size as carracks. Rather than looking for any one ancestor, it is probably better to consider the galleon as developing from an amalgam of Mediterranean and Iberian shipbuilding styles. Shipowners and shipbuilders saw the need for a new type of vessel that combined the speed and maneuverability of the carvel with the cargo capacity of the nao and the carrack. They used the best of both styles of sailing rig, and abandoned features seen as a liability, such as the high superstructure of the carrack. The result was a ship type perfectly suited to Spanish and Portuguese needs.

By the late 1530s the galleon had become a recognizable ship type in its own right, and in 1538 a Venetian galleon took part in the Battle of Prevesa, where it successfully held its own against a squadron of Turkish galleys. Unlike many other Mediterranean sailing ships, this vessel had been designed from the keel up as a warship, and it carried a powerful broadside battery of heavy guns. This is the period when galleons first start appearing in artwork, and we can begin to build up a picture of these iconic ships. Similarly, a Spanish votive model of a galleon from about 1540 shows just why these early galleons were so special. This wooden model shows a small ship of about six hundred tons, with a high but streamlined sterncastle sloping upward toward the stern. The ship has a small but pronounced forecastle, ending in a beak that looks like those on contemporary Mediterranean war galleys. The ship itself has a pronounced tumblehome, with the hulls sloping inward above the waterline—a feature that would have made the ship far more stable than a contemporary carrack such as the *Mary Rose*. The overall impression is one of a powerful but graceful ship, reasonably well armed, and appearing thoroughly seaworthy. This is exactly what made the galleon the ship of choice for Spain's treasure flotas.

The reason that the Spanish so enthusiastically embraced the galleon can be traced to a maritime encounter off Cape Sagres, on the southwestern tip of Portugal, in May 1523. Three Spanish caravels had just completed the last leg of their transatlantic voyage from Cuba, and their crews were looking forward to the delights of Seville. They had been sent to Spain by the famous conquistador Hernando Cortés, and their commander carried a report to the king describing the conquest of the Aztec empire. Better still, the holds of the ships were filled with Aztec gold—the plunder of the Aztec capital of Tenochtitlán. Within hours they would pick up their naval escort, a pair of armed naos waiting for them off nearby Cape St. Vincent. Then a lookout spotted five strange sails approaching them from the north. The Spanish captain wisely decided to head away from them and set a course directly toward the waiting escorts. Unfortunately for the Spanish, the five ships were much faster than their own weed-encrusted caravels.

Within hours the strangers had overhauled two of the Spanish ships and threatened to board them. Outnumbered and outgunned, the Spanish had no choice but to surrender. Then the identity of the attackers was revealed. They were French corsairs—privateers—commanded by Jean Fleury (or Flores) of Honfleur. As France and Spain were at war, the French crown had issued a privateering letter of marque to Jean Ango, a Dieppe shipowner, who ordered Jean Fleury to sea in search of Spanish plunder. That day he hit the mother lode. When the corsairs returned to Dieppe, the full extent of the haul was revealed—Aztec statues, emeralds the size of a human fist, shining ingots of gold and silver, bejeweled cloaks and headdresses . . . even a live jaguar. The entire treasure was valued at about 800,000 Spanish gold ducats—the equivalent of $320 million today. While this loss was bad enough for the Spanish, what was probably worse was that the other European powers now knew just how lucrative their shipments from the Americas had become. It was inevitable that Jean Fleury would be followed by other corsairs and pirates, all eager to steal their own share of this fabulous wealth.

As for the Spanish Crown, this stream of gold and silver from the Americas was a fantastic windfall, and it allowed them to pursue their own aggressive military campaigns in Europe, funding armies that would be the envy of less fortunate rulers. The Emperor Charles V couldn't afford to lose any more shipments. Whatever else they might have claimed, the main driving force behind the Spanish conquest of the New World was the quest for gold. While the conquistadors and the administrators kept the bulk of this for themselves, the Spanish Crown was entitled to a *quinto*, or fifth. This was the treasure being shipped, along with the private wealth of those lucky adventurers who had made their fortunes in the New World and were now transporting it home. Until the encounter off Cape Sagres the Spanish had sent their specie in single ships, or else in small groups, such as the one encountered by Jean Fleury. However, from 1527 all shipping sailing to or from the New World did so in highly organized convoys—the treasure flotas.

For almost two centuries the routine would be the same. The first of two convoys, the New Spain flota, sailed from Seville in April, followed in September by the Tierra Firme flota. Both followed the same

Drake attacking the Spanish treasure ship "Cacafuego"

route as far as the Spanish Main, but then they headed in different directions. The Tierra Firme flota spent the winter in Cartagena, where its ships collected Venezuelan gold and Colombian emeralds. In the spring it continued on to Nombre de Dios, where piles of Peruvian silver were waiting on the quayside. These had been shipped up the Pacific coast as far as Panama and then transported across the isthmus to meet the flota. After Francis Drake raided Nombre de Dios in 1572, the silver terminus was moved up the coast to the more easily defensible Porto Bello. From there the flota sailed to Havana, where it prepared to voyage home. The New Spain flota headed straight for Vera Cruz in Mexico—the place where the 1568 fleet ran into John Hawkins and the *Jesus of Lubeck*. There it collected the king's quota from the silver mines of Mexico, and even more specie, which had been transported across the Pacific from the Philippines and then carted across Mexico to the Caribbean coast. The flota then joined its companions in Havana, and the two fleets sailed home together.

The beauty of this flota system was its organization—one of the largest and most complex maritime ventures ever devised during the age of sail. The outward-bound flotas were powerful enough to resist most attacks, and once in the Caribbean their firepower was probably more than a match for any interlopers they might encounter. The firepower was ably demonstrated at San Juan de Ulúa. However, the joint homeward-bound fleet was practically invincible. During this period only one homeward-bound flota was ever intercepted and captured, and that was at the hands of the Dutch in 1628. What made these convoys so powerful was that although the bulk of them consisted of regular merchant ships, the core of the fleet—the royal warships—and the transporters of all the specie were all powerful galleons. The early convoys might have used armed naos, but from 1537 onward the guard ships operated by the Casa des Indies were small, purpose-built galleons. Consequently by the mid-1550s onward the galleon and the treasure flotas had become inextricably linked.

The Spanish excelled at administration. Every little detail of their flota operation was recorded, and today it remains wrapped in red ribbon and filed neatly in Seville's Archive of the Indies. In 1536 and again in 1543 the Spanish produced detailed lists saying exactly how these galleons should be armed, equipped, and manned. Fortunately we can judge just how closely these instructions were followed because we have archaeological evidence to compare to the documents. In 1554 the homeward-bound New Spain fleet was overtaken by a hurricane, and several ships were lost along the coast of what is now Padre Island, Texas. One of these unlucky ships was the 300-ton galleon *San Esteban*. The finds recovered from her included wrought-iron breech-loading guns, swivel guns (*versos* in Spanish), and even crossbows. What was missing from both the inventory and the shipwreck were the more modern guns that were already appearing in other fleets of the period. The Spanish seem to have been latecomers in the adoption of bronze muzzle-loading ordnance on their ships, which is probably why they were so impressed when they examined the armament of the *Jesus of Lubeck* after her capture.

The *San Esteban* was a small ship, and the documents suggest that she was typical of many of the Spanish galleons that plied the waters of the Spanish Main and the Atlantic during the mid-sixteenth century. During the 1540s it seems that most galleons run by the Casa des Indies were smaller than naos, with an average burden or cargo size of 120 *toneladas* (Spanish tons). However, just two years after the hurricane of 1554, galleons were listed as having an average burden of 334 toneladas, while galleons operating as guard ships in the waters of the Spanish Netherlands were listed as being 367 toneladas. Galleons seemed to have been getting bigger. The Spanish shipbuilding records also specify the length-to-breadth ratio of the perfect galleon as 4:1, which made them much sleeker than a typical nao, which had a 3:1 ratio, or even a carrack, which averaged 3.5:1. While in theory a wider ship would have made a more stable platform for artillery, this was countered by the height of the typical carrack, which tended to make the ships roll more. Therefore the galleon offered an excellent compromise between speed, armament, and seakeeping qualities.

In other words, for the most part galleons were well-designed ships, with an agility and grace that belie their later reputation as huge, lumbering leviathans. This bad reputation was largely the result of English propaganda, produced in the wake of the Spanish Armada campaign of 1588. Certainly some galleons—most notably those captured from the Portuguese in 1580—were large and probably a little unwieldy. However, others were smaller and as maneuverable as Oquendo's 350-ton Indies galleon *Juana*, which he handled the way a cavalryman handles his horse during the Battle off São Miguel in 1582. That certainly isn't the description of a lumbering and ungainly warship. What changed slightly was that during the second half of the sixteenth century galleons kept growing. By 1570 galleons of 500 toneladas had become commonplace, while during the 1588 campaign all three leviathans of the Portuguese squadron—the *San Martín*, the *San Juan de Portugal*, and the *Florencia*—exceeded 900 tons, while another six galleons in the fleet were more than 700 tons, and a group of eight galleons diverted from the Indies flota each displaced about 530 toneledas.

The English galleon White Bear

Strangely enough, these were matched by almost as many large ships in the English navy, two of which—the *Triumph* and the *White Bear*—exceeded 1,000 tons burden, making them similar in size to the largest of the Portuguese galleons. What really gave the Spanish a reputation for lumbering ships were not the galleons but the dozens of naos, carracks, and hulks, which made up the bulk of the fleet. The Armada's strength lay in its ability to maintain a tight defensive formation as it sailed up the English Channel. Therefore its speed and maneuverability were dictated by its slowest ships. The fight, which was hailed as a test between two different types of warships, was really nothing of the kind—it was more a clash between two groups of armed merchantmen supported by some of the finest warships in Europe. Ultimately what let the Spanish down was a combination of uncharacteristic bad planning, an inordinate amount of bad luck, and English superiority in gunnery.

In the decades following the Spanish Armada debacle, the Spanish tended to favor smaller galleons, so for the rest of the period the average Spanish galleon was no more than 500 toneledas burden. This was the size of the *Nuestra Señora de Atocha* (Our Lady of Atocha), the Spanish galleon that wrecked off the Florida Keys during a hurricane in September 1622. Some three and a half centuries later, in 1980, her remains and those of her sister ship, the *Santa Margarita*, were discovered by the treasure hunter Mel Fisher. Altogether some $200 million worth of treasure was recovered from the shipwrecks, making them one of the richest salvage sites in history. Fortunately, Fisher employed a team of archaeologists to record what they could of the ships themselves, and enough information was gathered to give us a clear idea of how these late Renaissance galleons were built and how they were manned, armed, and operated.

It seems that by this stage the Spanish had learned their lesson, and the galleons were equipped with the latest bronze guns, although they still carried a company of soldiers and a battery of swivel guns in case anyone was foolish enough to try boarding them. The galleon had reached the end of its evolutionary road, and within two decades of the sinking of the *Atocha* the Spanish would abandon centuries of maritime tradition and opt for a warship that closely aped the ships developed by their northern European rivals. It is therefore ironic that these seventeenth-century sailing ships of war were themselves a development of the Spanish galleon. While the Spanish simply refined the design, their English rivals were prepared to develop the design so completely that the result would usher in a whole new era of warship design.

John Hawkins and the Race-Built Galleon

The popular misconception about the Spanish Armada of 1588 is that the fighting was a David and Goliath affair, where small but nippy English ships were able to run circles around the big, lumbering Spanish galleons. The reality was a little different. We have already seen how many of the Spanish galleons weren't that big and that some of the English fleet were just as large as the Spanish flagships. However, the veteran English captains knew they held the decisive advantage in two key areas. First, their ships were better equipped to engage in a gunnery duel than their Spanish rivals.

Second, the handful of royal warships that made up the cutting edge of the English fleet were more than a match for any ship in the Spanish Armada. These ships—the so-called race-built Elizabethan galleons—were purpose-built to combine speed, maneuverability, and firepower. These represented a development of naval warfare—the prototypes of the ships of the line that would dominate the age of fighting sail for more than two centuries.

Late in the evening of July 6, 1553, King Edward VI died of tuberculosis in Greenwich Palace. The country he left behind was immediately plunged into crisis. Like his father, the teenage son of Henry VIII had been a Protestant, a stalwart defender of the new faith. While he lay dying, a fight for the crown had swirled around the bedside, ending—according to legend—when the Earl of Northumberland seized the crown and thrust it into the hands of his daughter-in-law Lady Jane Grey, a cousin of the dying teenage king. This coup lasted fewer than two weeks, and on July 19 Henry VIII's eldest daughter swept into London at the head of a triumphal procession, and the unfortunate Jane was consigned to the Tower of London. The coup had been one last desperate attempt to keep the Catholic Mary from the throne.

The English Protestants had every right to be concerned. One of Queen Mary I's first acts was to look for a husband who would help ensure a Catholic succession. The Emperor Charles V proposed his son Philip, soon to become King Philip II of Spain. When the less than glamorous English queen saw a portrait of the dashing Hispanic prince, who was eleven years her junior, she declared herself "half in love with him" already. The wedding took place in Winchester Cathedral on July 1554, well away from London, where the mob had already taken a dislike to the Spanish consort. Philip himself viewed the marriage as a political act, and even went so far as to claim that he had "no carnal love for her." However, Catholic Spain and Tudor England were now allies, and Spanish warships became regular visitors to ports such as London, Portsmouth, and Southampton. For the first time English shipbuilders had the chance to examine the Spanish galleon at close quarters, and it was inevitable that they would learn what they could from these visitors.

As England descended into something akin to a Catholic police state, Mary I ordered construction of three new warships—galleons, built in the Spanish style. This represented the first departure from the types of ships built by her father, Henry VIII, and so the 550-ton *Philip and Mary* (1554), the 600-ton *Mary Rose* (1556), and the 600-ton *Golden Lion* (1557) constituted a new phase in English warship design. The importance of these vessels has long been overlooked by historians, largely because of a combination of English pride and Elizabethan propaganda. However, the unsavory truth is that the English race-built galleons that saved the day during the Spanish Armada campaign of 1588 were all based on these three prototypes, which in turn were copied and adapted from the Spanish galleons brought to England by Philip and Mary.

There seems to be no indication that these ships weren't built along purely Spanish lines, only with English dimensions and

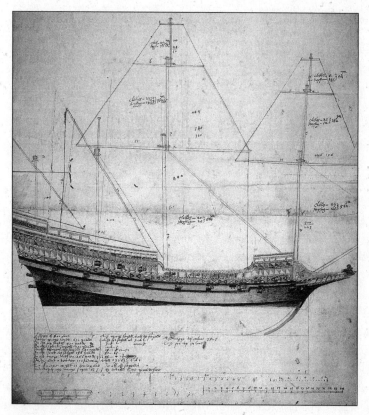

Plan of a race-built galleon, from Matthew Baker's Fragments of Ancient English Shipwrighty, *c.1582*

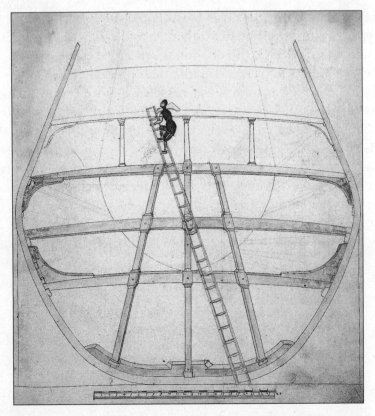

Cross section of a race-built galleon, from Matthew Baker's Fragments of
Ancient English Shipwrighty, *c.1582*

New Forest timber. The one big difference lay in their armament.
Quite correctly the English preferred their own system, which
placed a greater reliance on bronze guns, on four-wheeled carriages, and on firepower rather than on boarding. Consequently
these three prototype English galleons were armed in the English
rather than the Spanish fashion. Just how successful the three galleons were is reflected by their longevity. The *Golden Lion* remained in
service until 1582, while the *Philip and Mary*—renamed the *Nonpareil*
in 1584—survived without a major refit until 1584. The *Mary Rose*
was refitted in 1589, the year after the Spanish Armada. That meant
that for three decades these three galleons were considered main-
stays of the fleet, and there was no need to modify them in line with
more modern ship designs. This pretty effectively demonstrates

that the English thought they were perfectly modern to start with. It is therefore not especially surprising that all three ships remained in service until well into the seventeenth century. In fact although she was renamed the *Lion* and was heavily rebuilt, the *Golden Lion* was only sold out of service in 1698, some 140 years after she was launched. In anyone's navy that represented a success story.

Amid the modern multicultural bustle of Stratford in East London stands a monument to the dozens of Protestants burned at the stake on the spot during the closing years of "Bloody" Mary's reign. While many Protestants fled the country, the queen's younger sister, Elizabeth, remained in fear of her life. Then in November 1558 Mary died, probably as a result of ovarian cancer. This same affliction had prevented the creation of a Catholic heir, so Elizabeth remained the unchallenged successor. As King Philip was already in Spain, the regime change was swift and effective, and while the people danced in the streets of London, Elizabeth and her Protestant advisers quietly assumed the mantle of state. After securing her throne the new Queen Elizabeth looked to the security of her state. On her accession the Navy Royal consisted of Mary's three galleons, as well as five large carracks, including the *Jesus of Lubeck* and a cut-down carrack called the *Great Bark*, which had been partially rebuilt in imitation of Mary's new warships. Once the smaller ships of the fleet were added this represented a small but relatively efficient navy more than capable of holding its own against the French or even the Spanish if it had to. However, many of the carracks were showing their age, and if Tudor England wanted to maintain its naval presence, it had to modernize and expand.

The need for a fleet was clear. Although initially relations between England and Spain were outwardly cordial, Elizabeth's religion meant that conflict was inevitable, and within a few years the two countries were locked in what modern historians have dubbed a cold war. Elizabeth I wisely decided to expand her fleet. She ordered construction of three new large galleons, all improved versions of those built at the order of her older sister. The first of these was the 750-ton *Elizabeth Jonas* (1559), which seemed to have followed the example set by Mary's English shipbuilders, as she was described as being built in "the old way." She seems to have been a fairly sleek warship, although with a length-to-breadth ratio of about 2½:1 she was beamier than her three predecessors. This may well have been an attempt to make her a more stable gun platform. The 740-ton *Triumph* (1561) was followed two years later by a sister ship called the *White Bear*. These were probably very similar to the *Elizabeth Jonas*, as all three ships shared very similar specifications after they were rebuilt and their dimensions were fully recorded. These three ships therefore represent the first full-blown adaptation of the Spanish galleon by English shipwrights, producing wider and more stable versions of their Spanish counterparts. All three ships took part in the Spanish Armada battles almost three decades later, and the *Triumph*, which remained in the thick of the action throughout the campaign, achieved fame as the flagship of Sir Martin Frobisher.

Then came the loss of the *Jesus of Lubeck*. Although the aging carrack had been converted by lowering her superstructure a little, she still proved a liability to John Hawkins. By the time he returned to England, the sea dog had come to two decisions. The first was that a war with Spain was inevitable and that he needed to help Elizabeth prepare the Navy Royal for the coming fight. Second, he decided that his experience could be used to help create an improved type of warship that would allow the Tudor fleet to hold its own against the Spanish. In 1570 Hawkins entered into partnership with master shipwright Richard Chapman, and together they designed a small 300-ton galleon called the *Foresight*. She had a 78-foot keel, a 27-foot beam, and a length-to-beam ratio of 3:1. The key to her success was the line of her hull below the waterline, which Hawkins had based on the sleek hull lines of the war galley. The superstructure was kept low, sweeping upward from waist to stern, while a long beak and a rakish stem were designed to improve her handling in rough seas. Finally, the foremast was placed farther forward than was usual, and was raked forward slightly, which slightly improved the vessel's handling.

Sea trials showed that Hawkins and Chapman had their calculations right. The *Foresight* proved easy to handle; she could sail closer into the wind than any other ship in the fleet, and her armament made her the equal of warships twice her size. During these sea trials a few other Hawkins innovations became apparent. The draft of the *Foresight* was deeper than on most other vessels her size, and this deep hull acted much like a centerboard on a sailing dinghy, a counterbalance to the force of the wind on the sails, which greatly reduced her tendency to heel over like the *Mary Rose*. This made the *Foresight* a very stable gun platform. Another innovation was the sheathing of the lower hull with a double layer of planks, with a mixture of hair and tar packed between them. This was an attempt to reduce hull corrosion caused by the teredo worm, and predated the introduction of copper-sheathed ships' bottoms by almost a century. Almost certainly this was the result of Hawkins's own experiences in the Caribbean Sea, where he had seen the hull of the *Jesus* pulled open by a combination of toredo worms and hurricane-force seas. Hawkins was finding solutions to problems that had preyed on shipbuilders for more than a century.

Just as importantly, the *Foresight* carried a powerful broadside armament of twenty-eight guns, arrayed on one continuous gun deck. The aptly named *Foresight* was the ship of the future. Still, describing her gun deck as "continuous" is a little misleading. The trouble was, the decks of a wooden sailing ship followed the lines of the wales, or the curve of the hull. This meant that they sloped upward toward the stern, and underneath the sterncastle the decks became too steep to mount guns on. Hawkins's solution was to break the run of the gun deck just behind the mizzenmast, stepping it down by half a level. This created a sort of lower mezzanine deck at the stern, which became known as the gun room. This meant that guns could be carried lower in the hull than before, so the center of gravity of the warship was lowered. Externally the effect was to produce what looked like a continuous row of gun ports. In later and larger ships Hawkins used the space above this mezzanine to add an upper gun deck, effectively half a step above the line of the main gun deck. This created a perfect place to mount stern chase guns. It also meant that there was less need for a towering superstructure, and by lowering it Hawkins further improved the sailing qualities of the ship. In effect he had created the closest thing to the perfect sailing battleship that the technologies of Tudor England would allow. This new type of vessel would later be dubbed the race-built galleon, a term that perfectly captured its sleek, powerful appearance.

In 1577, Hawkins—now Sir John Hawkins—was appointed the new treasurer of the navy, and for the next decade he rebuilt the Tudor fleet, using the *Foresight* as his template. He survived the

jealousies of the court, and several charges of corruption and profi-
teering, largely because he was indispensable. The cold war with
Spain was fast turning into an undeclared open conflict, and what
followed was a race against time to prepare the fleet for the coming battle. Three more small galleons were built, all less than 500
tons—a size Hawkins saw as perfect for a warship that combined
speed, maneuverability, and firepower. The 460-ton *Revenge* was
built at the royal shipyard at Deptford in 1577, followed a decade
later by the 380-ton *Rainbow*. This last ship was built under the
supervision of Peter Pett, the patriarch of a shipbuilding family who
will reappear later in our story. In 1587, the same year the *Rainbow*
was launched, the master shipwright Matthew Baker was building
the 450-ton *Vanguard* just down the River Thames, at Woolwich. All
three ships were powerful, well-armed, race-built galleons, built
using the 3:1 ratio advocated by Hawkins.

While these new ships were being planned and built, Hawkins
was also kept busy rebuilding the existing fleet. It was customary to
rebuild a wooden warship halfway through its life—after, say, a couple of decades. However, for Hawkins this didn't just mean replac-
ing her rotten timbers with new ones. His vision was to rebuild
the fleet into race-built galleons. He began in 1570 with the small
royal warships *Tiger* and *Bull*, and by the time Hawkins was done
they were no longer recognizable as the oar-powered craft built
for Henry VIII back in 1546. As the cold war turned hot during the
1580s, the rebuilding process picked up pace. The *Elizabeth Bonaventure* was one of the first to be completely rebuilt along the new lines
in 1581, followed by all three of Queen Mary's galleons—the *Golden
Lion* in 1582, the *Nonpareil* in 1584, and finally the *Mary Rose* in 1589.
The real test of strength for these ships came in the summer of 1588,
when they sailed out to do battle with the Spanish Armada. The
ships performed perfectly, and without them history might have
taken a different course.

Sir John Hawkins retired the year after the Spanish Armada campaign, but Tudor warships continued to be built according to his
design for another generation. One of these was the 530-ton *Garland*,
built at Deptford in 1590—one of four new race-built galleons to
enter service in the years following the defeat of the Spanish. She was
built by Peter and Joseph Pett, members of a Deptford shipbuilding

dynasty that can be traced back to John Pett, who was paid to caulk Henry VII's *Regent* in 1499. Together with Matthew Baker, these shipbuilders turned Hawkins's vision into reality. In 1570 Peter Pett had a son, Phineas, who was schooled in Kent but who was forced to abandon his subsequent university education when his father died just weeks before the *Garland* was launched. The young Pett would eventually adopt his father's trade and so became the guardian of the Hawkins legacy. Some four decades later Phineas Pett and his son Peter would draw on Hawkins for inspiration when they produced the plans for their own perfect royal warship, the *Sovereign of the Seas*.

8

The Invincible Armada

The Plan

On paper the plan looked perfect. All Don Alvaro de Bazán, the Marquis of Santa Cruz, had to do was gather a force of some 150 major ships in Lisbon Harbor to transport an army of 55,000 men to England. This force would include artillery, engineers, and supplies—everything the army needed to fight its way ashore, defeat the English, and then march on London. Once it sailed the Armada would form itself into a tight defensive formation, designed to prevent the English from attacking the transports or picking off stray ships. When it reached the beachhead the army would be carried ashore in 200 specially built landing barges, while a force of 40 galleys and 6 galleasses (a strange cross between a galley and a sailing warship) would provide the landing ships with fire support. Once the veteran Spanish troops reached dry land it was assumed they would have little difficulty dealing with the hastily assembled militias raised by Queen Elizabeth of England. However, like so many plans in so many wars, someone decided to cut a few corners.

In 1585, as conflict between Catholic Spain and Protestant England became inevitable, King Philip II asked Don Alvaro to draw up a plan for the invasion of England. Since the San Juan de Ulúa incident in 1568, relations between the two countries had deteriorated fast. From 1572 on, Queen Elizabeth openly encouraged privateering attacks on Spanish ships. Francis Drake led raids against the Spanish Main, and when he returned home after a voyage of circumnavigation in 1580, the hold of his ship was filled with Spanish plunder. The Spanish ambassador protested, but Elizabeth's response was to knight "her pirate" on the deck of his own ship. In that same year the Spanish conquered Portugal, two years before Don Alvaro's naval victory in the Azores. These two events presented the Spanish with a powerful Atlantic fleet and the perfect base from which they could launch their "great enterprise of England." However, what finally turned the cold war into open conflict was the Treaty of Nonsuch, a pact between Elizabeth and the Protestant rebels in Holland in August 1585. For more than a decade the Spanish had been struggling to contain this Dutch-led revolt in the Spanish Netherlands, and now the English were openly offering the rebels military and financial aid. As soon as he heard about the treaty, Philip II sent the orders to Don Alvaro that would set the "great enterprise" in motion.

Unfortunately for him, the Spanish king also asked his foremost general, Alessandro Farense, the Duke of Parma, to submit his own plan. He proposed a landing in Ireland by way of a distraction, and when the English were diverted he would make a dash across the English Channel from Flanders. In April 1586 Philip reviewed the two schemes with his military advisor Don Juan de Zúñiga. The result was a compromise. Don Alvaro had already begun assembling the ships he needed, but he found that the scale of his enterprise had been scaled back to just 100 ships, plus 30 small dispatch vessels. Worse still, instead of embarking the entire invasion force in Spain, he was expected to sail up the English Channel to the coast of Flanders, where he would escort the Duke of Parma's troops across the narrow waterway to their English beachhead. Thirty-five thousand troops were to launch the invasion, half of whom would sail from Spain and the rest from Flanders. What had been a simple plan had been turned into a disjointed and overly complicated one,

Philip II of Spain, from a late-sixteenth-century satirical cartoon

a scheme that relied on perfect timing and the cooperation of two commanders a continent apart.

The fleet that gathered in Lisbon came from all over Europe—from Spain and Portugal, from Spain's Mediterranean allies—and it even included neutral ships that had been impounded and commandeered to make up the numbers. For administrative more than tactical reasons it was divided into squadrons, each named after an Iberian province. For the most part these squadrons were composed of ships of a particular type. However, once the fighting started, the fleet commanders rearranged their force based on the fighting abilities of the ships. The exception was the squadron of Portugal—those large and well-armed oceangoing galleons captured in Lisbon Harbor in 1580. They were the core of the fleet, and they stayed at the forefront of the action throughout the Armada campaign. Similarly, the Castille squadron was made up of treasure flota galleons, and while their ships lacked the firepower of the larger Portuguese ships, at least the ships themselves were well built and maneuverable. Less useful was the Levant squadron, made up of large Mediterranean grain ships—mostly hulks and naos that had been hastily converted into warships. The squadrons of Andalusia, Biscay, and Guipúzcoa were made up of Spanish merchantmen, while the squadron of hulks was gathered from all over Europe and was used to transport the men, stores, and equipment needed for the land campaign. Altogether this polyglot armada represented the largest concentration of sailing warships ever assembled during the Renaissance.

Over in England, a fleet was gathering, too. In 1587 Queen Elizabeth issued a decree that stopped English ships from leaving port, and all along the southern coast, small English merchantmen

Elizabeth I of England

were being hastily armed with whatever ordnance was available. The problem was that of the 163 private ships that took part, 108 were less than 100 tons burden. As the English naval captain Sir William Wynter put it, "If you had seen what I have seen of the simple service that hath been done by the merchant and coast ships, you would have said that we had been little helped by them, otherwise than that they did make a show." Like the Spanish, only a small portion of the English fleet consisted of proper warships. In 1588 the Royal Navy included 21 warships of 200 tons or more, and only 4 of these had been built in the past ten years. However, the four exceptions—the *Revenge*, *Vanguard*, *Rainbow*, and *Ark Royal*—were purpose-built "race-built" galleons. Several of the others had been heavily modified, and all carried greater firepower than their Spanish counterparts. Although these royal warships made up less than a fifth of the entire English fleet, they and the largest of the Spanish galleons would decide the fate of Elizabethan England.

The Finest Ships in Europe

The coming battle would be a test of two different approaches to shipbuilding and to the way ships were used in battle. The Spanish commanders learned their trade in the Mediterranean, and their tactics would reflect the way galley fights were organized—which in turn was largely a maritime version of a battle on land. It would be fought with a center, two wings, a vanguard, and a reserve. The aim would be to pin the enemy in a bitterly fought melee, while the rest of the force would concentrate against part of the enemy force, hoping to crush it before help could arrive. This was going to be a brutal fight, fought at close quarters, and where cold steel rather than roundshot would decide the day. But the English had never fought in the Mediterranean, and so they wrote their own rule book.

The different approaches to naval warfare were reflected in the two flagships that were the center of a frenzy of activity in their home ports of Lisbon and Plymouth. One, a proud Portuguese galleon, would already have stood the test of battle in the sea fight off the Azores six years before. The *San Martín* might have begun life as a Portuguese warship, but she was now armed and equipped with Spanish guns, troops, and seamen. She represented the ultimate in galleon design—a floating leviathan that was every bit as powerful as James IV's *Michael*, Henry VIII's *Henri Grace à Dieu*, or Gustav Vasa's *Elefanten*. In fact, the *San Martín* probably should be seen as the proud inheritor of that shipbuilding tradition where the greatest of warships were too powerful to board, and whose guns could sweep an enemy's decks before her own troops took the fight to the enemy.

The other would be a completely new departure—an English adaptation of the galleon that would combine size with agility, speed with firepower. Unlike her Spanish counterpart, the *Ark Royal* had not undergone a baptism of fire. These two flagships represented the most powerful warships in either fleet, and the coming clash would be as much a prizefight between these two greatest ships in Europe as a fight between two rival maritime powers. Don Alvaro de Bazán was delighted with his 1,000-ton flagship, whose full name was officially recorded as the *San Martín de Portugal*. She began life as the *Sao Martin*, having been laid down in Lisbon in 1577. She had barely been completed when the port was captured by a Spanish army in February 1580. Her crew opted to surrender her rather than fight their way through the Spanish fleet that blocked the mouth of the River Tagus. Therefore the brand-new galleon fell into Spanish hands.

She had an overall length of approximately 150 feet and a beam of 40 feet, which made her considerably leaner than most Spanish galleons of the period. She was a three-masted vessel, and in typical galleon fashion had a low forecastle with a pronounced beak extending in front of it, while farther aft her superstructure sloped gently upward toward her narrow stern. Her length on the waterline was less than 125 feet, which shows the length her towering sterncastle overhung the rudder, or how far her beak extended underneath her bowsprit. For all her size she apparently was maneuverable—at least compared to the naos and hulks in the fleet—although her high sides and large sterncastle sometimes made it hard for her to steer a straight course.

The *San Martín* was also very crowded. On May 11, 1588, when she sailed out of the mouth of the River Tagus at the head of the

Armada, she carried more than 500 men and boys, including 308 veteran Spanish soldiers—mostly armed with small arms—and 161 sailors. In her role as fleet flagship she was also crammed with noblemen, priests, officers, and gentlemen, including the king's illegitimate son the Prince of Ascoli; Don Jorge Manrique, the Armada's inspector general; Captain Marolin de Juan, its chief navigator; and at least a dozen other senior officers, plus their servants. She was armed with 48 guns, of which just over half were modern bronze muzzle-loading pieces; the rest were swivel guns. While this represented a relatively modern collection of ordnance, compared to the larger warships in the English fleet, she was seriously undergunned. Of course, that mattered very little as long as the veteran soldiers could do their job.

By contrast, the *Ark Royal* was a floating arsenal. She had been built just two years before, at the Royal Shipyard in Deptford, although her building was a completely private venture. Her owner was Sir Walter Raleigh, the queen's favorite courtier, commander of her guard, explorer, poet, writer—and one of the most hated men in England. The queen had granted him so many favors, so many forms of income and privileges, that he was widely resented, both at court and by the people whose taxes supported his opulent lifestyle. In 1586 it seemed he was riding for a fall, but this wouldn't happen until after the death of his royal patron. When he asked the master shipbuilder Robert Chapman to produce a private warship based on John Hawkins's race-built design, he was at the crest of his royal popularity—hence his free use of the royal shipyard when the country was gearing for war.

She was originally called the *Ark Raleigh*, and she was an improved version of the royal warship *Revenge*, built almost a decade earlier, and an enlarged sister of the 380-ton *Rainbow*, which Peter Pett was building in the same shipyard. She was listed as being of 550 tons burden, although this tonnage varied considerably from record to record, with an overall length of 140 feet, a beam of 37 feet, and a draft of about 15 feet. As her keel length was 100 feet, if we apply the standard formula for tonnage, she comes out at exactly 555 tons. Raleigh planned to use her to hunt down Spanish treasure ships in the Caribbean, probably using his newfound colony on Roanoke Island in what is now North Carolina as a base. He never got the chance, as in early 1587, before the ship could be completed, she was compulsorily purchased by the queen, renamed the *Ark Royal*, and added to the strength of the fleet.

She carried 50 tons of ordnance—56 guns—a total that probably included 38 large bronze muzzle-loading pieces, ranging from demicannons to sakers. Although her gun inventory was drawn up after the Armada campaign, the figures tally exactly with the numbers of guns she carried in 1588. The assumption is that her armament stayed the same. For the record, this small but powerful warship carried 4 demicannons, 4 cannon perriers (firing stone shot), 12 culverins, 12 demiculverins, and 6 sakers. Also listed are 4 port pieces and 2 fowlers. Unusually, the records describe these smaller guns as being made from brass rather than wrought iron, suggesting that by this time the two gun types had become little more than large antipersonnel swivel guns. She also carried up to 12 more conventional swivel pieces, and during 1588 her guns were served by 32 gunners supported by 100 soldiers and 268 mariners, giving her a total complement of 400 men.

She was such a well-designed ship that during the campaign of 1588 she became the flagship of the English fleet, flying the standard of the Lord High Admiral, Charles Howard, Baron of Effingham. He said of his new flagship, "I think her the odd [best] ship in the world for all conditions, and truly, I think there can be no greate ship make me change and go out of her." The fifty-two-year-old nobleman had some sea experience, but like General Eisenhower in a much later war, his real ability lay in his skill as a diplomat. His main job was to keep Elizabeth's sea dogs, such as Hawkins, Drake, Raleigh, and Frobisher, in check, involving them in his Council of War, pandering to their egos, preventing their rivalry, and making the most of them as veteran naval commanders.

Rather than simply waiting for the Spanish to arrive, Howard decided to take the initiative, and in 1587 he ordered the launch of a preemptive strike against the enemy. In April 1587 Sir Francis Drake launched a major raid against the packed harbor of Cádiz, an attack the sea dog claimed had "singed the beard of the King of Spain." However, although the Spanish lost twenty-four ships in the attack, most of these were armed merchantmen that could easily be replaced. The Cádiz attack did little more than delay the inevitable.

A more serious blow to Philip's plans was the unexpected death of the sixty-two-year-old Don Alvaro de Bazán. He was soon replaced by another nobleman, Don Alonso Perez de Guzmán el Bueno, the seventh Duke of Medina Sidonia. His contemporaries described him as rich, brave, intelligent, honest, pious, and magnanimous. The word "experienced" wasn't mentioned. He was appointed because his exalted social rank allowed him to keep the other noble commanders in line, which was expected to count for more than his lack of naval experience. After all, even the English had described the great armada as "invincible." What could possibly go wrong?

The Guns of the Armada

The answer lay in the black art of gunnery. The English had a greater number of good-quality guns, their weapons were mounted more effectively, and their crews were trained. The Elizabethan sailors enjoyed two major advantages. The first was simply qualitative: they had a larger number of reliable modern guns. The second was all down to tactical doctrine: the Spanish relied on the old-fashioned method of firing a broadside, then boarding the enemy in the smoke. By contrast, the English had developed the ability to keep their distance from the Spanish and to pound their ships with roundshot. The coming battle would be a contest between two fighting doctrines as much as a testing ground between the Spanish and the English versions of the galleon.

Although both the Spanish and the English made good use of the latest bronze muzzle-loading pieces of ordnance, the bulk of the Spanish fleet—all those armed merchantmen and some of the warships—were still armed in part with obsolete wrought-iron breech-loading guns. While some of these pieces were probably still carried on some of the English armed merchantmen, most English merchant captains had replaced them with cast-iron muzzle-loading pieces. Cast-iron guns had been produced in the area known as the Weald in southeastern England since 1545. While for the most part royal warships continued to be armed with bronze guns, cast iron became increasingly popular with the owners of merchant ships.

Cast-iron guns were significantly cheaper than bronze ones; they were readily available, and recent developments in gunfounding technology meant that they were virtually just as reliable as bronze pieces.

The guns were only part of the equation. Although the Spanish had started experimenting with more mobile gun carriages, most of their bronze guns were mounted on two-wheeled carriages, just like the typical gun carriages of the period on land. The only real difference was that naval carriages tended to be a little shorter, and often the wheels were built from solid pieces of timber rather than being spoked. The carriages used for wrought-iron breech-loading guns were also just like those used half a century before, with heavy wooden beds, and mounted on two wheels. This meant that in gun mounting, the Spanish were half a century behind the English. One of the most interesting finds from the wreck of the *Mary Rose* (1545) were the carriages designed to carry the Tudor warship's big bronze guns. Unlike the later Spanish carriages, or those from the *Carta Olaus Magnus*, these English gun carriages had four small wheels rather than two big ones. These four-wheeled gun carriages had more in common with the gun carriages used by the British at the Battle of Trafalgar some 260 years later than with those used by the Spanish in 1588.

These *Mary Rose* gun carriages consisted of a thick rectangular wooden base plate, with two side pieces, or cheeks. These were set on the two long sides of the rectangle and fitted into grooves in the base. These cheeks were linked by iron bolts and supported at the back by a second set of side pieces, which were stepped so they were far lower at the back than the front. To give them extra strength the main cheeks were ringed with iron bands. The trunnions of the gun barrel—the lugs that protruded from either side—rested in semicircular cutouts on top of the cheeks, while the rear of the gun barrel rested on the base of the carriage—or more accurately, on wooden wedges that were inserted between barrel and carriage. The whole carriage sat on two axles, each of which was fitted with small, solid wooden wheels called trucks. This contraption was perfectly designed for the gun decks of a wooden sailing ship. It took up much less space than the taller two-wheeled carriages used by the Spanish, and the smaller wheels were better able to absorb the recoil when the gun was fired. They could be trained and elevated relatively easily, or rolled back from the gun port for loading. This was the key. The four-truck-wheeled gun carriage could be reloaded in the middle of a battle with relative ease. The Spanish guns couldn't.

Before a Spanish muzzle-loading gun was fired on board a wooden sailing ship, the two-wheeled gun carriage was tied to the side of the ship. In effect the timbers of the ship absorbed the recoil, which placed a huge strain on the hull of the vessel. By contrast, the English gun carriages were only loosely secured, so that some of the force of the recoil could be absorbed by the wheels of the carriage scraping across the deck, while a rope secured to the side of the ship prevented the carriage from careering too far back across the gun deck. This also meant that the gun was already pulled back from the side of the ship and ready to be reloaded. Once the gun crew had prepared the gun for firing, all they needed to do was move it forward to the gun port again; it was simple and straightforward. By contrast, to reload one of the Spanish guns it had to be untied from the side of the ship and then rolled backward. The longer carriage made it hard to move the gun around on the gun deck. Once the piece was reloaded it was then rolled forward again and retied to the side of the ship. Experiments with replica carriages of both types demonstrated that the English system was far faster than the Spanish one, which meant that the English were able to keep up a far heavier rate of fire.

Worse, the organization of the gun crews on board the Spanish ships made the reloading of the guns all but impossible once a battle had started. Each large gun was commanded by a gunner, assisted by a number of "sea soldiers." Once the gun was ready for action, these soldiers picked up their pikes, halberds, or handguns again and rejoined the rest of their company. It was all a matter of doctrine. The Spanish were completely geared up to fight a boarding action. The gunners would fire off one big broadside, and then the Spanish soldiers would board the English ship before the smoke had cleared. Even if this wasn't possible, the Spanish planned to get so close to the enemy that their superiority in soldiers would allow them to clear the decks of the enemy using swivel guns, grenades, and small arms. The superiority of the Spanish soldier was legendary—during the late sixteenth century they were widely regarded as the finest troops in Europe. Once they managed to grapple and board an English ship, victory was virtually assured.

This Spanish advantage dictated English tactics. By keeping out of close range the English ships could avoid being boarded, and their advantage in gunnery meant that they could batter the Spanish ships without much risk of any serious return fire. If the Spanish wanted to match the English and fire more than once, then they would have to rethink the way their ships were organized, pulling soldiers away from their boarding stations and sending them back to their assigned guns. Even then the reloading process would take much longer than it did on board the English ships. The Spanish must have seen English gun carriages on board the *Jesus of Lubeck* when they captured her off San Juan de Ulúa in 1568. They had plenty of time to adopt the system for themselves if they thought it worthwhile. The fact that they stuck with their clumsy two-wheeled carriages shows just how much faith the Spanish placed in their infantry rather than in firepower.

This faith and the problem of reloading are borne out by the archaeological evidence from Spanish Armada shipwrecks. As the Spanish kept detailed records of every detail of the Armada's preparation, when archaeologists excavated the wreck of the Spanish hulk *El Gran Grifón*, which ran aground on Fair Isle off northern Scotland, they were able to compare the shot they found with the number of shot the ship had been issued. The large bronze *media culebrinas* (demiculverins) were hardly fired at all, while the smaller bronze *sacres* (sakers) used about half their ammunition. By contrast, the larger wrought-iron breech-loading guns used all but a quarter of their ammunition, while the small swivel guns fired off virtually every shot they had.

The only time the English came close enough for these obsolete muzzleloaders to be effective was during the final battle of the campaign off Gravelines. This suggests that by then the Spanish had tried to change their tactics, but their cumbersome gun carriages meant that their biggest guns still had a pitiful rate of fire compared to their English counterparts. When the English finally closed to within close range, the obsolete breech-loading guns of the Spaniards proved just as effective as the more modern English guns. However, by that time the Spanish Armada was already in serious trouble.

The Campaign

According to the legend, after lunch on Friday, July 29, 1588, Lord High Admiral Thomas Howard, Earl of Effingham, and Sir Francis Drake were rowed ashore from their ships anchored in Plymouth Sound. Accompanied by other senior captains they walked up the slope to the grassy eminence of Plymouth Hoe, which overlooked the harbor, and there they spent an hour playing a game of bowls. In midafternoon the scout ship *Golden Hind*—a different one from Drake's ship of circumnavigation—raced into the harbor under full sail. Shortly afterward her captain, Thomas Fleming, appeared on the hoe and reported that the Spanish Armada had been spotted that evening off the Cornish coast. Drake's response was to keep playing, and—so the story goes—he declared that, "We have time to finish the game, and beat the Spaniards too." The game reached its leisurely conclusion, and the commanders then returned to their ships. This example of English sangfroid might just have been part of the Drake legend, but it was grounded in reality. In the face of an onshore wind the English fleet would have been unable to work its way out of Plymouth Harbor until the tide turned that evening.

As dusk fell, Lord Howard and Sir Francis were still supervising the warping of their fleet out of the harbor—a tricky feat of seamanship that involved laying out anchors, then hauling the ship forward, repeating the process until the vessel had reached the open sea. This backbreaking work continued throughout the night, but by dawn the bulk of the fleet—some fifty-four ships—lay riding in the rough swell off the Eddystone Rocks, some ten miles south of the harbor entrance. The Spanish were still some fifty miles to the southwest, off the Lizard, the southern tip of the Cornish coast. The Duke of Medina Sidonia had spent the forenoon of Saturday waiting for stragglers, using the time to deploy his ships into their battle formation and to confer with his captains. He realized that success depended on keeping his ships in a tight formation and preventing the English from delaying his progress. Rain squalls kept visibility to a minimum, and as the two sides approached each other that evening neither commander had any real idea where the enemy was. In fact, the English fleet had divided into two groups—an inshore squadron and an offshore squadron—but both had sailed past the Spanish in the rain-swept darkness.

As dawn broke on Sunday, July 31, the two fleets saw each other through the rain. The wind was blowing from the west, which meant that the Spanish could maintain a stately four knots throughout the day. Lord Howard's offshore squadron lay southwest of the Spanish, while Drake's inshore squadron was immediately west of the Armada. An English sailor later wrote that the Spanish ships looked "like a half-moon, the wings thereof spread out . . . sailing very slowly, with full sails . . . and the ocean groaning under their weight." The first shot was fired at a little after 9:00 A.M. Howard led his fleet into the attack *en ala* (line astern), and as each ship came in range of the Spanish, it opened fire. Meanwhile the straggling inshore squadron took on the northern wing of the Spanish half-moon. All this long-range firing was largely ineffective—on Juan Martines de Recalde's *Santiago*, the flagship of the Biscay squadron, only fifteen men were killed or wounded by enemy fire throughout the day, and his ship had been in the thick of the fighting. However, as Howard's line of ships moved north, the Spanish commander saw that the enemy was now concentrating on his northern flank. He ordered Don Alonso Martínez de Leiva to lead a group of the more powerful Spanish ships to reinforce that flank, and the English respectfully kept their distance. Lord Howard later justified this apparent lack of aggressiveness by the English: "We durst not adventure to be put in amongst them, their fleet being so strong." So far the battle was going Spain's way.

Then disaster struck. At 1:30 P.M. an explosion ripped apart the sterncastle of the 950-ton nao *San Salvador*, probably because a spark had ignited in the powder store. The rest of the Spanish fleet heaved to as they picked up survivors and helped fight the fire, but by late afternoon the fleet was under way again, the smoking wreck of the *San Salvador* having managed to raise sail. That was when the second disaster struck. As the English continued to fire on the northern flank of the Spanish formation it veered toward the center, crowding the Spanish ships together. At about 4:00 P.M. the *Nuestra Señora del Rosario*, commanded by Don Pedro de Valdés, collided with another ship, and the *Rosario*'s bowsprit was damaged. As Don Pedro reduced sail to sort out the mess, another ship—the *Santa*

Catalina—collided with her, bringing down the *Rosario*'s foremast. The seas were becoming rougher, and the Duke of Medina Sidonia decided that the safety of the many outweighed the needs of the few. The stricken *Rosario* was left behind.

Darkness brought the fighting to a close. During the night the English tailed the Spaniards, who altered course to the northeast under cover of the darkness. Lord Howard had ordered Drake to lead the pursuit, and the rest of the fleet was supposed to follow the stern lanterns of Drake's *Revenge*. However, the sea dog was following his own agenda. The stern lanterns were extinguished, and the *Revenge* quietly altered course to starboard. Drake had been unable to resist the opportunity for plunder offered by the *Rosario*. As the English fleet became scattered in the darkness, Drake shadowed the *Rosario* and bided his time. As dawn broke on Monday, Don Pedro saw that Drake's *Revenge* lay to windward, her guns trained on his ship. After some discussion the Spanish nobleman surrendered his ship, and Drake's men took possession of their prize and of the 50,000 gold *escudos* she carried—the pay chest of the Andalusia squadron. In today's money the haul would be the equivalent of $18 million. Drake later expressed surprise at finding the *Rosario* within gunshot range at dawn. His fellow sea dogs knew better, and as Sir Martin Frobisher retorted, "Ay marry, you were within two or three cables length [at dawn, as] you were no further off all night"!

Sir Francis Drake's dereliction of duty had cost the Tudor fleet half a day, which is how long it took Lord Howard to heave to and gather together his scattered ships. The Spanish also used this chance to reorganize their formation as it slowly cruised past Start Point in Devon. Rather than forming his fleet into a crescent shape— a tactic from textbooks on galley warfare—Don Alonso decided to group his ships closer together, forming a tight defensive box. Don Alonso Martínez de Leiva in *La Rata Santa María Encoronada* was given command of the rear guard, comprising some of the best ships in the fleet, including most of the Portuguese galleons. The Spanish commander also decided to cast loose the *San Salvador* after taking off all her unwounded crew. At 4:00 P.M. Sir John Hawkins and Lord Howard both came alongside the stricken nao, and a witness described what they saw: "The deck of the ship had fallen down, the steerage broken, the stern blown out and about 50 poor creatures burnt with powder in most miserable sort. The stink in the ship was so unsavory, and the sight within board so ugly that Lord Thomas Howard and Sir John Hawkins shortly departed." The crippled Spanish ship was towed into Weymouth by Captain Fleming's *Golden Hind*.

The wind died as the afternoon wore on, and by nightfall both fleets were doing little more than drifting eastward. By that time Drake had rejoined the fleet, having made sure that the *Rosario* was towed safely into port. A few miles to the east a fast pinnace broke away from the Spanish formation, taking a message from the Duke of Medina Sidonia to the Duke of Parma. The naval commander wanted to make sure the army was ready to embark as soon as he arrived off the Flemish coast and that local pilots would be on hand to help him navigate his fleet through the shoals. Dawn on Tuesday, August 2, brought a light breeze from the east, which meant that for the first time the Spanish were to windward of the English fleet. Unable to steer directly into the wind, the Armada steered a north-easterly course toward the English coast near Portland Bill. Lord Howard gave chase, hoping to beat the Spaniards to the coast and so gain the weather gauge. As the two fleets crept inshore, it looked as if the campaign was about to be decided in one climactic sea battle.

The Spanish reached Portland Bill first, and the English commander ordered his fleet to veer to the southeast, clawing their way back out to sea. However, six English ships, including the *Triumph*, commanded by Sir Martin Frobisher, found their path to seaward blocked by tidal rips that lay off the promontory of Portland Bill. In effect they were cut off from the rest of the fleet. Don Alonso seized the opportunity and ordered Don Hugo de Moncada to attack. He commanded the four galleasses attached to the fleet—powerful ships that combined the oar power of a galley with the firepower and rig of a sailing ship. These calm winds and inshore waters made for their perfect hunting ground. Unfortunately, Don Hugo was used to the virtually tideless waters of the Mediterranean, and he shied away from crossing the tidal rip. The attack degenerated into some desultory long-range shooting, prompting Don Alonso to send a pinnace with a message for his galleass commander, involving "certain words which were not to his honour."

Farther to the south the fighting elements of the Armada had split into three groups: the main body commanded by the Duke of Medina Sidonia; a vanguard led by Martín de Bertendona; and a rear guard controlled by Juan Martinez de Recalde, which was charged with protecting the transports and supply ships. Howard's change of course had put his leading ships on a converging course with the Spanish vanguard, and by 9:30 A.M. the two straggling lines of warships were within musket range of each other. The two sides fired their broadsides, at which point Lord Howard in the *Ark Royal* turned away from the enemy line, no doubt trying to avoid a boarding attempt. The rest of the English line followed his lead, and the fighting degenerated into another desultory bombardment at long range. Howard then turned inshore again, still keeping his distance from the Spanish but moving to support Frobisher. The Spanish were still strung out to the east, heading south. Just when it seemed the fighting would die away completely, the wind shifted.

The wind was now coming from the southeast, which gave the Spanish a slight advantage. Howard was now to leeward—downwind—of the Spanish, and therefore it would take time for his ships to claw their way back into the fight. Meanwhile, Drake's squadron, at the rear of the long English line, found itself to windward—upwind—of the main Spanish line, and grasped the opportunity this presented of falling on Recalde's Spanish rear guard and the supply ships it was protecting. By 11:00 A.M. Drake and Recalde were fighting their own private battle, while the Duke of Medina Sidonia sent a handful of his best ships to reinforce his rear guard while the rest of his fleet regrouped into their tight defensive formation. Lord Howard turned back toward this group of Spanish ships, prompting the duke to lower the topsails of the *San Martín*, a chivalric challenge to Lord Howard in the *Ark Royal* to fight him in a single ship-to-ship combat. The English commander ignored the challenge, and instead his line of ships poured shot into the Spanish flagship at the range of half a musket shot.

A Spaniard on board the flagship described the fighting:

> The galleon "San Martin" being to windward of the Armada and near the enemy's ships, the latter attacked her with the whole of their cannon, she returning the fire

with so much gallantry that on one side alone she fired
of hundred shots, and the enemy did not care to come to
close quarters with her although she was alone, and her
consorts were unable to aid her for one and a half hours.

He was missing the point. The English had no intention of getting any closer to the Spanish galleons than they needed to. Finally,
Don Alonso and a fire brigade of Spanish galleons managed to
work their way forward to support the flagship, and the English
veered off, pulling back to the southwest to regroup. They were
low on ammunition and their crews were exhausted. When he saw
the rest of the fleet pulling back, Drake also broke off his action and
rejoined Howard's main force. The fighting was clearly over for the
day. Despite all this firing, the Spanish lost only fifty men during
the battle, while English casualties were negligible. A lot of powder
and shot had been fired, but the Armada was still on course, and
still heading toward its rendezvous with the Duke of Parma.

The next few days were an anticlimax. The English fleet was desperately short of ammunition, so the only fighting flared up when
Spanish ships lagged behind the rest of the Armada. On Thursday
morning, August 4, Drake, in the English vanguard, found that
the hulk *El Gran Grifón* had fallen astern of her companions, and
he swooped in to attack her. The Spanish captain, Juan Gómez de
Medina, held on until the galleass squadron could come back and
rescue him, at which point Drake pulled back. The same thing happened at dawn the following day when the English found that the
Portuguese galleon *San Luís* and the nao *Duquesna Santa Ana* had
fallen astern of the Spanish formation. This time it was Frobisher who
led the attack, the light winds forcing him to tow his ships into action.
Once again Don Hugo de Moncada's galleasses saved the day, and
the two stragglers were safely returned to the fold. Later that morning a breeze sprang up, and Frobisher's squadron worked its way
between the Armada and the English coast. Don Alonso responded
by leading some of his best ships into the attack, but soon the *San
Martín* found herself isolated, and as one Spanish participant put it,
"if the Duke had not gone about with his flagship . . . we should have
been vanquished that day." However, as night fell, the Armada was
back on track, and drawing ever closer to Flanders.

Spanish Armada battle off Dungeness, August 5, 1588

Spanish Armada battle off Gravelines, August 8, 1588

By late afternoon on Saturday, August 6, the Armada had reached the northern French port of Calais, where it dropped anchor. Their rendezvous with the Duke of Parma at Dunkirk lay just forty miles to the east, and the Duke of Medina Sidonia planned to continue the voyage as soon as he could embark local pilots. The trouble was, the Spanish army was far from being ready. The duke was still at his headquarters in Bruges, and his men hadn't embarked on their invasion barges. Worse, a squadron of small Dutch warships lay off Dunkirk, so the barges would have to make their way to Gravelines, a few miles east of Calais, using the Flemish canal network. All told it would probably be two weeks before Parma and his men were ready. Meanwhile, the Spanish Armada was anchored in an unsheltered roadstead, off a neutral port, with the English fleet to windward and a mass of sandbanks known as the Flemish Banks to leeward. It was an extremely unenviable position for any naval commander to be in.

Meanwhile, the English fleet had dropped anchor a few miles to the west, still to windward of the Spanish. That evening the English fleet was joined by reinforcements—the Downs squadron, commanded by Sir Henry Seymour, which brought Lord Howard's strength up to 140 ships. For the first time he had numerical parity with the Spanish. Even more important, Seymour's squadron had been accompanied by a convoy of ammunition ships. The following morning Lord Howard held a council of war and asked his captains for suggestions. So far his English had performed well, but they had been unable to break up the Spanish formation or to prevent it from sailing up the English Channel. Clearly Howard needed to change tactics. The solution the English commanders proposed was certainly novel.

Later that day, Sunday, August 7, work began on the conversion of eight small armed merchantmen into fireships—expendable vessels stuffed with anything that would burn, which would be set on fire, then sailed into the midst of the enemy fleet. Skeleton crews would wait until the last minute before tying the rudder fast, clambering into a longboat, and abandoning ship. That night the wind veered again, so that both wind and tide were working in favor of the English. The Duke of Medina Sidonia had placed a screen of small craft between the two fleets, and shortly after midnight these scout ships spotted the fireships bearing down on the Spanish fleet. The alarm was raised, and the Spanish admiral ordered his captains to cut their anchor cables, raise sail, and stand out to sea. It is a testimony to the seamanship of the Spanish that they managed to avoid the oncoming fireships. The only casualty was Don Hugo de Moncada's flagship, the galleass *San Lorenzo*, which broke her rudder in a collision and drifted onto a sandbank.

However, the rest of the Spanish fleet had been scattered in the darkness. Only the *San Martín* and four other galleons managed to regain their old anchorage by morning, and as dawn broke on Monday, August 8, the Spanish ships were spread out over several miles. While the fleet commanders tried to rally their ships, the more experienced seamen realized that with their best anchors gone the fleet had little chance of regaining an anchorage on the French or Flemish coast. Until now the tight defensive formation adopted by the Spanish Armada had kept it relatively safe from harm, but now that cohesive unity was lost. Until the ships could be gathered into some semblance of a formation, the fleet remained painfully vulnerable. All that now stood between this straggling mass of ships and the English fleet were the *San Martín* and her four consorts. Shortly after dawn the English fleet began closing in. Their first victim was the *San Lorenzo*. Lord Howard led a squadron of some thirty ships into the attack, leaving the rest of his fleet to engage the Duke of Medina Sidonia. The shallow water prevented the English from boarding the galleass, so they poured shot into her. When Don Hugo was killed, the fight went out of the Spaniards and they abandoned ship and raced to the shore. English boats were lowered and the galleass was plundered, but then the Spanish rallied and drove the looters off with small-arms fire. Meanwhile, the fighting around the *San Martín* was reaching a crescendo.

Don Alonso needed to buy time for the rest of his fleet to pull together. His small force—*San Martín, San Juan de Portugal, San Marcos, San Juan Bautista*, and *San Mateo*—were all powerful galleons, the elite of the fleet, but the admiral was willing to sacrifice these fine ships to save the rest of his armada. The English fleet played their part by ignoring the other ships and concentrating on this small rear guard. Drake led the first attack in the *Revenge*, followed by Hawkins in the *Victory* and Frobisher in the *Triumph*. At one point all three of these flagships lay within musket range of the *San Martín*, pouring fire into her at point-blank range. During the next two hours the hull of the Spanish flagship was hit by more than two hundred roundshot, her rigging was badly damaged, and her decks were awash with blood. The other Spanish ships of Don Alonso's "forlorn hope" were equally battered, but somehow all five galleons held the English off, and they slowly managed to creep northward, toward the rest of the fleet.

By 9:00 A.M. Don Alonso Martínez de Leiva had managed to pull the rest of the Armada together, and he even managed to create a rear guard. Then, shortly after 10:00 A.M., the five battered galleons passed through the cordon of the Spanish rear guard and soon were ensconced in the comparative safety of the Armada's defensive box. The English pulled back to regroup, but the respite was only temporary. The battle proper was about to begin. What followed would be a running battle, with the Spanish heading northeast, away from the coast and its treacherous sandbanks. The English nipped at the edges of the Spanish formation, trying to pull it apart. Drake led his squadron toward the Armada's left, supported by Hawkins's squadron on his right. Hawkins led his squadron against the Armada's center. The *Mary Rose* was in the thick of the fighting, and an observer on board her later wrote with some detachment, "As soon as we that pursued the fleet were come up within musket shot of them, the fight began very hotly." He probably wasn't exaggerating. At close range the English superiority in firepower was really making its mark, and the Spanish ships were literally being shot to pieces.

The worst damage was being suffered by the most powerful Spanish ships—the galleons that served as the rear guard, or that tried to protect the poorly armed supply ships. This force was led by Don Alonso Martínez de Leiva in *La Rata Santa María Encoronada* and Juan Martínez de Recalde in the battered *San Juan de Portugal*, which had returned to the thick of the fight. The problem was that the English could simply fire three or four times as quickly as the Spanish, and although the English ships managed to fire at point-blank range, they still managed to avoid being grappled and boarded by the Spanish. As Sir William Wynter put it afterward, "When I was furthest off in discharging any of the pieces, I was not out of the shot of their harquebus, and most times within speech of one another."

On the Armada's west flank the *San Felipe*, commanded by Don Francisco de Toledo, tried to board one nameless English ship, and she was close enough for his Spanish soldiers to fire onto her decks before the English vessel veered away.

The nao *La María Juan* sank from the battering she received, and her crew was reduced so much that all her survivors fitted into one longboat. Another of the rearguard ships, the *San Juan de Sicilia*, was so badly holed that according to one of her officers her carpenter worked throughout the battle to "repair the damage from many shots which the ship had received below, and from the prow to the stern." Another witness claimed that "the enemy inflicted such damage upon the galleons *San Mateo* and *San Felipe* that the latter had five guns on the starboard side and a big gun on the poop put out of action." By dusk these two Portuguese galleons were so battered that they were abandoned by the rest of the Armada. That night they drifted onto the Flemish Banks, and the following morning their demoralized crews were captured by the Dutch. By nightfall it was clear that the "invincible Armada" had been badly battered, but it still hadn't been beaten.

That night the Duke of Medina Sidonia considered he could renew the battle. He knew that the English must be desperately short of ammunition again, and if he could only hold his ground—and his formation—he still had a chance of working his way back to Calais or Gravelines. As Tuesday morning dawned, the two fleets lay about two miles apart, some twenty-five miles northeast of Calais and east of the Goodwin Sands, where the Scottish Sir Andrew Barton had met his end three quarters of a century before. However, morale in the Armada was low, and several captains refused to renew the fight. Then the wind changed again—a strong offshore breeze that began driving the battered Armada into the North Sea. Whatever else he could do, the Duke of Medina Sidonia was unable to harness wind and tide. He called another council of war, and this time the course was clear. Any rendezvous with Parma's army was now impossible. The admiral had little choice but to order his fleet to continue to the north and to head home by circumnavigating the British Isles.

By August 12 the Spanish had passed the level of the English-Scottish border, and Lord Howard's ships returned to port. The wind increased, and two days after the English returned home, a storm scattered the Spanish fleet. While some ships were blown almost as far as Norway, most managed to work their way between the Orkney and Shetland islands and out into the Atlantic Ocean. *El Gran Grifón* was less fortunate as she smashed into the rocks of Fair Isle, while another battered survivor, the *San Juan de Sicilia*, was forced to put in to the Scottish harbor of Tobermory in Mull, where she sank at her moorings. By September some sixty ships had managed to regroup, although by this time supplies were running low. A week later, a second series of gales raged across the Atlantic from the west, driving several ships onto the Irish coast. Those who survived this storm were caught by a third tempest nine days later, and yet more ships foundered or were driven ashore. Although the Duke of Medina Sidonia and the *San Martín* arrived safely in the Spanish port of Santander on September 21, many others were less fortunate, and over the coming weeks the full extent of the disaster became apparent.

Some sixty-five ships eventually made it back to Spain, which meant that forty-five had been lost, including four of the most powerful galleons in the fleet. The Armada had been an unmitigated disaster, and it provided Protestant propagandists with a fantastic opportunity to demonstrate that God was on the side of the reformed faith. The battle has long been billed as a great clash between two maritime empires, two types of ships, or two methods of fighting. The Spanish Armada campaign was all of those, and more. As probably the most significant naval battle of the Renaissance, it pointed the way toward the future for naval warfare—for those willing to learn from it. It demonstrated the superiority of the English system of gunnery, and to a lesser extent the superiority of Hawkins's race-built galleons over their Spanish counterparts. It also proved, at least with the benefit of hindsight, that the best plans are probably the simplest ones, especially when they involve the vagaries of wind, tide, and the English.

9

Phoenix from the Ashes

Juan de Benavides, knight of Santiago and captain-general of the New Spain flota, must have cut a sorry figure as he stood on the palm-fringed beach at Matanzas. It was September 8, 1628, and a series of errors had just led to the loss of his treasure fleet to the Dutch. Six years later he would answer for his mistakes with his life when he faced the public executioner in Seville. He must have realized that King Philip IV of Spain wouldn't be merciful to an admiral who had lost him his entire annual revenue from the New World. The flota was small that year—just eleven merchantmen, escorted by four galleons. While the merchantmen carried trade goods—silk, logwood, cocoa, animal hides, and indigo dye—the holds of the galleons were filled with treasure: silver ingots, gold finger bars, chests of coins, and bags of pearls and emeralds. This represented the king's *quinta*—his 20 percent share of the output of the mines of Mexico, as well as the specie owned by individuals shipping their fortunes to Spain.

In September 1628 the Thirty Years' War had been raging in Europe for a decade and the Spanish had been heavily involved, fighting on the side of a coalition of Catholic states. In 1621 a twelve-year truce between Spain and the Dutch ended, and within months the fighting spread to the Netherlands. While the veteran Spanish commander Ambrosio Spinosa laid siege to Dutch cities and the artist Diego Velázquez was on hand to capture the inevitable Spanish triumphs for posterity, a very different war was raging on the far side of the Atlantic Ocean. In 1624 the Dutch seized and captured the Portuguese port of Bahia—now San Salvador in Brazil. The port was recaptured by the Spanish the following year, and this time the painter Juan Bautista Maino recorded the victory in oil and on canvas. However, the Dutch would return. In 1626 the Dutch commander Piet Heyn raided and plundered the port again and returned home to a hero's welcome. Starved of successes at home the Dutch public willingly embraced Heyn as the new Drake. He was given ships, men, and a new mission: the capture of Captain-General de Benavides and his flota. It was hoped that if the Spanish were starved of their New World specie, their campaign in Holland would halt for lack of funds.

By the end of August 1628 Piet Heyn's fleet was lying off the northern coast of Cuba—thirty-six well-armed Dutch privateers crewed by thirty-three hundred experienced seamen. The Dutch blockaded Havana, trying to prevent word of their presence from reaching Captain-General de Benavides. However, dispatch boats sent from Cuba's southern coast managed to warn off the Tierra Firme fleet in Cartagena, which effectively halved the size of the coming disaster. Then somehow the commander of the New Spain flota also was tipped off. Presumably a fishing boat from Mariel or some other little port down the coast had brought him the unwelcome news. He decided to avoid Havana completely and put into the smaller port of Matanzas instead, some seventy miles farther east. Unfortunately for the admiral, his pilots didn't really know the area and his galleons ran aground on an uncharted sandbar as they entered Matanzas Bay. Worse was to follow. The Dutch had discovered that de Benavides had slipped past them, and they gave chase, arriving to find his four galleons stuck fast, unable to turn their guns on the approaching enemy. To Piet Heyn and his men it must have looked as if God favored the Protestant cause after all.

The Spaniards were hopelessly outnumbered and outgunned. The Dutch closed in and began firing into the exposed sterns of

Early-seventeenth-century Spanish galleons under attack

the galleons, their shot smashing through the whole length of the
Spanish ships—overturning guns, crushing seamen, and bringing
down masts. De Benavides ordered the ships abandoned and began
ferrying his men ashore. As the Dutch finally closed in to board
the enemy ships, the Spanish admiral abandoned his own flagship
and had his men row him ashore. His last act was to order a fuse
lit, intending to explode the powder magazine and deny the Dutch
their plunder. However, his order was never carried out, and soon
the jubilant Dutch privateers were firmly in control of the treasure
galleons. De Benavides's deputy, Juan de Leoz, remained behind to
surrender his sword, but the captain-general watched impotently
from the beach as the victors plundered all fifteen ships. While half
of them were burned, the rest were escorted to Holland, their holds
filled with plunder valued at a staggering 12 million pieces of eight:
$1.8 billion in today's money.

The execution of Juan de Benavides in the Plaza de San Francisco in 1634 was inevitable. He became a scapegoat for a maritime
disaster that many blamed for the subsequent collapse of Spain's
position as a European superpower. While the Matañzas incident
certainly highlighted the decline of Spain's ability to project its

maritime power, the simple truths were that the resources of the Spanish crown had been stretched too thin by a global war against the Dutch and the defenses of her flota system were woefully inadequate. The unfortunate Juan de Benavides had too few ships, armed with too few guns, although since 1588 the Spanish had done their best to improve the quality of their ships and the effectiveness of their naval armament. In fact, this process was already well under way when the disaster at Matanzas took place, and a new breed of Spanish galleons was being built that could better cope with the heavy demands on them. It seemed that the Spanish were at last trying to learn the lessons taught to them by the English in 1588. It just never had the chance to make a difference in time to spare the captain-general his misery.

This process of introspection began almost as soon as the remains of the Spanish Armada struggled back into port in 1588. Several reports were drawn up and fault was laid with the way the operation had been planned, the way its logistics had been organized, the lack of experienced Spanish seamen available, and the design of the ships themselves. Worse, it seemed that the Spanish could no longer protect their sea lanes between Spain and the Spanish Netherlands, or maintain a fleet capable of projecting Spanish power in northern waters. The Spanish naval planners clearly needed to go back to the drawing board. Actually, during the decade that

Battle at Matanzas, 1628

followed the Spanish Armada campaign it became apparent that strategically the Spanish still could hold their own against the English. They showed that they were able to maintain the integrity of their flota system despite these attacks, and ultimately it was the English rather than the Spanish who decided that these assaults were both financially and strategically unprofitable. The shipment of American specie would continue unimpeded until the Matanzas disaster.

The English launched three major maritime attacks on the Spanish in the aftermath of the Spanish Armada campaign. In 1589 they landed at La Corunna and near Lisbon, then lay off the Azores in the hope of intercepting the returning treasure flota. Although this expedition proved a complete failure, a similar enterprise was attempted two years later, when Lord Thomas Howard led a fleet of twenty-nine ships back to the Azores. This time the English were driven off by a larger Spanish fleet, although the engagement has lived on in naval history and English romantic poetry as "the last fight of the *Revenge*." A slightly more successful venture, the expedition to the Spanish Main in 1595–1596, was jointly commanded by Sir Francis Drake and Sir John Hawkins. The sea dogs successfully attacked Las Palmas in the Canary Islands but were rebuffed in their attempts to assault San Juan in Puerto Rico and Porto Bello, near Panama. However, both of these aging Elizabethan heroes died during the venture and ultimately this last English incursion into the Caribbean ended in failure. Finally, an Anglo-Dutch fleet successfully attacked Cádiz in 1596, destroying six Spanish or Portuguese galleons and plundering the city in the process. However, none of these assaults managed to interfere with the annual shipment of specie from the New World to Spain.

The Spanish began looking at the way their ships were designed and armed, but just how far they lagged behind the English was demonstrated during that sea fight off the Azores in 1591, where an entire Spanish fleet was hard-pressed to overwhelm a single Elizabethan race-built galleon. On August 30, 1591, Lord Thomas Howard's English fleet was lying off the island of Flores, where it hoped to intercept the homeward-bound annual treasure flota. One of the six large royal warships in the fleet was the five-hundred-ton Hawkins-designed galleon *Revenge*, commanded by Sir Richard

Grenville. Lookouts on Flores would have been searching the ocean to the west, hoping to see the sails of the approaching Indies flota. Instead they saw a fleet of thirty-one Spanish warships, the majority of which were large galleons, approaching from the southeast. This fleet had sailed from Lisbon to intercept the English and they had caught Lord Howard's fleet completely by surprise. Scores of the English sailors were sick and had been landed on Flores to recover. In the pandemonium some of these unfortunate men were left behind, while the English began an unholy scramble to escape from the approaching Spaniards.

One of the last ships to raise its anchor was the *Revenge*, as many of Grenville's 260-man crew were sick, and he refused to leave until they had all been brought on board. The Spanish force split into two, with roughly half the fleet passing on each side of Flores. To the English the formation resembled two horns, and the *Revenge* looked as if it would be caught between them. All but one of Howard's fleet escaped to the north, but Grenville proved less willing to cut and run. Instead he ordered the *Revenge* to turn toward the nearest easterly horn of the enemy formation. Grenville forced his way into the middle of this formation, which was made up of the powerful Castilian squadron—seven galleons, commanded by Marcos de Aramburu. The *Revenge* fired both broadsides as it crashed its way through the Spanish formation, and it broke through. The *Revenge* altered course to the north, toward the safety of the rest of the English fleet. Meanwhile, the Spanish gave chase, led by the General Admiral (fleet admiral) Alonso de Bazán in the *San Pablo*, followed by the venerable *San Martín de Portugal*, that veteran of the fight off Gravelines three years before.

Finally, the newly built 1,500-ton galleon *San Felipe* overhauled the *Revenge* on her starboard side, which meant she took the wind out of her sails, causing the English ship to slow. Her commander tried to come alongside the *Revenge*, but Grenville fired a broadside into her at point-blank range and the Spanish leviathan fell away astern, her hull pierced above and below the waterline. However, the exchange had delayed the English warship long enough for another galleon to overhaul her. She was the modern, 876-ton *San Barnabe*, commanded by the Armada veteran Martin de Bertendona. She managed to grapple the *Revenge* on her port side, and de

Bertendona ordered his gunners to keep firing into the masts and rigging of the English ship, in an attempt to cripple her. Meanwhile, his marksmen were sweeping the decks of the *Revenge* with small-arms fire. The smaller English ship was unable to fire into the hull of the *San Barnabe* for fear of sinking the Spaniard, which probably would have meant that the *Revenge* would be pulled down with her. Grenville was unable to escape.

The fighting had been raging for several hours by now and dusk was beginning to fall. In the failing light the 700-ton Armada veteran *San Cristóbal* crashed into the stern of the *Revenge* and a rush of Spaniards scrambled onto the English quarterdeck, waved on by Marcos de Aramburu. These handpicked Spanish soldiers hacked their way as far forward as the stump of the English vessel's mainmast. Somehow Grenville rallied the defenders and forced the Spaniards back, and as night fell the attackers were driven back over the poop and onto the *San Cristóbal*. Meanwhile, two decks below, English gunners fired their stern chasers into the Spanish galleon, holing her in the bows, just below the waterline. The crippled *San Cristóbal* dropped astern of the *Revenge* and would take no more part in the fight.

The English respite was a short one, as it was now the turn of the 530-ton galleon *La Asunción*, another veteran of 1588. Her soldiers boarded the *Revenge* over her port bow, but the attack was driven back, as were several more attempts to storm the *Revenge's* shot-wrecked forecastle, whose defenders held their ground with grim determination. The Spanish galleon was soon joined by another—possibly *La Serena*—which sent her men across to join the boarding parties from *La Asunción*. Meanwhile, de Bertendona, in the *San Barnabe*, coolly used his galleon as a bulwark for his soldiers and gunners, who were turning the upper decks of the *Revenge* into a charnel house.

Only the starboard side of the *Revenge* remained clear of Spanish ships, and belowdecks the English gunners continued to fire on any galleon that had the temerity to come within range. Gunners manning the bow pieces of the *Revenge* even managed to hole *La Asunción* below the waterline in several places, and soon after 3:00 A.M. the Spanish galleon pulled alongside the *San Barnabe* and her crew scrambled aboard her as their old galleon sank beneath them. More than a hundred of their shipmates were still on board when she slipped beneath the waves. Martin de Bertendona ordered his flagship to disengage, waiting for more light before he renewed the fight.

As dawn broke, it was clear that the *Revenge* was a complete wreck. Her masts had long since been shot away, and her upper works were shot away almost to the level of her main deck. Just a few splintered timbers were all that remained of her forecastle, and her decks were covered with the dead and wounded of both sides. Sir Richard Grenville was one of these, having been mortally wounded during the attack of the *San Cristóbal*. The *Revenge's* guns were firing only intermittently now, as very few of the English crew were still able to man their posts. The Spanish kept their distance and a ring of ships poured small-arms, artillery, and swivel-gun fire into the English wreck. Realizing that further resistance was impossible, the dying Grenville ordered his men to blow up the ship "so that no Spaniard could boast that he had taken a Queen's war galleon."

His officers argued that she was sinking anyway and that his duty lay in saving what remained of his men. Grenville and his badly wounded deputy, Captain William Langhorn, were still arguing when the master rowed over to the Spanish flagship, the *San Pablo*, and surrendered the ship. The Fleet Admiral Alonso de Bazán offered the English full honors of war, and the still reluctant Grenville had little option but to accept. The English sea dog died two days later and was buried at sea with full naval honors. After all, his *Revenge* had held its own for sixteen hours against a fleet of more than thirty Spanish warships, including the most powerful galleons ever to fly the Spanish flag. Of these, two galleons had been sunk, and two more were so badly shattered that they were barely able to limp into a friendly port.

Worst of all, the Spanish fleet had included five of the most modern galleons in the fleet—warships of the Apostle class, a group of a dozen war galleons ordered by Philip II in the immediate aftermath of the Spanish Armada fiasco. The whole incident demonstrated that the Spanish still had a long way to go before their warships were able to stand up to the English. The Apostles had been built as Spanish copies of Hawkins's race-built galleons, and ranged in size from 776 to 1,480 toneladas. These ships were meant to be an effective counter to the English fleet, but the battle off Flores revealed that although powerful in close-range action, they lacked the firepower of their English counterparts. However, the performance of the *San Barnabe* did at least prove that if well handled, they could be just as fast and maneuverable as ships like the *Revenge*.

A model of this new breed of Spanish warship was presented to King Philip II by his Flemish subjects in 1593—a beautiful replica of one of the galleons that had just been built in the shipyards of Antwerp. Although the model wasn't built to scale, it still reveals the way these post-Armada Spanish galleons had copied the shipbuilding styles of Sir John Hawkins's race-built warships. From her lines one might have thought she represented a ship built in Woolwich or Deptford rather than in the Spanish Netherlands. Although her hull below the waterline is too small to accurately represent what she would have looked like, and her superstructure and sailing rig were exaggerated for dramatic effect, anyone looking at the model today will be struck by the clean, fast lines of her hull, and the way her guns were mounted on a single, long, lower gun deck. The Spanish had shown themselves capable of adapting to suit the times—it was just a question of whether these modern galleons were enough to counter the threat posed by the English, the French, and the Dutch.

During the reign of Philip III (1598–1621), attempts were made to examine the whole business of Spanish shipbuilding, and three sets of shipbuilding ordnances were drawn up—in 1607, 1613, and 1618—each of which attempted to create an improved form of galleon, using a combination of state and private funds. Not all of these new galleons proved successful. For example, in late 1602 the Spanish crown signed a contract with the army commander Martín de Bertendona to build ten new galleons in Bilbao. In the end only seven galleons and two *galeoncetes* were actually produced, all modeled on the privateers produced in Dunkirk. Bertendona reckoned these were "the best design for warfare currently sailing the seas." These ships ranged in size from 125 to 900 tons burden, and entered service during 1604–1605. They clearly weren't as well suited for naval warfare as the commander had hoped, as two were captured by the Dutch in 1606, while three more foundered in a storm in the Bay of Biscay later that same year. Still, it showed that the Spanish were trying to come up with a way of dealing with the English and Dutch warships that had gotten the better of them.

In December 1607 a royal decree specified exactly what the new breed of treasure galleons should look like. This demonstrated that the tendency was to build ships that looked a lot more like Hawkins's race-built galleons than anything the Spanish had produced before the twelve apostles. It specified that hulls would be longer and narrower and that the ships would have a greater depth in the hold. The regulations suggested a keel-to-beam ratio of just under 2.6:1, which made for a ship that was maneuverable yet had a good cargo capacity so it could hold all those silver ingots and gold bars. However, the proportions were those of a warship rather than a merchantman, and if the cargo was anything other than heavy specie these narrow ships would have rolled and wallowed to the point of being unstable.

The maximum size now suggested for flota galleons was 567 tons—significantly smaller than some of the warships built in Philip II's reign. The thinking behind this was that many of the older ships were too large and deep-drafted to navigate their way up the shallow, twisting Guadalquiver, which led to Seville. If ships had to put into other ports, then the Casa de Contratación (House of Trade), which organized the Indies flotas, would be less able to prevent smuggling and the landing of contraband. It seems that for the most part these new regulations were ignored, so a slightly more flexible decree was issued six years later, in 1613.

Shipbuilders still weren't happy—the flota galleon was meant to be a compromise ship, part warship and part merchantman. Many felt the balance was skewed in favor of her fighting potential, which meant that profits would be reduced. The result was a 1618 decree, a compromise that kept shipbuilders, merchants, and naval commanders reasonably happy. Although the keel-to-beam ratio was still set at 2.6:1, the size restriction was increased to 624 tons, which gave these new ships a larger cargo capacity.

An example of this new type of flota galleon was the *Nuestra Señora de Atocha*, built in Havana in 1620. This Indies flagship was designed by master shipwright Alonso Ferreira, and although she had a burden of less than 550 tons, she was reasonably commodious, weatherly, and fast. This was well under the size restriction introduced by the Crown, and probably reflects the growing realization that these smaller ships were ideal for the job they were asked to perform—escorting convoys, fighting off pirates and interlopers, and negotiating narrow harbors and waterways. It was hardly the fault of Alonso Ferreira that within two years his galleon would be smashed against a reef off the Florida Keys, her hull would be ripped apart, and her precious cargo of specie be deposited in a neatly stacked pile on the seabed. Three and a half centuries later, this mother lode of treasure would be rediscovered by the legendary treasure hunter Mel Fisher.

However, the needs of the Indies flota were not necessarily the same as those of the naval commanders who tried to defend Spain's interests against the growing power of the Dutch. The trend among foreign fleets was usually toward larger and more powerful warships, and by the early seventeenth century it was clear that where once Spanish galleons had been noted for their size, now they were being increasingly dwarfed by their rivals. A list of Spanish ships operating out of Seville in 1625 revealed that while some vessels were registered as having a burden of 736 toneladas, the average was just over 500 tons. Typical of these ships were the six galleons built by Martín de Arana for the Spanish crown in 1625–1628, based on the guidelines of the 1618 decree. The *San Felipe, Nuestra Señora de Begoña, Los Tres Reyes*, and *San Juan Baptista* were all listed as 450 to 550 tons, with a keel-to-beam ratio of just under 2.5:1. Two smaller galleons—the *San Sebastián* and the *Santiago*—were just under 350 tons. Although these vessels might be maneuverable and fast, they would be at a serious disadvantage if they encountered a larger and better-armed Dutch warship on the high seas.

This problem was typified in a letter sent by the Spanish admiral Don Antonio de Oquendo to King Philip IV in 1637 during a naval campaign against the French. "We have news that the enemy's armada is of seventy ships, forty of them large, and some of such excessive size that they are over 2,000 toneladas, a thing never before seen on the sea . . . and of the ships that I have here, only the two that came from Vizcaya are as much as 700 toneladas, plus the *Capitana of Marmbradi* at 600, and the *San Carlos* and *Begoña* at 500. None of the rest exceeds 400 toneladas, and some are 300, the size of the dispatch ships that the enemy has." The only thing poor

Oquendo had going for him was that unlike the French, the Spanish had learned from the lesson in gunnery that the English had given them in 1588. By the second decade of the seventeenth century the Spanish had gone over to four-wheeled truck carriages, just like the English, and when Piet Heyn captured those Spanish galleons of Matanzas in 1628 he noted that all the Spanish warships carried modern bronze guns, mounted on modern truck-wheeled carriages. The French still used a mixture of four-wheeled and two-wheeled gun carriages.

This growing confidence in the art of gunnery was demonstrated in 1639 when the Spanish took on a Dutch fleet in the two-stage engagement known as the Battle of the Downs. Oquendo commanded the Spanish fleet, and during the first part of the battle, on September 16, his Spanish galleons held their own in savage exchanges of broadsides with a smaller Dutch force commanded by Maarten Tromp. What let the Spanish down was their lack of tactical finesse—the smaller Dutch force formed a line of battle and concentrated their fire on the head of the straggling Spanish column. The closest Oquendo came to issuing an order was to declare, "The flagship will set a good example." The Dutch avoided all Spanish attempts to board them, and although the Spanish gunnery was

Battle of the Downs, 1639

proficient enough to destroy one of the Dutch ships, by the end of the fight it was clear that the Spanish had come off worse.

Sir Henry Mainwaring, whose English squadron linked up with the Spanish the following morning, reported that they had "been shrewdly torn and beaten by only seventeen of the Holland ships in their first encounter." The battle would be resumed, but meanwhile both sides patched up their ships and restocked their powder magazines, the Spanish buying theirs from the neutral English. Unfortunately for Oquendo, the Dutch admiral managed to add another hundred ships to his fleet, including sixteen fireships. This time the Spanish would be outnumbered two to one. On October 21 Tromp struck again, using fog as cover. While a portion of his fleet screened a small English squadron, the rest of the Dutch fleet trapped the Spanish against the English coast, just in front of Walmer Castle, Kent. Several of Oquendo's ships simply ran aground to escape the fight, and the Dutch sent in fireships to finish them off. However, Antonio de Oquendo was made of sterner stuff. He ordered the rest of his ships to fight their way past the Dutch and out into the open sea.

The battle moved slowly to the southeast as a running fight developed, the compact group of about twenty Spanish galleons managing to keep the Dutch at bay. Finally Tromp sent in more fireships, and two became entangled with the *Santa Teresa*, the Portuguese-built flagship of Oquendo's deputy, Don Lope de Hoces. Oquendo remained as long as he could, but eventually the blazing *Teresa* had to be abandoned. The flight continued, with Oquendo's thousand-ton flagship, *Nuestra Señora de la Conception y Santiago*, forming the rear guard. Somehow he managed to keep the Dutch at bay until nightfall, and he was able to lead the survivors of his fleet to the safety of the Flemish coast under cover of darkness. However, the battle had been a complete disaster, and the Spanish losses had been catastrophic—as many as forty ships being driven ashore, captured, burned, or sunk during the fighting. Oquendo's spirit had been broken, and the valiant but rash admiral died soon after his return to Spain.

The Dutch victory at the Downs was not merely the result of numbers and luck. Like the Spaniards, they had been busy building a navy that befitted its role as a growing global power and designing warships and armed merchantmen that best suited their needs. From 1595 onward the Dutch had sent armed trading ships around Africa and into the Indian Ocean. After the foundation of the Vereenigde Oostindische Compagnie (Dutch East India Company) in 1602, the Dutch specialized in producing large armed merchantmen able to defend themselves during the long round-trip voyage between Holland and the East Indies. Although the Spanish and the Dutch were both concerned with building vessels with a similar function—oceangoing cargo carriers that could defend themselves— the Dutch developed their own style of ship, which was notably different from the Spanish galleon.

The *Duyfken* (Little Dove) was typical of these early Dutch East Indiamen. She was built in the Netherlands in 1595 and was originally intended to be either a privateer or a fast cargo ship. Instead she was selected to join the Moluccan Fleet—a five-ship trading expedition to the Spice Islands of the East Indies. These ships arrived off Bantam in Java on Christmas Day 1601, only to find that the small Dutch settlement was being blockaded by a Portuguese squadron. After a weeklong battle the Portuguese were driven off— a small sea battle with immense global consequences. It effectively ended the Portuguese monopoly of the spice trade and allowed the Dutch East India Company to establish a firm foothold in the East Indies. The *Duyfken* returned to Holland in 1603, then made a second voyage to the East Indies later that year under the command of Willem Janszoon. On this second voyage she entered the history books, when in 1606 Janszoon discovered and charted the northern coast of Australia, becoming the first European to discover this new continent. The little ship was finally decommissioned in 1608, when the damage incurred during a sea battle with the Portuguese was deemed too extensive to repair.

In 1997 work began on a replica of the *Duyfken*, the design based on contemporary artwork, early-seventeenth-century Dutch records, known shipwrecks, and modern computer analysis. The result was a small ship of 110 tons that was broader in the beam than the Spanish galleons of the era, and shallow enough to negotiate the coastal waters of Holland and the East Indies. The hull was maneuverable, and when fully rigged the ship was fast. The replica easily made four knots in moderate winds and frequently sailed at more than seven knots. The Dutch had classified the original *Duyfken* as a *jacht* (yacht, or scout), so her performance was probably exceptional. However, this little craft shared many of the design features of her larger and better-armed contemporaries. The experimental archaeologists and replica shipbuilders had stumbled across the secret of Dutch maritime success.

A study of Dutch warships and East Indiamen shown in engravings produced during the 1590s reveals that Dutch ships of this type were generally similar to the race-built galleons of the English. However, these Dutch ships tended to have a shallower draft—a limitation imposed by the need to navigate the shallow coastal waters and inland waterways of Holland. By the late seventeenth century English and French ship designers were regularly producing sailing ships of war far larger than anything the Dutch could build. This draft limitation effectively ended Holland's bid for global naval supremacy and left the field clear for the French and the British to fight it out for mastery of the seas throughout most of the eighteenth century. However, in the last decades of the Renaissance the Dutch were still ahead of the game.

By the 1620s the Dutch East India Company was producing East Indiamen that were both as large and as well armed as major warships had been just a decade or so earlier. Most of these were more than a match for the Spanish or Portuguese galleons they might encounter on the high seas, and in 1628 a portion of Piet Heyn's fleet was made up of similar large vessels, supplied by the short-lived Dutch West India Company. However, even these powerful Indiamen were poorly armed in comparison with the new breed of specialized Dutch warships built to project Dutch maritime power in the waters of northern Europe. These vessels were mainly single-decked, modeled on the sleek new breed of frigates built by the Flemish privateers of Dunkirk. Although they were generally more lightly constructed than their English or Spanish counterparts, these ships were broader in the beam, which helped to counteract the stability effects of their shallow draft and made them very effective gun platforms.

Then there was the *Aemilia*, Maarten Tromp's flagship at the Battle of the Downs. She was built in Rotterdam by the master shipwright Jan Salomonszoon van den Tempel, who began work on her in 1632. She was the second large warship to be built for the Dutch—she was preceded by the thirty-gun *Eenhoorn* in 1625. However, when she was built, the *Aemilia* was the largest warship in Holland and one of the most powerful in Europe. She carried a powerful armament of 486 guns—24 culverins and demiculverins on her lower gundeck, and 24 lighter guns (probably a mixture of demiculverins and sakers) on her second, upper deck. She may well have carried as many as 9 other smaller guns mounted high in her sterncastle or forecastle. She had a length overall of about 122 feet, a beam of 32½ feet, and a draft of just 14 feet. No other Dutch ship of that period—not even the *Eenhoorn*—carried her guns on two continuous decks, and so despite her small size and tonnage she was a considerably more powerful warship than any of the galleons commanded by Don Antonio de Oquendo in 1639. Put simply, Tromp's *Aemilia* was a ship of the future, while Oquendo's *Santiago* was a ship of the past.

The Battle of the Downs was the last great attempt by the Spanish to intervene in northern European waters, and the defeat represented the end of her maritime ambitions beyond the defense of her own sea lanes. This important sea battle was also something of a last hurrah for the Spanish galleon, the end of a tradition of Iberian shipbuilding that had lasted for more than a century. By the time Don Antonio de Oquendo's battered flagship reached the safety of the Flemish coast, the technology of shipbuilding had moved on, and the galleon was fast becoming a thing of the past. The launch of the *Sovereign of the Seas* had that same year ushered in a new era of naval shipbuilding, one that would be dominated by the heavily armed ship of the line rather than the smaller, multipurpose galleon. The galleon—an iconic ship type that helped to define Spain's imperial ambitions during the Renaissance—would finally sail off into the sunset.

10

Prestige over Practicality

The Jacobean Legacy

The procession of black-draped barges made their stately way down the River Thames, watched by thousands of mourners who lined the riverbank. In the center of this melancholy convoy was the royal state barge, where blazing torches illuminated a lead coffin carrying the body of Elizabeth I, queen of England. The funeral cortege was making its way from Richmond to Westminster Palace, where the body would lie in state while preparations were made for the most lavish state funeral England had ever seen. The whole country was stricken with grief—the English antiquarian and historian William Camden later claimed that even the fish in the river "wept out their eyes of pearle." In his entry two days previously, on March 24, 1603, the diarist John Manningham recorded, "This morning, about three o'clock her Majesty departed from this life, mildly like a lamb, easily like a ripe apple from a tree. . . . Dr Parry told me he was present, and sent his prayers before her soul; and I doubt not but she is amongst the royal saints in heaven in eternal joys."

On her deathbed the seventy-year-old virgin queen named her successor. According to Camden, when asked about the succession, she whispered, "I said that my Throne was a Throne of Kings, I would not that any base should succeed me." When her council asked her to clarify, she continued; "I will that a King succeed me; and who but my nearest kinsman, the King of Scots?" The historian went on to claim, "The most sorrowful misse of her, which she left to the English, was assuaged by the great hope conceived of the virtues of King James her successor; who after a few hours was proclaymed King with the most joyfull shouts and acclamations of all men." William Camden was being generous. King James VI of Scotland (reigned 1567–1625) lacked the charisma of Elizabeth I. He was dominated by suspicions and phobias, and it was unlikely that he would endear himself to his new English subjects overnight.

James VI of Scotland and I of England

However, at least his succession meant there would be no power struggle for the throne, and the dynasty of the Tudors passed its mantle to that of the Stuarts without a hitch.

The body of Queen Elizabeth lay in state for a month, waiting for King James to travel south from Edinburgh, and she was finally buried on April 28, the funeral procession winding through the crowded streets of London to Westminster Abbey. Four horses draped in black velvet pulled the funeral carriage, where the coffin was decorated with a life-size effigy of the queen dressed in her ceremonial robes. Thousands of courtiers followed behind, many of whom wept openly, as did the onlookers. The English historian John Snow captured the scene: "Westminster was surcharged with multitudes of all sorts of people in their streets, houses, windows, leads and gutters, that came to see the obsequy, and when they beheld her statue lying upon the coffin, there was such a general sighing, groaning and weeping as the like hath not been seen or known in the memory of man, neither doth any history mention any people, time or state to make like lamentation for the death of their sovereign." Historians often claim that the queen's death marked the end of an era, the passing of an Elizabethan golden age. It was little wonder that so many mourned their collective loss.

One of the new king's first acts was to negotiate a peace with Spain. The terms of the Treaty of London, signed in 1604, were generally favorable to Spain—it maintained its trade monopoly in the Americas and was given a relatively free hand to continue its war against the Dutch. However, the English treasury was all but exhausted, the naval war had reached a stalemate, and the country desperately needed a period of peace. In return James pledged that he would avoid interfering in Continental affairs, which effectively meant helping his Protestant Dutch allies. This coincided with the end of a long-running rebellion in Ireland, so for the first time in decades England had little need of a costly standing army. The Navy Royal remained the most powerful deterrent for any would-be invader, a wooden bulwark behind which Jacobean England could live in peace and growing prosperity.

The Elizabethan fleet bequeathed to the new king included twenty-three warships of 300 tons or more, most of which had either been built by Hawkins or rebuilt as his race-built galleons. Another nineteen smaller ships—tiny galleons, pinnaces, dispatch boats, light-ers, galleys, and hulks such as the *Nuestra Señora del Rosario*—brought the total to forty-two vessels. It was commonplace to survey the fleet when a new monarch took control of it, and this was always seen as a good opportunity to dispose of obsolete or badly rotting ships. The clear-out of the Navy Royal included two Spanish galleons captured at Cádiz in 1595—the *San Andrea* and the *San Mateo*; the 330-ton galleon *Swallow*, which had been built in 1544; and Hawkins's 300-ton *Foresight*, the first small race-built galleon. This wasn't any selling off of the "family silver," as some historians have suggested. It was a routine review of what was essentially an aging fleet.

Since the loss of the *Revenge* off the Azores in 1591, several new galleons had been built, all of which followed the Hawkins model. Sir John Hawkins retired as treasurer and comptroller of the navy in 1589—the year after the Spanish Armada—but ships were still being built according to his specifications. The most important of these new warships in terms of our story were the 440-ton *Defiance* and the 530-ton *Garland*, both of which were built in Deptford in 1590. The first was the work of Richard Chapman, while the second, larger ship was constructed by Peter and Joseph Pett. In the same year the master shipwright Matthew Baker built an even larger galleon, the 690-ton *Merhonour*, in the royal shipyard at Woolwich.

The business of shipbuilding was also becoming more organized. In his *Fragments of Ancient English Shipwrightry* (1582), Matthew Baker published a treatise that laid out the geometric proportions he used in ship construction. This formula revealed just how scientific the art of shipbuilding had become. While many shipbuilders continued to work on their own secret formulas of proportion and hull shape, or followed their own rule-of-thumb ideas about stability, the leading shipwrights were trying to codify the general ideas proposed by Hawkins. Hawkins himself had introduced his design innovations based on his extensive practical experience, and there is no evidence that he ever defined exactly what constituted a race-built galleon. It was up to the shipbuilders—men such as Richard Chapman, Matthew Baker, and Peter Pett—to interpret Hawkins's wishes and to build the ships. Baker's *Fragments* therefore represents an attempt to explain the Hawkins design so there was no room for mistakes—a move from art toward science.

The death of Sir John Hawkins off Puerto Rico in November 1595 was a serious blow to the navy. For more than two decades he had been the power behind the fleet, the man responsible for its modern warships and the maintenance of high standards of ship construction and gunnery. There was nobody else who could assume his mantle, and inevitably standards began to slip. However, the ships he had commissioned were still being built. In 1595 the 620-ton *Due Repulse* was built at Deptford as a replacement for her namesake lost in action four years earlier. She was followed by the *Warspite*, a 520-ton galleon built in Deptford in 1596 under the supervision of Edward Stevens. In addition, three older galleons were rebuilt—the *Triumph* in 1596, the *Elizabeth Jonas* in 1598, and the *White Bear* the following year. This meant that by 1603, apart from those two Spanish prizes, every major warship in the new Jacobean fleet had been rebuilt to Hawkins's design.

Some historians have criticized James I and VI as being a pacifist—a man who made peace with Spain and who neglected the navy. This simply isn't true. While he made peace with the Spanish, this was a decision even Elizabeth would have made had she lived. The long war had effectively bankrupted the country, and only peace could have saved the navy. Moreover, if we discount those two Spanish prizes, of the twenty-one major warships in the fleet—the race-built galleons of three hundred tons or more—eleven were still in service when the king died in 1625, and of these, all but the *White Bear* would still be in service by the time the English Civil War began sixteen years later. Most of these ships were rebuilt during the Jacobean era—the majority in 1608–1610 or in 1614–1617. Eight major ships were decommissioned during the reign of King James, four of which—the *Elizabeth Jonas*, *Triumph*, *Garland*, and *Mary Rose*—were condemned and broken up following a second extensive survey of the fleet in 1618. The *Victory* and the *Elizabeth Bonaventure* met the same fate in 1608 and 1611, respectively, while the *Swiftsure* (renamed the *Speedwell* in 1607) was lost at sea in 1624.

To replace these ships condemned in the 1618 survey King James embarked on a major shipbuilding program that saw the construction of nine major warships in the royal shipyard at Deptford, all built under the supervision of William Burrell between 1619 and 1623. These included five ships with a burden of 850 tons or more, and a 750-ton experimental frigate, the *Constant Reformation*, which was effectively the prototype of a whole new kind of warship. James even had an eye on consistency when he named these ships—they included the *Triumph*, *Victory*, *Garland*, and *Bonaventure*, new ships designed to replace their Elizabethan predecessors in name as well as in effectiveness. Therefore the argument that the Navy Royal was run down during the Jacobean period flies in the face of the evidence.

The one legitimate criticism that can be laid was of corruption in the dockyards, which is a different matter entirely—a problem that developed because there was no Hawkins to take overall charge. The fact that Hawkins himself was accused of corruption is conveniently ignored. Perhaps his own skills in this area meant that he was better able to detect corrupt practices in the shipyards than the lesser men who succeeded him—Sir Fulke Greville and Sir Robert Mansell. It was not until the appointment of Sir William Russell as treasurer of the navy in 1618 that King James found someone capable of dealing with the problem. This aside, it can be argued that the Jacobean period saw a move toward the creation of a more modern fleet, through rebuilding older Elizabethan galleons or the construction of a new breed of even more powerful warships. Then there was the *Prince Royal*, the ultimate royal warship of the Jacobean age. This magnificently revolutionary warship was a major shipbuilding gamble that provoked a storm of controversy when she was built, and whose launch became a seventeenth-century media circus. She also would be a major step toward the creation of the ultimate Renaissance warship.

Pett and the *Prince*

It all began with a small boy's model ship. In 1607 the young Deptford shipbuilder Phineas Pett made a scale model of a warship, a large and ornate vessel in miniature he hoped would result in a contract to build the real thing. Fortunately, Pett had friends in high places. His late father had known Lord Howard of Effingham, the man who led the English fleet to victory against the Spanish Armada. The seventy-one-year-old nobleman was now Charles, Earl of Nottingham, and he still held the title of Lord High Admiral of England. In what amounted to a stroke of marketing genius, Phineas Pett arranged that the earl would present him to the king's eldest son, Henry, Prince of Wales. When he arrived at Richmond Palace, the shipbuilder gave his model to the young prince. The ten-year-old "entertained it with great joy" and immediately showed it to his father.

James was almost as impressed by it as his son, as Pett himself later recorded: "His Majesty (who was present) was exceedingly delighted with the sight of the model, and passed some time in questioning the divers material things concerning it." The king then asked Pett whether he could build such a ship. Pett assured him he could. A delighted James immediately ordered him to begin work on the real thing, although he cautioned him to make the warship just like the model, "for I will compare them together when she

Phineas Pett, Jacobean master shipbuilder

shall be finished." Pett was therefore awarded a contract to build the first warship of the Jacobean reign, a ship worthy of a king who rules two kingdoms.

Phineas Pett was accused of many things during his early years, but he was no fool. He realized that since the end of the war with Spain the Navy Royal had been somewhat neglected. Although several existing ships had been rebuilt since James's accession, no new shipbuilding contracts had been issued. It was a lean time for the royal shipbuilders, and Pett's model was his attempt to pull the shipbuilding business out of the doldrums. While he succeeded in securing a profitable contract, he also incurred the wrath of his fellow artisans. The problem was, these other master shipwrights had far more practical experience, and were unconvinced that Pett could deliver what he'd promised. The thirty-nine-year-old shipbuilder was obviously gifted, but the suggestion that he could build a twelve-hundred-ton leviathan was met with howls of derision and protest. Nothing in Phineas Pett's past had prepared him for the political storm that now raged around him.

When Phineas Pett's shipbuilding father, Peter, died in 1589, his comfortable world fell apart. His mother, Elizabeth, decided she could no longer afford to maintain her middle son at Cambridge University. Instead he was apprenticed to the master shipwright Richard Chapman of Deptford, who had once served under Phineas's father. This apprenticeship lasted for two years, until Chapman's death in 1593. Pett's elder brother, Joseph, was already a master shipwright at the small yard at Limehouse, but he refused to take on his overeducated young brother. Phineas had no other option but to go to sea. He returned home in 1594, having decided that a sailor's life was not for him. This time the begrudging Joseph employed him as a carpenter, and so the twenty-five-year-old Phineas worked on the refitting of the modern race-built galleon *Defiance* and the rebuilding of the older *Triumph*. His big break came in 1595, when he was hired by Matthew Baker to work on a new ship in Deptford, the *Due Repulse*. Baker encouraged his apprentice, who showed an aptitude for Baker's more scientific approach to shipbuilding.

In Deptford in 1597 Baker introduced his protégé to the Earl of Nottingham, who in 1599 recommended Phineas Pett for the job of inspecting East Anglian timber, to see if it was good enough to be used in the royal shipyards. On the completion of the assignment in 1600 the earl appointed Pett as the keeper of the plank yard at Chatham Dockyard, where Joseph Pett had become the new master shipwright. This time Joseph was more supportive: he appointed Phineas as his assistant, and the younger brother eventually succeeded him. He worked on the rebuilding and refitting of two small royal warships, and was still there in 1603 when James I succeeded to the English throne. Nottingham commissioned Phineas to build a miniature sailing replica of his Armada flagship the *Ark Royal*, a project completed in early 1604. The admiral presented the twenty-eight-foot boat to James's ten-year-old eldest son, Henry, Prince of Wales, who was delighted with the present. This plaything was the first vessel that Pett had built from scratch. Although he would build another the following year—a three-hundred-ton merchantman—this hardly amounted to a wealth of shipbuilding experience. It is hardly surprising that his critics rounded on him so fiercely when King James commissioned him to build the *Prince Royal*.

A combination of cronyism, nepotism, bribery, and downright corruption was rife in His Majesty's royal dockyards. Since the death of Hawkins the industry lacked a firm controlling hand, and his successors as treasurer of the navy failed to keep a proper check on expenditures and accounts. Sir Robert Mansell was one of the worst, appointed through his friendship with the Earl of Nottingham, and set the tone by awarding himself lavish expenses from the public purse. Ships that should have been condemned were maintained to provide work for friends and dependents, and dockyard posts were created for the same reason. It was little wonder that everyone seemed furious that Pett had bypassed the system and secured a contract directly with the king. A hurried inquiry into his affairs and lack of experience failed to derail the project with what Pett described as their "malicious proceedings," and on October 20, 1608, he laid the keel of the new ship in Woolwich Dockyard.

The sheer scale of the new vessel was impressive—the largest warship built in England since the *Henri Grace à Dieu* almost a century before. More important, she was the first to boast a second complete gun deck. Her keel was 115 feet long, while her main deck extended for 135 feet. She had a 43½-foot beam, and a depth of hull of 18 feet, which made her broader and deeper in proportion than many of her contemporaries. She was estimated as having a burden of 1,200 tons, although as the way this was being calculated was changing, this figure is only an estimate. Under the new rules that came into effect in 1632, she was classed as being 1,035 net tons—without her guns—and 1,330 tons when fully laden. However you calculated her size, she was going to be an impressive ship—and an ambitious undertaking for an inexperienced master shipwright.

To make the job even harder, his jealous peers where doing what they could to prevent her from being built. Rivals and officials alike complained that the new ship would never work, or that Pett was the wrong man for the job. In an official protest one rival claimed of Pett that he was "no artist, and that he was altogether insufficient to perform such a service." Another claimed that her construction included "gross errors and absurdities," and during one of three official investigations into the project it was claimed that among other things her frames were dangerously weak, having been cut incorrectly (across the grain rather than with it), her planking was green and unseasoned, and old and rotting timbers were used where they wouldn't be seen. She "had too much floor"—meaning her decks were too heavily reinforced, and the scarf joints linking the sections of her keel and keelson together were too short and cut the wrong way, thereby fatally weakening the whole structure. None of this managed to prevent Pett from continuing to build her, and none of the allegations was ever supported by hard evidence. He was heartened by a visit to the shipyard by the prince royal himself, the teenage Henry, Prince of Wales, who viewed the dry dock where his model was being turned into the real thing, then dined with Pett afterward.

The third and final inquiry into the building of the *Prince Royal* was chaired by the king himself in an attempt to end the business once and for all. During the investigation in Woolwich, Captain Weymouth of the Navy Royal testified that the inclusion of a second tier of guns, together with what they regarded as her excessive top hamper, would render the finished ship unstable, unweatherly, and difficult to maneuver. Pett later described his evidence as "a long, tedious discourse . . . an infinite rabble of idle and unprofitable speeches, clean from the matter." Even Pett's former mentor Matthew Baker stated that he thought the ship objectionable in design and proportion. Finally, a report by other master shipwrights who inspected the ship—although they contradicted Baker's measurements—concluded that she was "unfit for any other use but a dung boat." They followed this up with a plea that Pett be forced to resign as a master of the Company of Shipwrights, and then publicly disgraced into the bargain. It probably ranks as one of the most vitriolic inquiries ever held in a dockyard, but in the end the sheer weight of the criticism worked in Pett's favor.

The king decided to see the ship for himself. Accompanied by the Earl of Nottingham and the members of the board of inquiry, the king toured the ship and had all the measurements checked. He peered at the cut of the timbers, examined the planking, and inspected the scarf joints. Once he had finished, he declared, "the cross-grain was in the men and not in the timber." Pett himself recalled what happened next: "His Majesty with a loud voice commanded the measures to declare publicly the very truth, which when they had delivered clearly on our side, all the whole multitude heaved up their hats, and gave a great and loud shout and exclamation." Not to be outdone, the young Prince of Wales piped up, "Where be now these perjured fellows that dare abuse His Majesty with these false accusations? Do they not worthily deserve hanging?" At the back of the crowd Captain Weymouth and Matthew Baker wisely kept their own counsel.

Phineas Pett had been fully vindicated, and the work continued. Finally, on September 24, 1610, she was ready to be launched. In what was intended to be a lavish ceremony the entire royal family arrived, accompanied by hundreds of courtiers, officials, and even the cynical shipwrights. The *Prince Royal* was draped in bunting, and her gilding caught the afternoon sunshine. Unfortunately, when the dock gates were opened and the mighty warship floated free of her supports, she was blown against the side of the dock gates, where she grounded. It was clear that there was no possibility of launching her that day, so a disappointed monarch and his entourage returned to Greenwich Palace. Weymouth, Baker, and their supporters must have been delighted.

Pett planned to try to free the ship on the next high tide, due at about 3:00 A.M. It was a bright, moonlit night, with intermittent light rain showers, and the master shipwright supervised the rigging of tow ropes and pulleys. At a little after midnight the Prince of Wales returned to the dockyard to watch the operation, accompanied by the Earl of Nottingham, and shortly after 2:00 A.M., as they stood on board her, the great warship floated free. This time there was no mistake, and within an hour she was safely moored in the middle of the River Thames. A delighted Prince Henry drank from a great silver cup, then tipped the rest of the claret over the quarterdeck, christening the ship *Prince Royal* as he did so. The nocturnal ceremony was accompanied by fanfares of trumpets and frenzied cheering.

The real proof of Phineas Pett's great warship came after she entered service. She carried an incredibly powerful armament of fifty-five heavy guns mounted on two complete gun decks, including six cannons, twelve culverins, and eighteen demiculverins. That meant she carried double the armament of most other ships in the fleet, and half as many again as her largest Spanish, French, or Dutch rival. This made her the most powerful warship afloat. The deck beams and "floors," which Weymouth and Baker had found too heavy, helped support the weight of these guns, while the draft they found too deep helped to steady the ship when she fired a broadside. In other words, she was a superbly designed fighting ship. However, some still questioned her value. One English admiral claimed that when she fired a broadside, the discharge from the extra bank of guns produced "so great a smoke within board that people must use their arms like blind men, not knowing how to go about their work, or having a sight of the ship whom they encounter." It seems there was no pleasing some critics, as the smoke-filled lower gun deck remained a feature of the sailing ship of war until the nineteenth century.

The design of the *Prince Royal* was innovative, but she wasn't completely revolutionary. The Dutch artist Hendrik Cornelisz Vroom painted her during a visit to Flushing, Holland, in 1613, and his eye for detail and knowledge of ships mean that the painting ("The Arrival of the Elector Palatine at Flushing, 1613") remains a valuable source of information. She was four-masted, the rear two masts—the mizzen and the bonaventure mizzen—carrying lateen-rigged sails, while her two larger masts were rigged with three square sails apiece. Her general appearance was that of a galleon, with a pronounced beak, a distinct forecastle, and a gently sloping

The Prince *entering Flushing—detail of "The Arrival of the Elector Palatine at Flushing, 1613," by Vroom*

sterncastle that narrowed significantly toward the stern. Compared to her consort, the *Red Lion*, which also appears in the Vroom painting, she looks sleek and graceful, her gently sloping quarterdeck giving her a flush appearance.

What stands out in the Vroom painting is the way the *Prince Royal* was decorated with carvings and a lavish use of gilding. Elaborate carvings and bas-reliefs cover her stern and beak, while gilded wreaths encircle the gunports of her upper gun deck. Her stern superstructure was dominated by a large painted bas-relief carving of a three-feathered plume—the symbol of the Prince of Wales—while her beak was crowned by the figurehead of an equestrian figure—St. George—charging into battle with the dragon with his sword held aloft. The dockyard accounts show that the London artist Sebastian Vicars was paid £441 to produce the wooden carvings, while a further £868 was spent on the painting and gilding. This was no mere piece of ostentatious frippery. The *Prince Royal* was meant to embody the power of Jacobean England, to be a floating symbol of seapower and naval might. In other words, she was a floating statement that under King James the Navy Royal was a force to be reckoned with.

The *Prince Royal* was the perfect vehicle for showing the flag. In early 1613 she was used to transport the Princess Elizabeth together with her new husband, Frederick, Elector Palatine, on the first leg of their journey to their palace in Heidelberg. Pett traveled with the young couple and declared that his ship "wrought exceedingly well, and was so yare of conduct that a foot of helm would steer her." Her arrival in Flushing was the occasion celebrated by Vroom in his painting—now on display in the Science Museum in London—and when she arrived in Holland, the entourage was greeted, in Pett's words, by "such a multitude of people, men, women and children, come from all places in Holland, to see the ship that we could scarce have room to go up and down till very night." One suspects that most of these spectators came to see the royal couple rather than their conveyance, but the point is clear that the *Prince Royal* played her part to perfection.

As a warship she was extremely successful. She remained in service for much of the seventeenth century, and when she was rebuilt in 1641, her armament was increased to seventy guns. During the English Civil War she became part of the Parliamentarian fleet, when she was renamed the *Resolution*. She was rebuilt again in 1663, and ended her days three years later, during a battle against the Dutch known as the Four Days' Fight. Having run aground on Galloper Sands off the coast of East Anglia, she was surrendered to the Dutch admiral Cornelis Tromp. Unable to pull her off, he ordered her burned—an ignominious end to a warship that had served England well for more than half a century. As for her builder, 1610 was a momentous year in another way, as in August—six weeks before the launch of Pett's great ship—his wife, Anne, gave birth to their fourth child, a boy named Peter. During the 1630s father and son would join forces to build an even greater warship for a Stuart king: the *Sovereign of the Seas*.

Henry, Prince of Wales, didn't live long enough to see much of his namesake ship. The much-loved teenager died of typhoid in November 1612, which meant that his less capable twelve-year-old brother, Charles, became next in line for the throne. British history might have taken a different course if the Scottish-born prince had survived. As for Phineas Pett, he enjoyed a revenge of sorts in early 1618 when King James cracked down on corruption in the dockyards. This led to the dismissal of the corrupt Sir Robert Mansell, and his replacement by Sir William Russell. The new treasurer of the navy sought Pett's advice over the replacement of several condemned ships with new ones, and in the commissioning of a new breed of warships. Pett was involved in the planning and building of the *Constant Reformation*, a Jacobean great ship whose basic design was based in part on the lines of the *Prince Royal*. He also rebuilt the old *Vanguard* to conform to the new notions of ship design. After Charles I succeeded his father to the throne in 1625, Pett remained in favor, and in 1631 he was appointed first commissioner of the navy, a position he held until his death in 1647.

The reign of King Charles I (1625–1649) would be dominated by the English Civil War (1641–1646), but before that he, like his father before him, would become involved in a new conflict raging across the mainland of Europe. The Thirty Years' War (1618–1648) was probably the most destructive war on the Continent until the twentieth century, but geography would protect the English from its horrors. The struggle began in 1618 when the Protestants of Bohemia revolted against the Holy Roman emperor. They asked Frederick, the Elector Palatine—the son-in-law of King James—to become the new King of Bohemia. This led to a military clash with a Catholic alliance led by the Emperor Ferdinand II, and Frederick lost both his lands in Bohemia and the German Palatine. He died in exile in Holland in 1632, survived by his widow, Elizabeth "of Bohemia." King James did what he could for his son-in-law, but it was clear that England lacked the army and the resources to intervene on the European stage. Instead, Gustavus Adolphus of Sweden would pick up the torch for the Protestant cause. Sweden was desperately trying to become a player on the European stage, and the Thirty Years' War provided their king—"the Lion of the North"—with the perfect opportunity to fulfill his political destiny.

The Lion of the North

The Lion of the North was not known for his patience. The twenty-seven-year-old King Gustavus Adolphus of Sweden had been besieging the city of Riga for six weeks, his warships blockading the port from seaward while his army encircled the city on its landward sides. The Swedish siege guns had knocked several breaches in the city's medieval walls, but so far every attempt to storm the walls had been thrown back with heavy losses. The Swedish king had given the defenders two chances to surrender, and he now awaited word from his negotiators, who three days before had delivered a third and final ultimatum. This time Gustavus's demand was accompanied by a deadly threat. Swedish engineers had dug a tunnel under the walls and packed it with enough explosives to demolish half the city. If his negotiators returned empty-handed, the Swedish king was prepared to order the fuse lit. His crack assault troops were ready to storm the city, and this time there would be no taking of prisoners. Finally, late on the afternoon of September 15, 1621, a messenger brought the news: Riga had surrendered. Sweden now controlled the largest city in the Baltic, and a bridgehead on the mainland of central Europe.

Although an independent city, Riga—the capital of Lithuania— had been under the protection of the Swedish king's cousin, King Sigismund III of Poland, a rival claimant to the Swedish throne. Sweden and Poland had been at loggerheads since the Swedish Parliament deposed the Catholic Sigismund in 1599 and gave the throne to Gustavus's father, Charles IX. The Vasa dynasty of Sweden was not known for its family unity. When Gustavus Adolphus succeeded his father in 1611 he inherited a country fighting wars on three fronts—against the Danes, the Poles, and the Russians. He quickly signed a peace with the Danes and arranged a truce with the Poles, thereby freeing himself to concentrate on the Russians. The Swedish-Muscovite War (1613–1617) that followed resulted in the securing of Sweden's hold over its eastern province of Finland and forced the Russians to the peace table. With the Russians knocked out, Gustavus turned his attention to Cousin Sigismund.

The siege of Riga was the opening move in a campaign that would propel Sweden into the heart of a pan-European war. The Swedes managed to secure most of Riga's hinterland and, more important, gained access to lucrative trade routes. However, Gustavus needed time to build up his military resources, so another truce was declared, and this time the peace lasted until 1625. The conflict the young Swedish king had inherited was part of the long-running struggle for dominum Maris Baltica—control of the Baltic—and the capture of Riga was a major step toward that goal. However, Gustavus Adolphus had even greater ambitions. The Thirty Years' War (1618–1648) had been going badly for the Protestants, and without Swedish help it looked as if the Catholic League, led by the Holy Roman emperor Ferdinand II, would emerge victorious, and so would unite Germany under the Catholic banner. While Gustavus still had to deal with the Poles, he also began thinking about intervening in the war in Germany.

For this he needed money, troops, and ships. The organization of the army had already been overhauled, and by the time the fighting renewed in 1625, the Swedes were regarded as one of the most efficient fighting forces in Europe. Money came through trade and the plunder of Polish cities. That left the problem of the Swedish navy, so Gustavus Adolphus began planning a major expansion of the fleet. The navy had suffered badly during the first two years of his reign. In 1611 the Danes besieged and captured Kalmar, in southern Sweden. The port was an important naval base, and almost half the ships of the Swedish fleet were trapped there, and had to be destroyed to prevent them from falling into enemy hands. This blow meant that until the Treaty of Knäred was signed in January 1613, the Danes enjoyed complete naval supremacy in the Baltic. After a truce signed with Poland in 1622, Gustavus seized the opportunity to rebuild the Swedish fleet.

The Swedish king was once quoted as saying that "next to God, the welfare of the realm depends on its Navy." He was well aware that before he could play a part in the military affairs of central Europe he needed to reestablish Swedish naval supremacy in the Baltic Sea. The navy he inherited from his father, Charles IX, was substantial—more than twenty-two major warships—but many of these were small and poorly armed. Most were also completely obsolete, having been built by the king's deposed uncle Erik XIV during the 1560s, while some even dated from the time of Gustav Vasa (reigned 1523–1560). The 1620s was therefore a boom time in the Swedish shipyards. In the autumn of 1624 the Dutch-born master shipbuilders Hendricks Hybertszoon de Groot and his assistant and brother Arendt were summoned to the Three Crowns, the royal palace in Stockholm. There the two shipbuilders met Admiral Carl Carlsson Gyllenheim and his staff, and discussed plans for a rapid expansion of the Swedish navy. The Dutchmen ran the royal shipyard at Skeppsgården in Stockholm on a contract basis, a system known as *holmarrendet* by the Swedes.

At the time the Skeppsgården shipyard was probably the biggest industrial site in Stockholm, where the Hybertszoon brothers employed more than four hundred carpenters, sawyers, blacksmiths, caulkers, coopers, ropemakers, woodcarvers, hemp spinners and other key tradesmen. In turn, the other businesses of Stockholm provided the shipyard with many of the things needed for ship-building or for running a busy shipyard—canvas, tallow, cast-iron tools, food, and domestic supplies, plus the whole service industry of taverns and eating houses that thrived on the trade from the ship-yard workers. The brothers rather than the state were responsible for running all this, and were paid—sometimes begrudgingly—by the king's treasurer in a series of staged payments. Gustavus Adolphus felt that this use of private contractors helped reduce costs to the state—an early example of privatization.

On January 16, 1625, the two shipbuilders contracted to build four warships for the Swedish crown within four years. The con-tract was then revised to just three ships—two small ones and one larger vessel, with a keel length of 120 feet. The Dutchmen began gathering materials—oak planks from Germany, seal blubber oil from Finland, compasses from Holland, and ironwork and tar from Sweden itself. The most important order probably was for the tim-ber from five hundred oak trees, felled on the estate of Dame Brita Bååt of Ängsgö on the shores of Lake Mälaren, west of Stockholm. Traditionally ship timber was cut in winter, when the trees con-tained less sap, which meant that construction of the new ships started in early 1626. By that time Sweden needed all the ships it could get. In September 1625 the Swedish navy lost ten ships in a storm in the Gulf of Riga—cast ashore and wrecked in what was probably one of the worst maritime disasters in Swedish history. This also affected the shipbuilding contract, as the king needed to replace his losses as quickly as possible. Initially he ordered the Hybertszoon brothers to start on the two smaller ships first, as they would be quicker to build.

The Swedes had one large replacement: the *Tre Kronor* (Three Crowns), launched in Stockholm in October 1625. She had a 108-foot keel, and was armed with 30 guns mounted on a single gun deck. However, Gustavus Adolphus then seemed to change his mind. A letter from the shipbuilder to the Swedish king in January 1625 stated that the timber he was gathering wasn't suitable for a ship as large as the one specified by the king, with a keel more than 130 feet long—an increase on the large ship specified in the contract.

The king replied that he wanted the bigger ship built, but if the timber stocks didn't allow it, then he'd prefer that the yard start work on the big ship specified in the contract—the one whose keel was 10 feet shorter. It seemed that during the winter the king had changed his mind, and now bigger was definitely better.

By the spring of 1626 Hendrik Hybertszoon and his principal shipbuilder, Hein Jacobsson, had already begun laying the keel of one of the smaller contracted ships—one about the same size as the *Tre Kronor*. They simply extended the keel and added extra frames, effectively lengthening the ship while she was still under construction. This probably was one of the main reasons why the new vessel—known as the *Vasa*—was poorly designed: she was built

Gustavus Adolphus landing in Germany, 1630

as a compromise, with a hull narrower than normal for a ship her size. However, as Jakobsson later claimed, "I worked with the measurements I was given by Master Henrik, and which the King had ordered. . . . I even added a foot and five thumbs to the width . . . and everyone said it was well built."

The building of the ship was completed in record time, mainly because Arendt Hybertszoon de Groot excelled in managing the shipyard and in gathering the men and materials his brother needed. The ship's name first appeared in the records in August 1626, when it was called the *Ny Wasan* (New Vasa), as there was already a *Vasa* in the fleet. As her frames rose over the industrial clutter of Skeppsgården it became clear that the *Vasa* was to be no ordinary vessel. She was 154 feet long from her stern to the end of her beakhead, and the top of her intricately carved and decorated sterncastle was 65 feet above her waterline. Her mainmast was 170 feet high, dominating the Stockholm skyline as she was being fitted out. Most important of all, she was built with two full gun decks, and an upper deck virtually devoid of weaponry, which made it ideal for fighting boarding actions. However, she had two flaws, both the result of her keel and frames being designed for a much smaller ship. First, her draft was only 15½ feet, which was fine for a smaller vessel but offered little counterresistance if the wind heeled the ship over. Then there was her beam: 38 feet, which gave her a length-of-keel to width-of-beam ratio of 3.5:1.

While this width was acceptable in a small, deep-drafted ship, it meant that the *Vasa*, with her high sterncastle and extensive sail plan, was pushing the limits of safety. Of course, it is easy to criticize these things with the benefit of hindsight. In those days there were few plans and specifications—shipbuilders worked using their own formulas, based largely on their own experience. Hendrik Hybertszoon kept his calculations a closely guarded secret, and by Christmas 1625 illness kept him bedridden much of the time, unable to supervise the work as closely as he might have liked. Instead he relied on Hein Jakobsson to carry out his wishes. Hendrik Hybertszoon finally died early in 1627, leaving his assistant and his brother to see the project through. The *Vasa* was launched later that year, and the long process of fitting her out began. As her masts were swayed into place, the great ship must have been a bustling hive of activity—although for one man the work still wasn't progressing fast enough. Gustavus Adolphus visited the shipyard in January 1628 to check on the work himself, and as the months passed he became increasingly impatient, ordering inspectors to send him weekly reports on the ship's progress. Finally he sent a missive to Jakobsson demanding that the ship be ready by the next Jacob's Day: July 25.

Workmen toiled around the clock, mounting the ship's 64 guns, filling her hold with ballast, and painting the last of the many sculptures that adorned her upper works. The guns themselves had been supplied by the royal gun foundry—48 large bronze demiculverins firing 24-pounder shot, with 12 guns on each side of her 2 gun decks. This gave her an impressive broadside of 576 pounds of metal. Finally, 8 small bronze 3-pounders—little more than signal guns— were mounted on either side of her quarterdeck, while 2 1-pounder pieces were carried in her forecastle alongside 6 small mortars, which were probably experimental pieces. This was enough firepower to make her a real force in the Baltic: she was significantly more powerful than anything the Danes, the Poles, or the Russians could send against her. If the *Vasa* had taken her place in the Swedish fleet she might well have achieved Gustavus Adolphus's goal of dominum Maris Baltica virtually single-handed.

Then there was the ballast. It was commonplace in wooden sailing ships to fill the bottom of the hold with ballast, which helped made the ship more stable by lowering her center of gravity. Hein Jakobsson calculated that 120 tons of round ballast stones would be needed, and workmen virtually filled her hold with them. Modern stability tests have shown that this wasn't enough, but there simply wasn't any more space to fill. Once the ballast, the guns, and the ammunition were stowed away, the Swedish admiral Clas Fleming felt that the ship was far from stable. He decided to test his theory by ordering thirty sailors to run from one side of the ship to the other to see if they could make her rock at her moorings. After three runs he stopped the experiment, as the *Vasa* was beginning to roll violently with the movement. He later claimed, "had they run more times, she would have keeled over." The naval boatswain who ran the test reportedly exclaimed to the admiral, "God hope it will stay on its keel." Fleming replied, "The master shipbuilder surely has built ships before, so you need have no worries of that kind." However, it was clear that something was badly wrong, but under pressure from the king neither the admiral nor the shipbuilder was willing to delay her commissioning until the problem could be investigated.

If Söfring Hansson, the captain of the new warship, and a guest, Captain Hans Jönsson, both had reservations, they kept their opinions to themselves. The maiden voyage of the *Vasa* began on Sunday, August 10, 1628, when there was very little wind, despite the summer being noted for its unusually stormy weather. It seemed that fortune was favoring the venture. The maiden voyage was hardly ambitious. After her launch the *Vasa* had been moved from the Skeppsgården yard across the harbor to Skeppsbron, the quayside in front of the Tre Kronor palace in the Gamla Stan (Old Town). Here the guns, ballast, and stores had been loaded aboard her. It was planned to sail her to Vaxholm, on the outer edge of the Stockholm archipelago, and several guests, wives, and other passengers were making the short trip in the warship before a chartered boat took them back to the city. What breeze there was came from the southwest, which was the perfect direction for the voyage.

Watched by thousands of spectators, the *Vasa* was warped away from the quayside using kedge anchors until she was well out into the channel and level with Tranbordana, now a suburb of Slussing. A little after 5:00 P.M. Captain Hansson ordered the foresail, maintop, and mizzensails set—four of the *Vasa*'s ten sails. The three-pounders fired a salute toward the royal palace, and the *Vasa* began picking up speed. As she did, Hansson noticed a gust of wind that had veered to blow from the south, but apart from making the warship heel slightly, it had little effect. For the most part the ship was sailing gently eastward out of the harbor, with the wind coming from over the starboard side of her stern. Then, as the ship reached the more open water beyond the fortified island of Kastellholmen, things started to go wrong.

A second strong gust of wind came from the south, and the *Vasa* gently heeled to port. The crew managed to right her, but then as the ship approached the island of Beckholmen, which marked the harbor entrance, another gust came, and the same thing happened. This time the ship heeled so much that the gun ports on her port side reached the level of the water. There was nothing Captain

Hansson or his men could do, and with a slow inevitability the lower sills of the open gunports dipped below the level of the water and the sea began to pour in. All attempts to right her failed, as the incoming water countered any attempt to correct the list. Still under full sail and with her pennants and flags flying, she sank to the bottom of the harbor.

Admiral Erik Jönsson was on deck when the ship began to heel, and immediately ran down to the gun decks to check that the cannons were lashed properly. If the ship heeled they could career across the deck, crushing anything and anyone in their path. He found that the water was already so high that the ladders and companionways had floated loose, and he only made it back to the upper deck with great difficulty. He was "so waterlogged and badly knocked about by the hatches" that it was several days before he recovered. Most of the crew would have been on deck, as all hands would have been needed to set the sails when the ship left the harbor. If they could swim or could grab something that floated, they had a reasonable chance of surviving the disaster. Several boats were on the scene within minutes of the sinking, and these began rescuing the survivors. Others were less fortunate.

The royal official Gabriel Oxenstierna claimed that "some thirty persons, with seamen, women and children" lost their lives, including Captain Hans Jönsson, one of the guests on board. Others claim that thirty to fifty people drowned in the disaster, so Oxenstierna's tally is probably correct. When the wreck of the *Vasa* was rediscovered, the remains of sixteen bodies were recovered from the hull, while eight more bodies dating from the early seventeenth century were found on the seabed close beside the wreckage. Recriminations began almost as soon as the survivors were brought ashore. A still bedraggled Captain Hansson was placed under arrest, facing charges of criminal negligence. Hein Jacobsson and his assistant Johan Isbrandsson, together with Henrik's brother Arendt Hybertzoon, had all watched the sinking, but for the moment the builders were in the clear. However, they all knew they would eventually be held accountable. Then someone—in this case, Oxenstierna—had the difficult task of telling the king.

Gustavus Adolphus was in the Prussian port of Pillau (now Baltysk) when the *Vasa* went down, and it took two weeks for the news to reach him. His first reaction was to blame the disaster on "imprudence and carelessness." In fact, this was only the first maritime disaster of several that would decimate the Swedish fleet. In late August Admiral Clas Fleming's flagship, the *Kristina*, collided with another warship in the Gulf of Riga, and with the *Kristina*'s bowsprit damaged, she was unable to prevent herself from running aground. She was then set on fire to prevent her wreckage from falling into the hands of the Poles. Then on September 6, the Swedish warship *Riksnyckeln* ran aground on the southern side of the Stockholm archipelago and became a total loss. Faced with the loss of three major ships through accident, the king wanted answers and a scapegoat.

An inquest was held in the royal palace on September 5, 1628. Captain Hansson was the first called to the stand. He was asked if he had remembered to secure the guns. He replied, "You can cut me in a thousand pieces if all the guns were not secured." His dramatic testimony was supported by Admiral Jönsson, who had checked that detail for himself. Then the captain was asked if he and his men were drunk. "Before God Almighty I swear that no one on board was intoxicated." This time he was supported by Per Bertilsson, the chief bosun, who added that as it was a Sunday such things would be frowned on. He was asked if the ship was rigged properly, if her cargo was properly stowed, and what helm orders he gave. No fault could be found with anything the experienced captain had done that morning. Then, when Captain Hansson was asked about the way the ship sank, he managed to shift the blame. "It was just a small gust of wind a mere breeze, which capsized the ship . . . the ship was too unsteady, although all the ballast was on board."

One by one his officers were called to the stand, and all repeated the same story. One officer reported, "The ship is top-heavy with her masts and yards, sails and guns." Then the ship master, Jöran Matsson, told the inquest about Admiral Fleming's stability test. Clearly human error wasn't to blame, so the board of inquiry turned its attention to the shipbuilders. When challenged, Hein Jakobsson replied, "The ship was built according to the specifications I was given." Johan Isbrandsson supported his employers, claiming that Jakobsson was simply finishing the job started by Hendrik Hybertszoon. His employer, Arendt Hybertzoon, added, "The ship was faultlessly built, as everyone can testify." Besides,

Arendt added, the design "pleased His Majesty." The buck was being passed all the way to the top—something that cannot be allowed in an absolute monarchy. When asked where the fault ultimately lay, Arendt answered, "Only God knows." It was clear that the matter could go no farther without criticizing God or the king, so no blame was ever assigned for the disaster.

With hindsight it seems obvious that the problem lay with the builders. Hendrik Hybertszoon had botched the original design by expanding the keel and frames of a much smaller ship. The king was in such a hurry that he forced this compromise on the builders, but they should have stood their ground and demanded that the job be done properly. Instead Hybertszoon made do with the timbers he already had. When he took over the project Hein Jakobsson should have said something, but he, too, was placed under intense pressure to finish the ship as quickly as possible. Then there was Admiral Fleming and his stability test. Like the builders, he was unwilling to incur the wrath of the king by imposing any delay. Swedish maritime historian Björn Landström placed the blame firmly with Gustavus Adolphus, as he had approved the design and loaded the ship with all the guns and weighty decorations he thought she could carry. Possibly Arendt Hybertzoon felt some responsibility, as in November 1628 he returned to Holland, accompanied by Hein Jakobsson. This could be assigned to guilt, or more likely to the realization that the chances they would ever be awarded another Swedish contract were exceedingly slim.

Even before the board of inquiry made its deliberations, a salvage team led by the English diver Ian Bulmer was hard at work pulling the ship onto an even keel, then trying to raise guns and recover the ship's pay chest. When Bulmer failed, the task was given to Admiral Fleming and Captain Hansson, who employed the Swedish diver Hans Olofsson, who used a diving bell to "walk under water." After a year the admiral admitted to the king that "this is a more onerous task than I could ever have foreseen." The work continued until the majority of the *Vasa*'s bronze guns had been recovered; then the enterprise was abandoned. The ability of these seventeenth-century divers to work underwater in such mind-numbingly cold and claustrophobic conditions is still a feat to be marveled at. However, only so much could be achieved using such crude diving machines, and

Raising the Vasa

eventually the wreck was abandoned and forgotten—left to sink deeper into the mud of Stockholm Harbor.

The *Vasa* was left undisturbed for more than three centuries. Then in August 1956 the Swedish engineer and amateur maritime historian Anders Franzén pulled up a core sampler filled with blackened oak. He had spent five years searching Stockholm Harbor using this primitive tool, and his search finally paid off. A diver confirmed that he'd found the remains of an old warship with gunports—a ship which could only be the *Vasa*. The wreck lay in a hundred feet of water in the main deepwater channel into Stockholm Harbor. Franzén knew that the Baltic was different from other seas and oceans—it was too salty to support the teredo worm, which ate away at exposed wooden timbers. There was therefore every chance that the warship would be well preserved. The Swedish navy became involved, and after an extensive underwater survey it was found that the ship was in good condition. It was decided to raise her—an operation the like of which had never been attempted before.

Several ideas were proposed, including filling the hull with table tennis balls, or freezing the ship in a giant block of ice. In the end the Neptune Salvaging Company opted for a straightforward approach. Divers tunneled though the mud underneath the warship's hull to run heavy steel cables beneath the ship. The divers used high-pressure water jets to tunnel through the mud—an incredibly dangerous task, carried out in total darkness. Above the hard-hatted divers lay a thousand tons of wooden ship, and behind them trailed their lifeline of air hoses, communication cables, and water hoses. Nobody was really sure if the scheme would work. In typical naval fashion, chief diver Per Edvin Fälting gave his men some practical advice: "if it feels like you're going to die down there in the darkness and cold, just don't give a damn about it, and find out what you're doing wrong!" This grim, determined work lasted for two years, but by late 1959 the tunneling was complete. Thanks largely to the professionalism of the Swedish divers, this had been achieved without any serious accident.

The idea was that the steel cables would form a cradle from which the hull of the *Vasa* could be suspended. These would then be attached to two mammoth salvage barges, and the ship towed to shallow water. The first move would be just a few feet, so the hull was lifted clear of the mud. After some hesitation the *Vasa* lifted clear, and her hull hung above the seabed. Very carefully the salvagers began a stage-by-stage move of the whole contraption to the side of the deepwater channel. Once in shallower water the divers were able to work on the hull itself, sealing the gun ports and filling in the thousands of holes the iron fasteners that held the ship together had eroded away. The stern was badly damaged, so this was patched with timber. The whole job took the best part of a year. Finally everything was ready for the final raising of the ship.

On April 24, 1961, the world's press lining the harbor looked on as the *Vasa* was finally raised to the surface after 333 years. As soon as her deck appeared, Anders Franzén and Per Edvin Fälting jumped on board her—the first men to walk on her decks in a third of a millennium. Then the bilge pumps were started and the business of pumping out the water began—a ten-day operation. By the end of it the salvors found that the *Vasa*'s hull was so well preserved that she was able to float unaided. It was therefore with some dignity that she completed her maiden voyage, towed into a waiting dry dock on the nearby island of Beckholmen, which would become her permanent home. Archaeologists could now begin the business of recovering the thousands of artifacts trapped within her hull—everything from cannons and carriages to clothing and personal possessions—and the remains of those seamen and passengers who went down with their ship.

Over the next five months some fourteen thousand objects were cataloged and removed. Of course that was only the start. All these finds had to be conserved—and in the early 1960s the science of the conservation of underwater archaeological finds was nonexistent; the team had to discover the principles of this delicate work as they went along. The testimony to their achievement can be found in the thousands of perfectly preserved objects on display today—the entire contents of the ultimate historical time capsule. Then there was the ship itself. Wood recovered from the sea starts to disintegrate when it becomes exposed to air. Therefore the hull had to be kept wet, and scientists figured out how best to preserve more than a thousand tons of waterlogged oak. The solution was to gradually replace the water in the timber with a chemical, polyethylene glycol, which was able to penetrate the wood and displace the water. The process began in 1962, and the spraying of the hull with the chemical, mixed with fresh water, continued around the clock for seventeen years. It took another nine years for the whole hull to dry, so it wasn't until 1988 that the *Vasa* was finally ready to be displayed in all her glory.

In the meantime, conservators had labored to replace all the timber that had been broken off during the seventeenth-century salvage attempts and over the intervening centuries. Steel pins replaced the old iron ones that held her hull together, and broken decorations were put back in place. This giant jigsaw puzzle took decades to finish, but by its end more than 95 percent of her original timbers, sculptures, and fittings were back in place. The remaining 5 percent were then replaced in a way that left it clear which bits were original and which were new. In all some 13,500 fragments were put back where they came from during two decades of restoration. The result is now a fully restored early-seventeenth-century warship. Like the *Mary Rose*, she represents a unique chance to pull back the curtains of the past and see exactly what a Renaissance warship looked like and how she worked.

Today the hull and the finds are on display in the purpose-built *Vasa* Museum, which opened in 1990. Visitors are greeted by the breathtaking view of the *Vasa*'s bow as they enter the building, and then get the chance to walk all the way around her hull, and even to peer down on her decks from galleries. The only drawback is that visitors are unable to enter her hull, and have to make do with a superbly reconstructed section of her decks and cabins. In a way

The Vasa

this is where the *Mary Rose* scores as a museum display, being effectively a cutaway version of a sixteenth-century ship. However, this
aside, a visit to Stockholm's *Vasa* Museum is a truly unforgettable
experience. The scale of the ship, the wealth of its decoration, and
its sheer majesty have to be seen to be fully appreciated. Nowhere
else in the world do we still have the opportunity to see such a spectacular and complete survivor from the age of the Renaissance—a
true sovereign of the sea.

King Gustavus Adolphus might have lost his great warship, but
he achieved his goal. In 1630 he led the Swedish Army into central Germany, embarking on a Protestant crusade to drive back the
forces of Catholicism. In September 1631 he won a sweeping victory over the army of the Holy Roman emperor at Breitenfeld, outside Leipzig, and so was hailed as the savior of Protestant Europe.
He then drove the Imperialists back into their southern German
heartland, and by the early summer of 1632 he managed to capture
Munich, the capital of Bavaria. The campaign culminated in the
Battle of Lützen, one of the most decisive engagements in European
history. On November 16, 1632, he attacked the Imperialist army,
commanded by Albrecht von Wallenstein. Although the Swedes
emerged victorious, Gustavus Adolphus died on the battlefield,
where his blood-stained and mutilated body was found when the
smoke had cleared. His body was taken back to Stockholm for
burial, and today his remains lie in Riddarholmen Church, just a
few steps from where his great warship began her first and final
voyage.

11

Toward the Holy Grail

The Duke of Buckingham

It was shortly before 10:00 A.M. on August 23, 1628. The assassin fingered his dagger beneath his doublet, and waited for the duke to appear from his private chambers. As he was wearing the uniform of an army officer, John Felton had little difficulty entering the duke's headquarters—a large house on Portsmouth's High Street. His claim that he carried important dispatches ensured he was sent directly to the duke's reception chamber. George Villiers, the Duke of Buckingham, was due to start the business of the day, and Felton was first in line to be received. A letter written by a courtier to King Charles I's wife, Henrietta Marie, described what happened next:

This day between nine and ten of the clock in the morning, the Duke of Buckingham, then coming out of a parlor, into a hall, was by one [John] Felton (a Lieutenant of this Army) slain at one blow, with a dagger-knife. As the Duke staggered, he turned about, uttering only this word, "Villain!" and never spoke a word more. But, presently

George Villiers, 1st Duke of Buckingham

plucking out the knife from himself, before he fell to the ground, he made towards the traitor two or three paces, and then fell against a table . . . the Duchess of Buckingham and the Countess of Anglesey came out into a gallery which looked into a hall where they might see the blood of their dearest Lord gushing from him. Ah, poor ladies, such was their screeching, tears and distractions, that I never in my life heard the like before, and hope never to hear the like again.

Just over two months later John Felton was hanged for his crime at London's notorious Tyburn Prison. His body was then returned to Portsmouth, where it was strung up again and left to rot as a warning to other enemies of the king. However, in many circles

Felton was regarded as something of a hero—a necessary Brutus, and a martyr to the cause of freedom. After all, the man he had killed was probably the most hated figure in England. The Duke of Buckingham had been a pampered favorite of two kings and had single-handedly plunged England into a war on two fronts. Worse, as lord high admiral he had led two expeditions to defeat and cost the lives of thousands of men. Felton was just one more wounded and embittered ex-soldier who felt that the national interest would be well served if Buckingham were killed.

George Villiers first rose to prominence in August 1614, when he was introduced to the court of King James VI of Scotland and I of England. The twenty-two-year-old was described as "the handsomest-bodied man in all of England," and the bisexual monarch had an eye for the lads as well as the ladies. Three months later the young Villiers was made gentleman of the bedchamber, much to the annoyance of the king's current favorite, Robert, Earl of Somerset. As the king and the youth became more closely acquainted, other favors followed—Villiers was made a knight, a baron, a viscount, an earl, and a marquis in quick succession before being named Duke of Buckingham in 1623. Arthur Wilson, a diarist and wag of the time, declared, "No one dances better, no man runs or jumps better. Indeed, he jumped higher than ever Englishman did in so short a time, from private gentleman to dukedom."

In March 1618 King James initiated an investigation into naval corruption, and removed the corrupt Sir Robert Mansell as treasurer of the navy. As Mansell's superior, the octogenarian Charles Howard, Earl of Nottingham, realized that he would be next. Consequently he sold his title of lord high admiral of England to the Duke of Buckingham for an undisclosed sum, plus a pension of £3,000 a year for the rest of his life. Buckingham embraced the challenge of naval reforms, and in September 1619 the naval commissioners reported to the king that they had managed to halve naval expenditure to just £30,000 a year, with no drop in the efficiency of the navy itself. Buckingham and his new treasurer, Sir William Russell, worked wonders, and completed a survey of the fleet that reported that several ships were completely unserviceable, having been kept on for no reason other than to provide an income for naval officials. As Europe was plunged into the Thirty Years' War, the Navy Royal was finally recovering from years of corruption and neglect—an improvement brought about largely by the king's favorite.

In 1620 Buckingham married Katherine, the daughter of the Earl of Rutland, and bought York House on the Strand, whose gardens overlooked the Thames River. From there the duke regularly visited the London offices of the naval commissioners, who by then had developed into a permanent administrative body charged with supervising the organization of the Navy Royal. This was Buckingham's great achievement—the development of a naval administration that would safeguard the efficient running of the fleet. During Charles I's reign it would evolve into the Board of the Admiralty and would actively steer the development of naval construction.

Buckingham's commissioners even issued what might today be called a business plan, establishing exactly how big the future fleet should be and what kind of ships it should include. The English fleet should contain an average of thirty seagoing ships, with a keel-to-beam ratio of 3:1 and a maximum draft of sixteen feet. These warships "must be somewhat snug-built, without double galleries and too lofty upper works, which overcharge many ships and make them loom fair but not work well at sea." They then suggested how new ships should be built: "For strengthening the ship we subscribe to the new manner of building—first, making three orlops, whereof the lowest being placed two feet under water, strengthening the ship though her sides be shot through; second, to carry this orlop end to end; third, the second or main deck to be sufficiently high to work guns in all weathers." In other words, they called for continuous gun decks and lower decks running the length of the ship—which probably was first introduced by Phineas Pett in 1610 when he built the *Prince Royal*.

As a naval administrator the Duke of Buckingham realized that Pett's design represented the way forward, and he was determined to provide his king with a modern and efficient fleet. During the first five years of Buckingham's tenure as lord high admiral nine powerful new warships were built, all of which conformed to these specifications. If Buckingham's activities had been limited to the court and the navy, then history might have regarded the dashing nobleman as a force for good. Unfortunately, he also considered himself a diplomat, and a doting King James gave him free rein to indulge himself on the European stage. In 1623 he escorted Charles, Prince of Wales, to Spain, where Buckingham played his part in the negotiations surrounding the proposed marriage of the prince to Maria Anna of Austria, the infanta of Spain. Not only did the talks fall through, but also Buckingham's crass and loutish behavior led to the Spanish ambassador's request that he be executed for his insolence. The request was ignored.

His next foray came in 1624, when he traveled to France to negotiate another marriage alliance, this time with the Princess Henrietta Maria. She was the youngest daughter of the late King Henry IV of France, and the sister of King Louis XIII (reigned 1610–1643). He also met the real power at court, Cardinal Richelieu, who was in the process of becoming the king's new chief minister. As a Catholic, Henrietta Maria was an unpopular match for a future king of England and Scotland, and consequently Buckingham's standing fell as a result of his association with the match. However, his actions helped secure the friendship of the young prince. Then in early March 1625 King James suffered a stroke, and his health declined rapidly. He died on March 27, with Buckingham at his bedside.

The twenty-five-year-old Prince of Wales, now King Charles I of England and Scotland, confirmed Buckingham's position as his chief adviser—the same role by which he dominated the court of his father. Charles also inherited the diplomatic problems engineered by his father and Buckingham: by dabbling in the European politics surrounding the outbreak of the Thirty Years' War, the two men had brought the two British kingdoms to the brink of war—and beyond. Under Buckingham's encouragement King James bankrolled a force that attempted to recover the Palatinate—the province of the king's son-in-law. Led by the mercenary general Ernst von Mansfield, this English volunteer army of "raw and poor rascals" achieved little apart from earning the English the enmity of Catholic Europe and provoking a war with Spain.

Buckingham's solution was to launch a naval expedition to attack Cádiz—an attempt to repeat Drake's "singeing of the King of Spain's beard." Instead it was Buckingham who was burned by the venture. In early October 1625 he sailed for Cádiz with a hundred ships and ten thousand soldiers. When they arrived, Buckingham landed the troops and secured control of the harbor entrance. However, the city itself remained firmly in Spanish hands, and the English lacked the siege guns they needed to batter the walls. After three futile weeks the soldiers were reembarked and the expedition returned home. This expensive failure left King Charles short of funds, and in 1626 he was forced to recall Parliament, which resented Buckingham's influence over the king. Members of Parliament led by Sir John Elliot tried to impeach Buckingham on a charge of treason—a prerequisite for raising funds to fight Charles's war. Rather than risk the censure of his favorite, the young king dissolved his Parliament. Unable to raise taxes, he forced his leading landowners to lend the Crown money, and pawned the crown jewels to replenish his war chest.

The failure of the Cádiz expedition meant that Buckingham needed a military success to save face. He saw his opportunity in France. Encouraged by Cardinal Richelieu, the young French king had revoked the rights granted by his father to the Huguenots. The power base of these French Protestants was the port of La Rochelle, on the coast of the Bay of Biscay. When a French royal army laid siege to the city, Cardinal Richelieu accompanied the troops—an indication of his determination to crush the Protestants once and for all. The Huguenots appealed to King Charles for help, and Buckingham persuaded him to mount a naval expedition to relieve the port. The operation would be another costly failure. The approaches to La Rochelle were protected by the Île de Rhé, a twenty-mile-long island whose eastern tip lay just two miles from the French mainland. It remained in the hands of the French Crown, which kept a strong garrison there. To relieve La Rochelle, Buckingham needed to capture the island.

This time Buckingham had eighty ships and six thousand men at his disposal, and in July, after fighting their way ashore, the troops laid siege to the island's main town, St. Martin-de-Rhé. After two months both sides were short of supplies, but the situation for the defenders looked grim. Then, under cover of darkness, a French squadron slipped past the English fleet and relieved the garrison. By October the besiegers were close to starvation, so Buckingham decided to gamble everything on a night assault. The attack was a complete disaster. The French had been forewarned, the English scaling ladders were too short, and the attackers were reputedly befuddled with wine. The result was a slaughter, and by daybreak the English were in full retreat, harassed by the French all the way back to their ships. Of the six thousand troops who sailed from England in June, fewer than a third made it back home. One of these wounded survivors was John Felton.

While the Duke of Buckingham set up his headquarters in Portsmouth and laid plans to lead a fresh expedition to France, Charles was forced to call another Parliament. This time he forbade any discussion of impeachment. When the members met in March 1628, they immediately declared that they would help him raise money only on the condition that he ratified a petition of rights. This demanded that there be no taxation without the consent of Parliament, and no imprisonment of English subjects without just cause. This was the opening shot in a battle for political power in England, a struggle that would only end in 1641, when the country had been plunged into the Civil War. The Duke of Buckingham was blamed for most of England's woes—foreign and domestic— but despite protests in the streets of London, Charles continued to back his father's favorite. That was the moment when John Felton struck his assassin's blow. While the king mourned the loss of his closest adviser, he failed to understand why many of his subjects celebrated the murder. This failure to grasp the mood of the country would lead directly to Charles's own death two conflict-strewn decades later.

The Cardinal's Fleet

In *The Three Musketeers*, first published in 1844, Alexandre Dumas père rightly named John Felton as the Duke of Buckingham's assassin, but Felton's motive for the deed was his infatuation with the sinister Milady de Winter. In the novel, Felton killed for unrequited love rather than for his idea of the national good. Milady is portrayed as a secret agent of Cardinal Richelieu, who ordered her to arrange the murder. Like all good historical novels, this incident in *The Three Musketeers* is grounded in fact. While there is no evidence that the cardinal had anything to do with Buckingham's death, he certainly stood to gain from the assassination. After all, the duke might have been a poor naval commander, but he was a gifted naval administrator. As Richelieu was rebuilding the French navy, the last thing he wanted was for the English Navy Royal to pull itself from its post-Elizabethan mire of corruption and torpor.

When King Henry IV's nine-year-old son became King Louis XIII (reigned 1610–1643), his mother, Marie de Médicis, became regent, and she remained the power behind the throne until the boy king reached manhood. Various rebellions against royal authority weakened the position of the monarchy, so the young king sought a strong adviser who could help him steer his kingdom through its troubles. He found the right man in Armand du Plessis, Cardinal Richelieu, who became the king's first minister in 1624. From the start he became the virtual dictator of French policy, pursuing two main goals: the centralization of political power in France, and opposition to the Hapsburg rulers in Germany and Spain. Although a devout Catholic, his campaign against the Huguenots was influenced less by religion than by that group's divisive influence within the kingdom.

The campaign against La Rochelle demonstrated the inability of the French state to exert much of an influence beyond cannon range of the shore. Granted, a French fleet had broken through the English blockade to relieve the French royal garrison on the Île de Rhé, but this was the fleet's sole achievement in the brief war against England. Similarly, although the cardinal wanted to assist the Dutch against the Spanish, France lacked the naval means to take on the Spanish at sea. In fact, a general lack of military preparedness meant that Richelieu would keep France out of the Thirty Years' War for another decade, buying time he used to build up its armed forces.

This policy involved rebuilding the French Royal Navy, a force that had been much neglected during a significant part of the previous century. The only effective French naval presence was in the Mediterranean, where they maintained a small galley fleet. By contrast, the French Huguenots had relied on privateering as a source of revenue and a means of harassing their religious enemies for the best part of a century. Consequently, ports such as La Rochelle were privateering havens, which meant that when their Catholic enemies threatened them the Huguenots could assemble a fleet of well-built warships crewed by experienced seamen. Before Richelieu the French state had nothing to match them.

By crushing the Huguenots at La Rochelle, Richelieu hoped to end the threat to French commerce posed by these privateers, and if possible to harness these Protestant naval resources for the benefit of the state. He also tried the privateering approach himself, which always offered a cheap alternative to building a large national navy. Regional admirals were given the power to issue privateering letters of marque, and these French privateers would then be used to augment the fledgling French Royal navy in time of need. Two years after he gained power, Richelieu appointed himself *grand-maître de la navigation* (grand master of navigation), which effectively made him head of the navy. In line with his grand strategic aims, he used this post to limit the power of the regional French naval commanders. This ensured that both the fleet and its auxiliaries such as privateers and armed merchantmen operated solely under his own central control. This was partly so no aristocratic admiral could use his own naval force in a rebellion against the state. Just to make sure, in 1634 Richelieu also appointed himself general of the galleys, which effectively gave him direct control of the Mediterranean fleet.

However, Richelieu's policy of centralization applied only to command of the navy. He actually limited government involvement in many other aspects of naval affairs, including shipbuilding, supply of guns and stores, and the hiring of crew. These were all either privatized or given to the various regional admirals to run on behalf of the Crown. There were no royal dockyards to speak of. The galley fleet had its own base at Marseilles, although by the 1630s this had moved to Toulon. The sailing fleet on the Atlantic coast was concentrated in three ports: Brest, Le Havre, and Brouage, a naval base established in the 1630s close to La Rochelle. While these ports were all administered by Richelieu through the regional admirals, most of the functions of the bases were contracted out to businessmen. That meant that private contractors played a key part in the development of the French fleet.

The most important area where contractors were involved was in shipbuilding. There was no equivalent of the English royal dockyards. Instead Richelieu was prepared to use private shipyards in France, or even in neighboring countries. At first there also was a lack of skilled shipwrights with experience building warships. The majority of French shipwrights with this kind of experience were

Huguenots, and it wasn't until the 1640s that these experts overcame their religious scruples and sought contracts with the French crown. The first of these French ships buit abroad was *La Grand Saint Louis*, a powerful warship with two gun decks. She was built in a Dutch ship-yard—probably Rotterdam—and therefore she was similar in style and appearance to many of the ships being built at about the same time for the Dutch navy or the Dutch East India Company. She appears in an engraving by the Dutch artist Hendrik Hondius, who shows a highly decorated vessel with a covered waist, a broadside armament of forty-six guns mounted on continuous decks, and a modern three-masted sailing rig with a lateen sail on her mizzenmast.

Some maritime historians claim that the *Saint Louis* was an inspiration for the *Vasa* and that possibly Hendrik Hybertszoon had a hand in building the warship for Cardinal Richelieu. The two vessels certainly have similar lines, although the timetable precludes any direct involvement by Hybertszoon—when the *Saint Louis* was ordered in mid-1624, the Dutch master shipbuilder was already in Stockholm. What is probably more accurate is that both

The Saint Louis, *Cardinal Richelieu's French "battleship"*

the *Saint Louis* and the *Vasa* were large, powerful warships similar in general appearance to the Dutch warship *Aemelia*, built by master shipwright Jan Salomonszoon van den Tempel in the early 1630s. If anything, the *Vasa* was the odd one out from this trio, as she lacked the wide beam of the other two warships. She had a length-to-beam ratio of 3½:1. By contrast, the 1,000-ton *Saint Louis* had a keel length of 120 feet and a beam of 42 feet, which was closer to 3:1, the same ratio as in the *Aemelia*. The *Vasa* should therefore be seen as an exception to the general rule—a warship whose design was fatally compromised while she was being built. The *Saint Louis* and other Dutch-designed ships of the time were probably better reflections of the state of northern European naval ship design during this period.

The lines of the *Saint Louis* suggest that the Dutch had fully understood the concept of the race-built galleon and had studied Phineas Pett's *Prince*. The height of the *Saint Louis*'s superstructure was kept low, while gratings were rigged over the main deck to create additional working space for both the sailors and the gunners, effectively creating a fully enclosed upper gun deck. In addition, her fairly wide beam made her a stable gun platform. She had a square rather than a curved stern, which was then a feature of Dutch shipbuilding, while her highly efficient sailing rig was a direct copy of those on contemporary Dutch ships such as the 700-ton *Batavia*, an East Indiaman built in 1620 that wrecked off the coast of Australia in 1629. Her remains are now displayed in the Western Australian Maritime Museum in Fremantle. A replica of the ship was built, and is now on display in the Dutch port of Lelystad. Her appearance is roughly similar to that of the *Saint Louis*, only with one less gun deck and a lot less decoration. She also was far more lightly constructed.

Later in the career of the *Saint Louis* more guns were added, which suggests that she was more strongly built than most Dutch warships. The majority of warships in Holland earmarked for Dutch use were built according to specifications of the States General or the Dutch East India Company. The stresses put on wooden hulls during voyages to the Indies were immense, and like the Spanish flota galleons, their ships had a relatively short working life—usually five to ten years. To lower production costs and shipbuilding times, the States General tended to build similar vessels, designed for effectiveness and speed of production rather than longevity. The French preferred their warships to remain in service for one or two decades; consequently their warships were built differently from those built by the Dutch and for the Dutch.

A later and even more spectacular example of a private shipbuilding venture was the building of *La Couronne* (The Crown) at a private shipyard at La Roche–Bernard in Brittany in 1636. This was a year before the commissioning of the English *Sovereign of the Seas*. *La Couronne* was probably the first French warship to be built in France using French shipwrights, which makes her something of a milestone in French naval history. She was designed by the master shipwright Charles Morieur of Dieppe, who learned his trade in Holland before returning to France. Almost certainly she was built in reaction to reports of the construction of this English leviathan, and she certainly came close to her in firepower. *La Couronne* carried seventy-two guns on two long decks, one gun deck less than her English rival, but the French emphasis was on maneuverability and seaworthiness. It was probably hoped that in a strong breeze the English ship would be unable to fire her lower guns, while with her guns mounted higher in the hull, *La Couronne* could fire all of her pieces at the enemy. The first true three-decker built for the French was the *Dauphin Royal*, which entered service in 1658.

This French reliance on foreign shipbuilders and shipyards continued until Cardinal Richelieu's death in 1642. It was only in 1639 that a state dockyard was established, on L'île d'Indret on the Loire, near Nantes. Even this operated only as a shipbuilding yard rather than as a fully fledged naval dockyard, as all repair work and refitting was still carried out by private contractors. Instead Cardinal Richelieu developed his own unique privatized approach to shipbuilding and repair, a model that was unique in Europe during this period. The drawback was that while the French Royal Navy could be rebuilt with reasonable economy, there was little quality control in the construction and maintenance of warships. It was not until Jean-Baptiste Colbert took over as the secretary of state of the navy in 1683 that the system was changed. The cardinal's system also was more open to corruption and nepotism; Richelieu often appointed men whose loyalty he could count on, regardless of ability or honesty. For example, as a regional admiral the marquis de Pont-Courlay proved singularly inept, although he did manage to lead a small French galley fleet to victory against the Spanish in September 1638.

Richelieu also never devoted the funds to the navy that it really needed to thrive. Between 1626 and 1642 some 50 million livres were earmarked for development of the French Royal Navy, while a staggering 317 million livres were spent on the army. The fleet always was of secondary importance in France—throughout history her geography dictated that the army was a far more important strategic tool of state. However, you would have expected more for the money—while France certainly developed a fleet of sorts, it never managed to do much with it. Certainly it campaigned against the Spanish, but its performance was lackluster, and demonstrated the fragility of French naval power. The attack of the English on the Île de Rhé demonstrated the need for Richelieu's new fleet, but when called to do anything it seemed constrained by a lack of good commanders and experienced crew. This in part was a result of the lack of cooperation by French Protestants, who had dominated the ports of the Atlantic seaboard for a century. These religious wounds would remain raw until after the death of Cardinal Richelieu.

A Matter of Science and Nationality

During the reign of King Charles I the English were a little jealous of their Continental rivals. In most cases these foreign ships left English-built ones standing, and ship design was fast becoming a national embarrassment. For example, during the Île de Rhé campaign of 1628 the English fleet encountered a squadron of Dunkirkers—Flemish privateers who sailed under the flag of Spain. Some sixty English warships gave chase, a force that included warships, privateers, and armed merchantmen. None of the English ships could come close to catching the Dunkirkers, and in the end only one small pinnace managed to overhaul the enemy when they reduced sail. She lacked the guns to take on the privateers, so she slipped away to safety in the darkness.

In 1634 Admiral Sir John Pennington blamed the lack of careening— the regular scraping of the hull. In a letter to the Admiralty he reported coming across a squadron of Dutch warships "All tallowed and clean,

The English fleet off the Île de Rhé, 1626

which is a course they duly observe every two months, or three at
the most . . . which is the only cause which makes them go and
work better than ours; whereas most of our ships are grounded and
graved two or three months before they come out, and never tallowed, so that they are foul again before we get to sea with them,
and then they are kept out for eight or ten months, whereby they
are so overgrown with barnacles and weeds under water that it is
impossible that they should either go well or work well . . . all men-
of-war of whatever nation, whether Turk or Christian, keep this
course of cleansing their ships once in two or three [months]."

While poor ship husbandry might be part of the problem, it was
also a matter of design. On several occasions Dutch ships of a similar size to English ones were able to sail right around them—a clear

demonstration that something was wrong with English ship design. A clue to the problem was given by a Dutch captain who described English warships as being "so full of timber." As late as 1636, Algernon Percy, the Earl of Northumberland, complained to the king that his ships were "clogged with timber." This problem was really an extension of the difference between Dutch and French ships. While the Dutch ships were built with light frames, beams, and decks, the French ships were more solidly constructed—ships built to take a pounding and to last. When he compared English ships with Dutch ones, Captain Nathaniel Butler, an English sea captain, said that the English built their ships to last seventy years while the Dutch built theirs to last seven. The English approach called for an even greater reinforcing of timbers. While this might indeed make their warships appear to be filled with timber, with less internal space, the English designers were attempting to build purpose-built warships, not part-time ones capable of carrying cargo when needed.

The heavy construction that made them slower and less maneuverable than their Dutch counterparts also gave them a solidity the Dutch ships lacked. During the Dutch wars of the later seventeenth century, the two maritime powers would fight three wars, and despite setbacks the English design would emerge triumphant. The lighter Dutch vessels were less suited to the rigors of naval combat, and in a gunnery duel this placed their ships at a significant disadvantage. In effect the English had taken the idea of the Elizabethan race-built galleon—a fast, well-built, and maneuverable ship design—and then had tilted the balance between speed and firepower. Certainly, by adding guns and making ships as robust as possible, the designers were sacrificing speed. However, this was a risk they were prepared to take. In other words, the English warships were designed for fighting a close-range gunnery action. English ship designers such as the Petts saw that the new arbiter of victory in naval warfare would be guns, not maneuverability.

That said, English designers were already looking at the problem posed by those fast-sailing Dunkirkers. The Duke of Buckingham asked for suggestions, and one of the first, produced in 1626, called for a fast, lean warship with a length-to-beam ratio of 4½:1. This ratio was unheard of, and the conservative Board of Admiralty rejected the idea outright. In effect, this solution had been the frigate, a ship type that would come into its own later in the century and that would remain a vital part of a sailing fleet for more than two centuries. The next suggestion was for a nimble 340-ton warship with a lower length-to-breadth ratio, but in the end the duke and his successor, Richard Weston, opted for a far smaller vessel known as a *whelp*. These were tubby little craft built along the lines of the type of small Dutch warship known as the *cromster*, which had a length-to-breadth ratio of about 2½:1. In effect they were setting a thief to catch a thief. These little English Channel guard ships would prove reasonably effective, but the problem would not be completely solved until the frigate idea was resurrected in 1645.

This reactive floundering was partly due to the malaise gripping the navy. It was disillusioned by the failures of Cádiz and the Île de Rhé, and despite his administrative successes the Duke of Buckingham achieved little to further the honor of the service. Since the accession of Charles I no new large warships had been commissioned, although five Huguenot warships of 250 to 530 tons had been captured off the Île de Rhé and added to the fleet. The only ships on the stocks in English shipyards were three tiny dispatch boats, built in 1626, and then ten 190-ton whelps, which weren't even given proper names, just numbered: *First Whelp, Second Whelp*, and so on. With no large contracts on offer, shipwrights began examining ways to improve their art. While they might have been spurred on by criticism that their ships were too slow and sluggish, they also realized that the move toward better-armed ships probably was the way forward.

In 1625 an anonymous English author published *A Treatise on Shipbuilding*. In it he gave a step-by-step guide to ship design, including guidelines about proportion, the size and placement of all the ship timbers, and the way the ship should be built. The emphasis was on planning—designs were no longer kept solely in the head of the master shipbuilder, but instead would exist in plans and models worked out using the latest scientific principles. In effect this was the first development in the science of English shipbuilding since the publication of Matthew Baker's *Fragments of Ancient English Shipwrightry* in the 1580s. Of course, Baker's influence was still felt. Speaking about his brief apprenticeship under Baker, Phineas Pett said that "in the evenings, commonly I spend my time in good purpose, as in cyphering, drawing and practicing to attain the knowledge of my profession, and I then found Mr Baker sometime forward to give me instructions, from whose help I must acknowledge I received my greatest lights."

In this period "cyphering" meant working out numerical calculations, while the "drawing" clearly meant the production of plans. Pett was clearly an advocate of scientific shipbuilding; he might even have been the anonymous author of the treatise. The book described the way a master shipbuilder should approach his task. First came the drawing out of the shape of the backbone—the keel, stem, and sternpost. Then came the drawing of "rising" and "narrowing" lines, which determined the shape of the hull, worked out section by section. These were developed using geometrical principles based on the arcs of circles of various radii. The first set of lines determined the width and height of the beam, while the second set determined the shape of the lower hull below the waterline. Then came the body plan, where all the frames were designed to fit the two sets of lines, starting with the midframe, then working out toward the bow and the stern. The result was a ship whose design was fully planned rather than based on experience, trial, and error.

Of course, other authors had already written shipbuilding treatises. In the 1550s the Venetian master shipwright Pre Theodore de Nicolò produced a guide to building Mediterranean galleons, while in the Spanish world Diego Garcia de Palacio's *Instrucción Náutica para Navegar* (1587) spelled out the need for better-designed galleons for the treasure flota. In Portugal Father Fernando de Oliviera produced two studies on shipbuilding, while João Baptista Lavanha's unpublished *Livro primeiro da architectura naval* (c. 1595) was clearly a thorough attempt to marry the new science of mathematics with the art of Portuguese shipbuilding. Then came Manuel Fernandes's *Livri de traças de carpintaria* (1616), which included detailed plans and cross sections similar to Matthew Baker's *Fragments*, produced more than three decades earlier. This may well have represented a Spanish attempt to quantify the English race-built galleon design and to turn it into something of their own. There were others, most notably Joseph Furttenbach's lavishly illustrated *Architectura Navalis* (1629), but the key thing about *A Treatise on Shipbuilding* was that it wasn't full of mathematical theories; it was a practical guidebook that attempted to turn the art of ship-building into a science.

This was a true Renaissance achievement. The main impetus of the Renaissance had been the revival of classical learning, and this inevitably involved the study of science and mathematics. Before the Renaissance, mathematics were limited to cumbersome calculations using Roman numerals. There was no plus or minus sign, and complicated equations were completely impossible. The breakthrough came when Arabic numerals were adopted during the fifteenth century. Mathematical books such as Peurbach's *Theoricae novae planetarum* (1472) and Ratdolt's reworking of Euclid's *Elements* (1482) paved the way for a new way of calculating numbers. Seafaring remained a major impetus, as rulers such as Portugal's Prince Henry the Navigator encouraged mathematicians to apply their skills to navigation and mapmaking. This led to the development of geometry and trigonometry. Bartholomaeus Pitiscus's *Trigonometria* was published in 1596, and by the time *A Treatise on Shipbuilding* was published, the tools were in place to apply this discipline to building the perfect Renaissance warship.

12

The *Sovereign of the Seas*

A Matter of Limits

It is one of those bizarre twists of history that the ultimate sailing ship of the Renaissance was built because of the musings of a Dutch lawyer. It all began in 1609, when a gifted twenty-six-year-old lawyer from The Hague called Hugo Grotius published a legal treatise, *Mare Liberum* (Freedom of the Seas). It expounded the right of the Dutch to travel the seas without hindrance and to trade where they liked. As he put it in a principle, "the spirit of which is self-evident and immutable, to wit: Every nation is free to travel to every other nation, and to trade with it." When he wrote this, Holland had been fighting for independence from Spain for the best part of four decades and it was about to develop its own sea trade routes to the Indies, a region that had been the province of Spain's Portuguese allies. Grotius was simply providing the legal justification for the Dutch East India Company's attempt to break this cozy monopoly. However, while *Mare Liberum* annoyed the Spanish and the Portuguese, it also was seen as a provocative declaration by the English.

In the treatise, Grotius advocated that the sea was international territory and that ships of all nations were free to use it to trade. Force was advocated only if a maritime power tried to maintain a trade monopoly—such as the Portuguese were doing in the Indies, or the Spanish enjoyed in the Caribbean. The problem was, as England had an East India Company of its own, Grotius's treatise could be seen as a justification for economic rivalry, as it was a call to end the monopoly of world trade. Worse, the English had long claimed sovereignty of the coastal waters around their own shores. Traditionally this extended as far as a man could shoot, which effectively meant long artillery range—some two miles on a good day. The English rightly saw this Dutch treatise as an attack on their own ancient rights.

The Dutch certainly made the most of their legal challenge. During the early years of King Charles I's reign they chased Dunkirk privateers to within hailing distance of the English shore, they refused to show the respect due to English ships in English coastal waters by dipping their ensigns, and Dutch fishermen freely operated within sight of English ports. In June 1633 the bailiff of the port of Yarmouth, on England's eastern coast, complained, "The Holland ships of war, while at anchor before the town, rode with their colours displayed, their ordnance lying out, their drums beating, and their soldiers and companies on their decks." Clearly something had to be done.

The answer was obvious: a legal riposte to Grotius's treatise. It was eventually penned by John Selden, a lawyer and brilliant scholar, who by the 1630s had already made a name for himself as one of England's leading intellectuals. He first penned a counterblast to *Mare Liberum* in 1619, but its publication had been suppressed by King James, who was worried that it might cause an international incident. However, the political climate had changed, and in 1635 *Mare Clausum* was published, with a dedication to King Charles on the inside cover. It argued that while Grotius's view had merit in international waters, in practice parts of the sea could be owned and governed by a sovereign power. Selden confessed that the boundaries of maritime sovereignty hadn't been set, but he declared an English and Scottish maritime claim on the waters of the North Sea, the English Channel, and the western approaches. This was more than just an argument for the establishment of territorial waters. Like the Monroe Doctrine of 1823, this was the creation of a defensive cordon, a sphere of influence. All England needed to back it up was a navy powerful enough to patrol these waters, and if necessary to contest their control with the Dutch, the French, or the Spanish.

When King Charles read Selden's treatise, he liked it so much it became a sort of state paper—an official statement of intent. In effect it awakened the king's interest in all things maritime, and in the need to project maritime power. In fact, it already tied in with one of his pet policies. For several years the king had been concerned with protecting British fishing fleets. As the joint king of England and Scotland, he realized that the livelihood of many of his subjects depended on fishing, and he saw the industry as an important source of national income. In 1632 he approved the foundation of the Society of the Fishery of Great Britain and Ireland, and he even enforced the creation of fish days, when coastal communities were forced to eat fish one day a week. Charles seemed oblivious that to many of his subjects this smacked of Catholicism and seemed like a ploy to reintroduce the old religion. While ultimately the Society of the Fishery proved a failure, it did demonstrate that King Charles was aware of the importance of the sea to the welfare of his kingdoms.

This coincided with a number of incidents that highlighted the decline of England's maritime status. In 1633 the English ambassador to the French court was returning home on the warship *Bonaventure* when he encountered eight Dutch armed merchantmen. Honor demanded that the traders dip their topsails in salute, but the Dutch refused. The English captain fired a shot across their bows, and the Dutch fired back. Outnumbered, the English warship was forced to back away from the fight. That same year a Dutch ship seized an English dispatch boat carrying letters for the Venetian court. Then there was the problem of the Dunkirk privateers. Despite England and Scotland being at peace with Spain, they continued their attacks. In 1635 they even captured a ship carrying the queen's French midwife, called to the court to help in the birth of the Princess Elizabeth, the royal couple's fifth child. In June he read Secretary of State Sir John Coke's report that "Our ancient reputation is not only cried down, but we submit to wrongs in all places which are not to be endured." There was only one solution: Charles had to expand the Navy Royal.

In 1636 he told the Dutch ambassador, "We hold it a principle not to be denied that the King of Great Britain is a monarch at land and sea to the full extent of his dominions, and that it concerneth him as much to maintain his sovereignty in all the British Seas as within his three kingdoms." He backed up his words with deeds. The trouble was, to build ships he needed money. The standard source of revenue was through taxes levied by Parliament on behalf of the king. However, Charles had dissolved his last Parliament in 1629, and instead he ruled the country directly—a policy that continued until 1640. His Parliamentarian enemies called this personal rule the "eleven-year tyranny," which indicates the strength of feeling in the country. Until 1636, Charles managed to govern by reducing his expenses and increasing his income. The man behind this fiscal policy was Richard Weston, the lord treasurer and the first lord of the Admiralty. He increased income by reviving long-abandoned medieval taxes and fines, granting monopolies to his favorites, and charging courtiers for their right to hold court positions. While all this was hugely unpopular, it allowed Charles to govern without recalling the elected Parliament.

However, this was all very well when it came to the day-to-day running of the realm, but this patchwork form of income didn't extend to building new warships. Weston's solution was to revive another ancient form of income, known as ship money. This medieval custom demanded that coastal towns contribute to the upkeep of the kingdom's naval defenses in time of need. Charles demanded the payment of ship money in 1634, the year before Selden's treatise was published. At first the taxation was limited to coastal counties, but in 1635 Charles decided that the entire kingdom should shoulder this new financial burden, and the ship money scheme was extended to cover the inland counties as well. The result was a political storm. Most people rightly regarded ship money as a major form of taxation, introduced without the legal consent of Parliament. William Fiennes, First Viscount Saye and Sele, led a nonpayment campaign, and in 1637 he was arraigned before the Court of the Exchequer together with his fellow protester, the Member of

Parliament John Hampden. What followed was a legal showdown that set the stage for the Civil War.

John Hampden had been called on to pay ship money for his lands in Buckinghamshire—an inland county. He refused to pay the full amount, and in court he argued that such a demand was illegal without the backing of Parliament. The trial of Lord Saye and Sele and John Hampden was very much a test case, and therefore the trial became a highly public contest between an imperious monarch and a righteous commoner. The case for the Crown was put by Attorney General Sir John Banks and Solicitor General Sir Edward Littleton. Their case was straightforward, and they simply demanded that the two defendants pay their dues or forfeit their liberty. Hampden was a gifted orator, and his legal team—Oliver St. John and Robert Holborn—knew their job. Their spirited defense caught the public imagination, but on June 12, 1638, the judges ruled seven to five in favor of the Crown. The judiciary knew who their paymasters were. However, the close verdict was regarded as a moral victory—a small blow against Charles's personal rule.

Hampden became a national hero, a defender of liberty. Charles emerged as an unpopular tyrant. The king was becoming increasingly at odds with his people—his seemingly pro-Catholic stance, his attempted imposition of High Anglican religious ceremony on the staunchly Presbyterian Scots, and the continued exclusion of the majority from the reins of power all contributed to the final break between the king and his people in 1641. John Hampden would die in defense of his Parliamentarian liberties, but ultimately the contest would be decided in favor of democratic rule by the people and for the people. It was an extremely high price to pay for a few warships, although out of this political maelstrom emerged the ultimate symbol of English sea power, a ship that completed the great Renaissance quest.

Through all this Charles maintained his belief that he needed a strong navy. The murder of the Duke of Buckingham in August 1628 led to something of a reshuffle in the Board of Admiralty. The title of lord high admiral died with him, and his successor, Richard, Baron Weston of Neyland, was given the new title of first lord of the Admiralty—a position that remains in use today. Charles I also awarded Weston the title of Earl of Portland in 1635. Weston was charged with raising money for the king and was the originator of the ship money scheme. His right-hand man in the Admiralty was Sir Sackville Crowe, who replaced Sir William Russell as treasurer of the navy. However, Crowe proved incompetent, and Sir William was reinstated in 1630. It was therefore to Weston and Russell that the king turned in 1634 when he wanted to use his new source of income to build new ships.

The *Sovereign* and the Ship Money Fleet

At least on paper, in 1634 King Charles already had a reasonably powerful fleet. On his accession nine years before, he inherited an aging fleet of twenty-one major warships. Seven of these were comparatively modern, built during the reign of his father, the oldest being the *Prince Royal* (1610). However, the rest of the fleet consisted of old, rebuilt, and patched-up Elizabethan warships, the oldest of which included the *Red Lion* (formerly the *Golden Lion*) and the *Nonsuch* (originally the *Philip and Mary*), two of the galleons built during the reign of "Bloody Mary" more than three quarters of a century before. The very oldest was the 450-ton race-built galleon *Antelope*, which had begun her active service in 1546, during the reign of Henry VIII. No less than eight of these ships had taken part in the Spanish Armada campaign just under half a century earlier. It was little wonder that English captains found that modern Dutch ships were able to run rings around them. It was a contest that matched a fit young athlete with an old lady nearing retirement.

As early as 1630, when King Charles visited Chatham to inspect the rebuilding of the venerable *Vanguard*, he declared his intention to commission two new major warships a year. It was an ambitious plan, particularly as the Treasury was virtually empty. This program was the impetus behind the adoption of the kingdom-crumbling ship money scheme. The first two ships of the new program were the 800-ton *Charles* and her sister ship, *Henrietta Maria*, both of forty-two to forty-four guns. Commissioned in mid-1630, the *Charles* was launched at Woolwich in late January 1633, followed a few days later by the *Henrietta Maria*, launched just up the river, at Deptford. The king and the queen watched both launches, and inspected the next batch of warships already under construction. Sir John Pennington privately declared the *Henrietta Maria* a poorly built ship, as was the *Unicorn*, launched in Woolwich the following year. It was even claimed that the only reason why officials at Trinity House gave the latter warships a certificate of seaworthiness is that the officials didn't want to disgrace the builder. (The corporation of Trinity House was charged with maintaining the safe navigation and the regulation of shipping in English waters.)

It seemed that the best ships were still those built by members of the Pett family. The *Charles* was built by Phineas Pett's son Peter, as was the 875-ton *James*, launched in 1634, and the 515-ton *Leopard*, which entered service the following year. Effectively that meant he launched a ship a year—one being laid down while another was still being built, a feat achieved by building the middle vessel—the *James*—in Deptford rather than in Woolwich. With a keel length of 105 feet and a beam of 33½ feet, the *Charles* had a length-to-beam ratio of more than 3:1. The other two were a little less elongated, but effectively all three ships were built according to the same formula. This is hardly surprising, as unlike his rivals, Pett was following a mathematical plan. This meant that all three ships performed well and proved highly successful additions to the fleet. The *Charles* was wrecked in 1653, while the *Leopard* was captured by the Dutch three years later. However, the *James* remained in service through the three Dutch wars and was finally decommissioned in 1682, after almost half a century of faithful service. Evidently the Petts knew how to build ships.

Shortly after the launch of the *Prince Royal* in 1610, Phineas Pett's second wife, Elizabeth, gave birth to a boy, whom they named Peter. The child was brought up at Woolwich, surrounded by the sights and sounds of dockyard life. It was almost inevitable that he would follow his father's profession, so in 1626, when his father was appointed as a commissioner "to enquire into certain alleged abuses of the Navy, and to view the state thereof," Peter began serving his apprenticeship as a shipwright. Four years later Phineas became the principal officer of the navy, an appointment ratified in January 1631. Later that year King Charles I visited Woolwich to witness the launch of the newly rebuilt *Vanguard*, a warship that had first been built by Matthew Baker in the same shipyard in 1586. The monarch honored the Pett family by dining with them after the ceremony, and it seems inconceivable that the master ship-wright didn't seize this opportunity to introduce his son to the king. Peter had already established a name for himself as a gifted shipwright, and had supervised his father's restoration of the old Spanish Armada veteran.

Peter's father must have suggested his next move, as it was an exact repeat of the trick that had worked so well with the king's father. Peter Pett built a ship model, and asked permission to present it to King Charles's eldest son, Charles, Prince of Wales—the future King Charles II. In early 1634 the two Petts were called to St. James's Palace in London, where they handed the model over to the four-year-old infant prince "who entertained it with great joy." We know nothing about this model, although we can presume it was a robust and basic version of the model of the *Prince Royal* that Phineas had presented to the king's elder brother almost thirty years earlier. The only difference was that this ship model almost certainly was of an even larger ship. All the Petts had to do was wait for the king to take the bait.

That moment came on June 24, 1634, when King Charles sailed down the River Thames to the Woolwich shipyard to inspect prog-ress on the *Leopard*. The warship was being built by Peter Pett, and her frames and beams had recently been fitted in place. The hull was being planked when the king arrived. During the royal tour of the ship, Charles inspected the vessel from all angles and then clambered aboard. When he reached the vessel's hold he managed to have a private word with the elder Pett. As Phineas Pett recalled, "Being in the ship's hold, his Highness, calling me aside, privately acquainted me with his princely resolution for the building of a great new ship, which he would have me to undertake, using these words, 'You have made many requests of me; and now I will make it my request to you—to build this ship.'" It was the shipbuilding commission of a lifetime, but the elder Pett allowed his son to have his head. It would still be a father-and-son shipbuilding team, but Peter would be the master shipwright. The chance to build this "great new ship" would be the greatest legacy a shipwright father could bestow on his son.

News of the commission leaked out fairly quickly, and in a repeat of the events surrounding the commissioning of the *Prince Royal* in 1610, the shipbuilding community rose in protest. One of the first groups to voice objections was Trinity House, the board set up by Henry VIII to look after safe navigation of the seas surrounding the British Isles. On August 9 they submitted their protest, "being informed that his Majesty is minded to build a great ship of these dimensions, viz., 124 foot by the keel, in breadth 46, and for draught of water 22 foot, these strange and large dimensions gave us cause to fall into discourse, and in our discourse [we] fell on these particulars following, namely that a ship of this proportion cannot be of use; nor fit for service in any part of the King's Dominions; and as unfit for remote service." They added that with the exception of the Isle of Wight, there was no port where she could safely anchor. They concluded that a warship with three gun decks was "beyond the art or wit of man to construct." Fortunately, the king ignored the critics.

The project was still in the planning stage. When the king met Phineas Pett at Woolwich the previous summer the king asked his venerable master shipwright to produce a model of the vessel—a real one this time, not just a child's toy. It was finished on October 29, 1634, and presented to the king the same day. As a reward, Charles renewed Pett's pension of £40 a year, which had been temporarily stopped due to financial constraints. However, ship money was starting to come in, and Charles was anxious to forge ahead. In January 1635 King Charles "with his own hand hath set down the burden," which was established at a mammoth fifteen hundred tons. The following month Phineas Pett hosted a planning meeting attended by Peter Pett; Vice Admiral Sir John Pennington; former treasurer of the navy and new charman of the Navy Board Sir Robert Mansell; and John Wells, the storekeeper at Deptford, who was an expert in the lading of ordnance. Together these men thrashed out the details.

The "new great ship" would have a burden of 1,466 tons, which increased to 1,661 tons once she was fully laden. Her keel would be 126 feet long, which was not markedly longer than that of the ill-fated *Vasa*. Her length overall would be 160 feet, while she would have a beam of 46½ feet. That gave her a length-to-beam ratio of 2.7:1, significantly less than that of the other great ships of the time. The reason for this was undoubtedly stability: she needed the extra beam to compensate for the weight of her ninety guns. Her depth in the water of just over 19 feet prevented her from entering smaller British ports, but it was significantly less than the estimate of the scaremongers at Trinity House. However, whatever way you looked at the figures, nothing like this had ever been attempted. One can hardly blame the experts for having doubts.

The term "great ship" was an old one, which had traditionally been used to describe the carracks of Henry VIII's navy. During the reign of King James it was revived to describe the new breed of English warships, the overgunned descendants of the Elizabethan race-built galleons. For the most part these Stuart great ships were warships such as the *James*, the *Charles*, and all those built during the Jacobean period. The typical great ship was six hundred to eight hundred tons, had a length-to-beam ratio of 3:1, and mounted about forty heavy guns in two gun decks. Naval experts argued that this was the optimal size for a warship—anything bigger would be too lumbering to be of much use in a sea battle. What they didn't take into account was the sheer weight of the new ship's broadside. With more than double the number of guns per side than most other warships afloat, it could literally blow the opposition out of the water.

The father-and-son team set about gathering what they needed during the early summer of 1635. They sailed to Whitby in northeastern England, inspecting the forests there until they found what they needed just outside the village of Brancespeth, near Durham. The local estate was owned by the king and was known for being "very plentyful of all things . . . and well replenished with woods and timber." An even better source was Chopwell Wood, some seventeen miles to the north, on the outskirts of Newcastle. The orders were given, and by November felled and trimmed oak was being shipped from Newcastle to Woolwich. In all some thousand trees were felled in Chopwell Wood, while another three hundred were supplied by the Brancespeth Estate. This was only part of it: the Petts also arranged the supply of thousands of iron fittings and fastenings from the Wealden foundries of Sussex, while timber for the masts was shipped from Finland.

Work began later that year. The keel was laid on January 16, 1636, and work continued steadily. And although costs mounted steadily, Phineas and Peter Pett seemed unconcerned about the budget. After all, that was what the ship money was for. Phineas Pett's original estimate for the ship was £13,680, but the wage bill alone came to £20,948, as the Petts' answer to the large scale of the project was to throw workmen at the problem. Shipwrights, caulkers, carpenters, blacksmiths, and other expensive skilled tradesmen were drafted from every other major shipyard on the Thames, regardless of the cost. Construction took twenty-one months, and while the project was big, Peter Pett proved up to the challenge. The scientific approach was paying off—detailed plans of frames, knees, and braces meant that these parts could be carved and constructed elsewhere in the dockyard, then brought to the building dock when required. It worked a bit like the construction of a modern prefabricated house, only with a lot more parts.

In early 1637 Charles I peremptorily set the launch date at September 25, and during the last few months, work continued at a frenzied pace. As with any construction project where time is a problem, the records show that overtime costs escalated sharply. Pett wanted the launch delayed until the following month, when the neap tides were more favorable, but King Charles simply replied, "I am not of your opinion." The launch would go ahead as planned. Almost inevitably, what followed was almost a repeat performance of the launching of the *Prince Royal* a quarter of a century before. Phineas Pett's diary recorded what happened. On the appointed day "His Majesty, accompanied by the Queen and all the train of lords and ladies, and their attendants, came to Woolwich, for the most part by water, landing at the dock-stairs about twelve of the clock." The royal party "went directly on board the ship where they stayed about one hour," inspecting the whole vessel. Then came lunch in the Pett home "prepared and furnished for their entertainment."

This was followed by the launch itself. "About two of the clock the tackles were set taut and the ship started as they heaved, 'till the tackles failed and the water pinched (being a very poor tide), so that we gave over to strain the tackles and began to shore the ship." In other words, the launch was a dismal failure, and the enormous hull refused to budge. A disappointed royal party returned up the river to their palace in Whitehall, where the king no doubt ruminated about his regal ability to harness the tide. Phineas hoped to repeat the attempt on the next high tide, but the ship still refused to move. It was decided to call the whole thing off and revert to Pett's original plan, launching the ship on the next spring tide.

The two master shipwrights called in the experts—none other than the members of the Board of Trinity House, the men who had ridiculed the project from the start. Having incurred the displeasure of the king, the Petts seemed to be fair game for their critics, who made the most of the farce. However, the Trinity House advisers said that a launch was impossible before Sunday, October 14, the date of the next spring tide, and that they rather than the Petts should oversee the proceedings. The date for the new attempt was set, but this time the king declined to watch. However, Phineas and Peter refused to be outmaneuvered. The evening before—Saturday, October 13—they rerigged the blocks and tackles, and lit the area using bonfires that burned throughout the night. High tide came at about midnight, and at approximately 10:00 P.M. Peter ordered

The Sovereign of the Seas, *the perfect Renaissance battleship*

the workmen to start hauling. In what was almost a repeat of the nocturnal launch of the *Prince Royal*, everything went smoothly, and this time the ship moved out of her dock. By 1:00 A.M. she was anchored safely in the middle of the Thames River.

The following morning Peter Pett sent messengers with the news to the king at Whitehall and to Sir Richard Mansell in the Navy Board's offices. Another messenger went to Trinity House, where he broke the news that the Board's expert services would no longer be required. At noon Mansell arrived at Woolwich and was rowed aboard the new ship. He had been authorized by the king to christen the vessel, and in a short ceremony he named the new ship *Sovereign of the Seas*, the declaration followed by a fanfare of trumpets and the wild cheering of all of Woolwich. The great wooden baby had been born, the Petts had triumphed, and naval history would never be quite the same again. A week later sheerlegs were raised over her hull, and during November her three great masts were fitted "with safety and expedition." She was then towed six miles down the river to Erith, "by reason there was a greater depth of water to ride in."

The business of rigging and fitting out the ship continued throughout the winter and spring of 1638. Finally, by the middle of May, the rigging was completed, and she sailed under her own power down the river for another six miles to Greenhithe, where she took on board her stores, guns, and ammunition. It was there that King Charles finally got to visit his ship, as on June 6, 1638, the king, queen, and members of the court all came aboard "and dined to their great content." Then on July 12 the *Sovereign of the Seas* weighed anchor and put to sea to conduct sailing trials in the tidal waters of the river. The king visited her again on July 21, when she lay at anchor off Gravesend, another six miles nearer the open sea. Having explored her from stem to stern, the king declared himself delighted with the new warship. Phineas and Peter Pett had been fully forgiven for the debacle of the launch.

With Phineas Pett on board, the *Sovereign of the Seas* finally headed toward open water. Once out in the Thames estuary, the warship conducted her sea trials, and her commander, Captain William Cooke, declared himself more than satisfied with her performance. It was later declared that "no great ship or smaller *barke* which ever

Charles I, the monarch who finally fulfiled the great naval quest

floated . . . can with more dexterity or pleasure play with the tide. She, though of that vast burden . . . hath proved somewhat above expectation, bearing the weight of 1,637 tun, besides her other tackling." On August 18 she arrived off the Downs, where Vice Admiral Sir John Pennington's Channel Fleet was riding at anchor. After another dinner Pett rowed ashore, and the *Sovereign of the Seas* became the latest operational addition to the Navy Royal.

Another naval officer who was delighted with her was her master gunner, Captain Taylor. Pett had originally designed the *Sovereign of the Seas* to carry ninety bronze muzzle-loading guns, but in early December 1638 the king demanded that her armament be increased to more than a hundred pieces. His reasoning was almost certainly based on prestige: his great ship would be the first vessel in the world to carry more than a hundred big guns, and he saw her as much a floating declaration of English sea power as a powerful warship. Consequently she was fitted with twelve new pieces, mounted on her quarterdeck, forecastle, and waist. By the standards of the day her firepower was phenomenal. She carried twenty forty-pounder cannons and eight thirty-two-pounder demicannons on her lower gun deck, thirty sixteen-pounder culverins on her middle gun deck, and thirty twelve-pounder demiculverins on the upper gun deck. Finally, another sixteen demiculverins and two culverins were mounted on her open quarterdeck and forecastle. Despite the fact that a few of the guns were mounted to fire over the bow or stern, that still gave her a broadside of around thousand pounds of iron roundshot. In terms of late Renaissance warships she was in a league of her own.

Then there were the decorations. The *Sovereign of the Seas* was probably the most highly decorated ship ever seen: some £6,691 had been spent on carvings and paintwork. These decorations were important parts of the vessel. After all, she was a showpiece. The decorations were designed by the sixty-five-year old playwright Thomas Heywood, and the carving undertaken by the sculptor brothers John and Matthias Christmas. Heywood had long been known for designing pageants and lavish stage sets, and this was exactly what King Charles wanted for his new warship. Heywood had a mixture of amateur and professional help, as King Charles sketched a few suggestions, and reputedly the Flemish-born court artist Anthony van Dyck improved on them, and passed them on to the designer. The resulting "gingerbread" or gilded carving on the hull was taken to extremes, and as a result the *Sovereign of the Seas* was a sparkling visual feast. Thomas Heywood was allowed to publish a description of the great ship, grandly titled *A True Description of His Majesties Royal Ship, built this yeare 1637 at Wooll-witch in Kent—to the great glory of our English Nation, and not paraleld in the whole Christian World*. What followed was little more than a glowing account of the decoration he had designed.

Heywood certainly knew how to wax lyrical. He started with the figurehead: "Upon the Beak-head sitteth Royall *King Edgar* on horseback, trampling upon seven Kings." King Edgar (reigned 959–975) was supposedly the founder of the Anglo-Saxon navy. Then "upon

the stemme-head there is *Cupid* . . . bestriding, and bridling a Lyon."
This symbolized the mercy of the king. "On the Bulk-head right
forward, stand six severall Statues in sundry postures." These represented Council, Industry, Virtue, Victory, Navigation, and Care.
"Upon the Hances of the waste are foure Figures with their severall
properties: *Jupiter* riding upon his Eagle . . . Mars with his Sword
and Target . . . Neptune with his Sea-horse . . . lastly *Aeolus* upon a
Camelion (a beast that liveth onely by the Ayre)." Aeolus was surrounded by allegorical depictions of the four winds.

The designer saved the best part to the end: "I come now to the
Sterne, where you shall perceive upon the upright of the upper
Counter, standeth Victory in the middle of a frontispiece, with this
generall Motto, *Validis incumbite remis* [lean upon strong oars]. . . .
Her wings are equally disply'd; on one Arme she weareth a Crowne,
on the other a Laurell, which imply Riches and Honour." The legend *Soli deo Glorium* (The glory only to God) was set above her,
flanked by the figures of a lion and a unicorn—symbols of England
and Scotland. Victory was supported on her right by "Jason, being
figured with his Oare in his hand, as being the prime *Argonaut* . . .
and shee pointeth to *Hercules* on the sinister side, with his club in his
hand." The central figure of Neptune surmounted the royal coat of
arms and the three-feathered plume of the Prince of Wales. Finally,
cartouches on the lower part of the stern bore the Latin inscription
*Qui mare, qui fluctus, ventos, naves [que] gubernat, Sospitet hanc Arcam
Carole magne tuam* (He who seas, winds, and navies protect, great
Charles, your great ship on her course direct). That was literally the
topping on the "gingerbread."

This florid description ended with something altogether more
practical—a description of what lay inside the ship: "She hath three
flush Deckes, and a Fore-Castle, an halfe Decke, a quarter Decke,
and a round-house. Her lower Tyre hath thirty ports, which are to
be furnished with Demy-Cannon and whole Cannon through out
(being able to beare them). Her middle Tyre hath also thirty ports for
Demi-Culverin, and whole Culverin: Her third Tyre hath Twentie
six Ports for other Ordnance, her fore-Castle hath twelve ports, and
her halfe Decke hath fourteene ports; She hath thirteene or foure-
teen ports more within Board for murdering peeces, besides a great
many Loope holes out of the Cabins for Musket shot. She carrieth

moreover ten peeces of chase Ornance in her, right forward; and ten right aff, that is according to Land-service in the front and the reare. She carrieth eleven Anchors, one of them weighing foure thousand foure hundred, &c. and according to these are her Cables, Mastes, Sayles, Cordage."

With no trace of sarcasm, Heywood finished by declaring that the *Sovereign of the Seas* "should bee a great spur and encouragement to all his faithful and loving Subjects to bee liberal and willing contributories towards the Ship-money." It was little more than wishful thinking, as by the time the great leviathan joined the fleet the ship money revolt was the least of King Charles's problems. Faced with what they saw as an attack on their religious freedom, the king's Scottish subjects rose in revolt. In February 1638 the "Solemn League and Covenant" was signed in Edinburgh, a declaration of Presbyterian opposition to the king and his bishops. By the end of the year the Scots were in open revolt, and the following summer a royal army sent north to teach them a lesson fell apart due to lack of funds. To raise more money, the king had no option but to recall Parliament in early 1640. It proved so hostile that Charles disbanded it after just three weeks. However, he would be forced to recall Parliament before the year was out, and this time there was no turning back. By then king and Parliament were set on a confrontation that had only one possible ending. The fate of Britain would be settled on the battlefield, a conflict that ended with the triumph of Parliament and the execution of the king as a traitor to his people.

Phineas Pett remained a master shipwright for four years after the launch of the *Sovereign of the Seas* but resigned all his offices at the outbreak of the First Civil War (1642–1646). He remained an ardent supporter of the king until his own death in August 1647, and was buried in Chatham, less than a mile from where the great warship lay at anchor. His son Peter sided with Parliament, and played his part in keeping the Parliamentarian navy in operation. He rebuilt his father's *Prince Royal* in 1641 and built several more warships, including the *Constant Warwick*, the first in a long line of British frigates. He became the commissioner of Chatham Dockyard, and served Oliver Cromwell during the Commonwealth. Peter Pett's skills allowed him to survive the transition from republic back to monarchy, and after the Restoration of 1660 he enjoyed the continued patronage of King Charles II.

However, he finally fell from favor at the end of the Second Anglo-Dutch War (1665–1667). He was blamed for not doing enough to save the fleet anchored off Chatham from the Dutch, who raided the port in June 1667. During the inquiry that followed he was accused of spending more energy on rescuing his plans and ship models than the ships themselves. The Dutch "raid on the Medway" had been a disaster beyond Pett's control, as he lacked the men and the time to move the fleet to safety. He was disgraced, fined, and stripped of his office. He withdrew to the country, and died five years later, in 1672. Ironically, although the inquiry ridiculed him for saving his models and plans, he was probably quite correct in seeing them as more valuable than the real thing. After all, it took two years to build a ship but a lifetime to work out how.

During the Civil War the *Sovereign of the Seas* was all but neglected, kept "in ordinary" at Chatham, at the mouth of the Thames estuary. The English diarist John Evelyn saw her there in July 1641, on the eve of the Civil War, when a lack of funds kept her in port. The navy declared for Parliament, and during the long years of conflict, Parliament's admirals had little use for such an expensive ship. After all, their war involved patrols, privateer-chasing, and blockades, not fighting a stand-up sea battle. It wasn't until the Commonwealth and Protectorate of Oliver Cromwell (ruled 1649–60) that she was recalled to service. The old Navy Royal had become the Commonwealth Navy, and this time she flew the flag of the English Republic. She was also renamed the *Sovereign*. In 1651 she was refitted, and her superstructure lowered slightly. During the First Anglo-Dutch War (1652–1654) she became the flagship of General-at-Sea Robert Blake. She fired her guns in action for the first time on October 8, 1652, during the Battle of Kentish Knock, when Blake led her into the very heart of the Dutch fleet, where her great broadsides caused mayhem. The battle ended in an English victory, and the Dutch learned to keep their distance. They even had a name for the great gilded ship: *De Gouden Duivel* (The Golden Devil).

The *Sovereign* was rebuilt in 1659–1660 by master shipwright John Taylor, and after the death of the Lord Protector Oliver Cromwell she formed part of the squadron that escorted Charles II back to

Britain. She served with distinction in what was now renamed the Royal Navy during the two Dutch wars that followed. Then, in 1690, when the *Sovereign* was more than half a century old, she took part in the Battles of Beach Head (1690), Barfleur, and La Hogue (1692). When the end finally came, it was an ignominious one. On January 27, 1696, she was anchored in ordinary at Chatham, with only a skeleton watch on board. Someone overturned a candle belowdecks, and the fire caught hold. Before anyone could save her, the *Sovereign* burned almost to the waterline.

The master shipwright Fisher Harding was given the task of rebuilding her, but as everything apart from parts of her keel had to be replaced, the rebuilt ship was not really the same as the one built in 1637. However, the new ship—the *Royal Sovereign*—was launched in 1701, and remained a mainstay of the Royal Navy until she was broken up in 1768. By that time the Royal Navy had become the undisputed master of the maritime world, her global power guaranteed by the massed firepower of her sailing ships of war. Somehow it is reassuring to think that even a few feet of the ultimate Renaissance battleship remained in her namesake's keel throughout the eighteenth century, extending the life of the *Sovereign of the Seas* to more than 130 years. This meant that the ship that sowed the seeds of Britain's naval supremacy survived long enough to see it come to fruition.

POSTSCRIPT

The Ship of the Line

The quest was over. For all intents the ultimate Renaissance battle-ship had finally been created, just in time for the era to give way to what historians now label the Early Modern Age. It had been a long journey, plagued by numerous dead ends and wrong turnings, one that saw its share of disasters and tragedies along the way. However, in the *Sovereign of the Seas* Peter and Phineas Pett finally managed to create a warship which lifted ship design onto a new plane; in effect they produced the prototype of a warship that would become the standard sailing ship of war throughout the age of fighting sail. The key difference between her and what came before was not in appearance, or sailing rig, or even hull shape. It was her fighting potential that was important—her latent ability to deliver a smash-ing broadside using her heavy guns. In effect the *Sovereign of the Seas* was the first ship of the line.

The word "potential" is important. While her 102 heavy bronze guns gave her the firepower she needed, the men who crewed and commanded her were still not ready to use her to best advantage. The crucial sphere of naval tactics had still not caught up with warship design. It is a well-known military axiom that armies are

perfectly trained and equipped to fight the last war their country was involved in. When the United States of America entered
World War II, its GIs were geared up for fighting the kaiser's army
in France rather than the Japanese in the Pacific. The British at Bun-
ker Hill followed tactics that had swept them to victory against the
French in Canada a decade and a half earlier. Strangely enough,
navies rarely worked that way. Their development was often based
on technology and design rather than combat experience; then they
used this innovative edge to secure victory. The Romans used the
corvus (beak) as a boarding bridge during their naval wars with
Carthage, while the U.S. Navy adopted the British invention of
radar to give them a fighting edge during their nocturnal battles
against the Japanese off Guadalcanal. The key was to identify this
crucial innovation and then to use it to best effect.

When Phineas Pett stepped from the *Sovereign of the Seas* into
a waiting rowboat off the Kent coast on August 19, 1638, he was
effectively handing his great warship over to the navy. The problem
was that neither the fleet commander, Admiral Sir John Pennington,
nor her own captain, William Cooke, really knew what to do with
her. Naval tactics were still mired in the past, based on the sea wars
fought against the Spanish half a century before. In 1634 Captain
Nathaniel Boeteler's *Dialogues about Sea Services* contained guidelines showing how a captain should handle his ship in action. While
gunnery was seen as important, the ideal coup de grâce was still the
boarding action, the perfect dramatic and decisive conclusion to any
hard-fought sea battle. Boeteler recommended that on meeting the
enemy, a captain should sail his ship toward them until they were
within point-blank range. He would begin the engagement by firing his chase pieces—guns that fired over the bow. He would then
turn his ship aside and fire his full broadside. To give his gunners
time to reload, the captain would complete the circle, presenting his
stern to the enemy so his stern chase guns could fire, then continue
around so the other broadside could be fired.

This was a tricky enough maneuver for a sailing ship, as it meant
either tacking into the wind, or wearing the ship around by falling away from the wind. Captain John Smith, the mainstay of the
Jamestown colony, offered the same tactical advice. His *Seaman's
Grammar* was first produced in 1627 and contained a fictional

account of a sea fight: "Give him a volley of small-shot, also your Prow and Broadside as before . . . he pays us shot for shot. . . . Try him once again, as before . . . and load your Ordnance again: Is all ready? Yea Yea; edge in with him again, begin with your Bow Pieces, proceed with your Broadside, and let her fall off with the wind, to give her also your full Chase, and also your Weather Broadside, and bring her round so the stern may also discharge, and your tacks close aboard again." This naval battle was a deadly pirouette, where both ships constantly maneuvered so all their guns could fire. If this was difficult in a single ship, it was nigh-on impossible if the ship was part of a fleet.

It is hardly surprising that those Spanish Armada galleons collided with each other, as the result would be utter confusion. Still, Captain Boeteler recommended that supporting ships in the fleet follow the same maneuver, to cover the first ship as it reloaded. This meant that a sea battle was little more than a free-for-all, where a loose gaggle of ships would engage the enemy in seemingly haphazard fashion. After these gunnery exchanges were out of the way, Boeteler advocated boarding the enemy. Size was important: "If you find her lower of board than your own, and withal an open ship, and not very much overtopping you with men, you may confidently board her." If she was bigger or better crewed, he sensibly suggested that captains keep their distance and keep firing. While this was all very well for small Elizabethan galleons, it hardly applied to big, lumbering ships such as the *Sovereign of the Seas*.

Boeteler argued that smaller and more nimble ships, if "well manned, well munitioned and sufficiently commanded," would always be able to outfight larger and more sluggish ones. "After they had bestowed one of their broadsides," these smaller ships "may speedily give the other," while their larger opponents, "being heavy and wieldy withal, they can never use save one [broadside], the same beaten side." In other words, nippy small ships could run rings around the *Sovereign of the Seas*, firing off all of their guns on every side while the larger ship managed to get in only one broadside. What Boeteler and his contemporaries failed to grasp was that this one broadside was probably all it would take to blow the smaller ship out of the water.

A naval battle of the First Anglo-Dutch War, 1652–54

Like many things that military minds failed to understand, the *Sovereign of the Seas* was tucked away—kept in mothballs until her potential could be unleashed. Actually, this is only partly true—more accurately, she was caught up by political events: a lack of funding and manpower, and then the outbreak of the Civil War. As the navy went over to Parliament en masse, there was little need for a big, prestigious, and costly warship. The naval campaign that followed was more of a police action, keeping the sea lanes clear of royalist privateers, blockading enemy ports, and intercepting enemy blockade runners. Unlike America's Civil War there was no mighty river to fight down, or innovative ironclads or submersibles to contend with. The only innovative warship spent the war riding at anchor off Chatham, near the mouth of the Thames estuary.

That all changed in 1652. By then the Civil War was over, King Charles was dead, and England was a republic. War between the English Commonwealth and the Dutch had been brewing for more than a year, ever since the publication of the Navigation Act in 1651, which restricted access of foreign shipping to English and colonial ports. The naval war that followed was therefore fought over freedom of maritime trade—an escalation of the intellectual clash between the legal stances of Hugo Grotius and John Selden a few decades before. What followed would be known in the history books as the First Anglo-Dutch War (1652–1654), a conflict that centered on a series of naval clashes between two admirals: Maarten Tromp and Robert Blake. Tromp first advocated a form of battle line during the Battle of the Downs, fought against the Spanish in 1637. During the first leg of that two-part battle he found that his Dutch fleet was outnumbered. Therefore, to make the best possible use of his firepower and to reduce the risk of having part of his force isolated and destroyed, he formed his squadron into a long line. Although this meant that only one broadside could be fired at a time, it reduced the risk of exposing the vulnerable bow and stern of his ships to Spanish fire.

General-at-Sea Robert Blake took this idea one stage farther. Blake is one of the great unsung heroes of naval warfare, airbrushed out of history by anti-Cromwellian post-Restoration historians. As an admiral of the English Republic, he was therefore an embarrassment to the pro-Royalist British establishment. However, he was the man who finally unleashed the full potential of the *Sovereign of the Seas*. On September 28, 1652, Blake fought a scrappy engagement against the Dutch at the Battle of Kentish Knock. During the engagement the *Sovereign of the Seas* (by then known simply as the *Sovereign*) is said to have had as many as twenty Dutch ships around her at one stage, but managed to fight them off. Blake was impressed by her firepower, and after his victory he began to think how he would use this to even greater advantage. After narrowly losing a battle to Admiral Tromp in December, Blake decided to lay down his tactical ideas on paper. The result was his *Sailing and Fighting Instructions*, published in early 1653.

They laid down that "Each squadron shall take the best advantage they can to engage the enemy next to them, and in order thereunto ships of a squadron shall endeavour to keep in a line with their chief." It was groundbreaking stuff. If the admiral was knocked out of the fight, then "every ship of the said squadron shall endeavour to get into a line with the Admiral, or he that commands in chief next to him and nearest the enemy." This didn't necessarily mean forming what naval tacticians still call a line-ahead formation. It meant keeping the ships in a line parallel to the line of the enemy.

A naval gun and carriage, from John Seller's The Sea Gunner, *1691*

There was a subtle difference. In Blake's instructions, prearranged signals allowed the whole line to alter course at the same time, maneuvering as a team before re-forming into a line-ahead formation. This was his answer to the maneuverability advocated by Captain Boeteler. A fleet could still maneuver, but once it got close to the enemy the matter would be decided by firepower alone.

In effect, Blake's *Fighting Instructions* meant that the naval broadside had come of age. It meant that the fleet made the best possible use of its firepower without the ships getting in each other's way. It achieved this while protecting every ship apart from the ones at the ends of the line. Tactics now revolved around battering the enemy until one side or the other decided to break off the fight. It was the kind of fighting for which the *Sovereign of the Seas* was perfectly suited, even if Charles I, the Petts, and the navy hadn't fully appreciated it at the time. Robert Blake went on to win two decisive victories over the Dutch, at the Battle of the Gabbard (June 1653) and the Battle of Scheveningen (August 1653), when the new tactics were tested in the heat of battle. Maarten Tromp, the man who first came up with the idea, was cut in two by a roundshot during this final battle. Although captains still tended to break formation, and fighting often degenerated into the old free-for-all, Blake's *Fighting Instructions* proved the key to victory.

New tactics meant new ships. When she was first launched, the *Sovereign of the Seas* might have carried 102 heavy guns, but 10 of these were arranged to fire over her bows, 10 over her stern, and 2 into her waist—ready to blast any enemy boarding party from her decks. When she was rebuilt in 1660, these would be remounted so they formed part of her broadside. After Blake, warships that stood in the line of battle had no need for all-round protection. Instead, everything centered on the broadside, and ships had to have the strength and the firepower to take their place in the line. Ships that didn't make the grade were used as scouts, or kept out of the fight. The battle line was now no place for armed merchantmen, or for warships that traded firepower for maneuverability. Those who remained soon came to be known as ships of the line, a term that remained in vogue throughout the age of fighting sail, until the advent of steam power. The quest had finally ended when Pett's design was married to Blake's tactics, so creating a new type of ship and a new style of fighting. The *Sovereign of the Seas* might have represented the end of a two-century quest, but she also marked the start of the two-century domination of the ship of the line. With her, the Age of Fighting Sail began, and the colorful and experimental era of Renaissance ships finally passed into history.

NOTES

Abbreviations

BL   British Library
Cott   Cotton Collection of Manuscripts, British Library
MM   *Mariners' Mirror*
PRO   Public Record Office, National Archives, London

Introduction. The Quest

1 *More than forty years ago*   Cipolla (1965).
3 *Leonardo da Vinci trained as a military engineer*   Rundle (1999), 245–246.
3 *In his book of the same name*   Parker (1988).
4 *The real winners in this naval arms race*   For a development of this theme see Padfield (1979), 1–6.
5 *As Dr. Colin Martin once put it*   Lecture course, Scottish Institute of Maritime Studies, University of St. Andrew's. His theme was developed in Martin and Parker (1988).

Chapter 1. Europe Comes of Age

10 *The turn of the seventeenth century is often cited*   For a general discussion of the dating of the Renaissance see Waley (1964), Rundle (1999), and Ritchie (2006).
10 *On the wider stage*   For an account of these developments see Cipolla (1965), Parry (1966), and Boxer (1977).
11 *Whichever way you define it*   Dupuy and Dupuy (1985), 444–470, 506–534.
12 *During the last half of the fifteenth century*   For a detailed discussion of these developments see Waley (1964), Hay (1966, 1976), and Tierney and Painter (1978).

12 *The arrival of the French in 1494* Oman (reprinted 1991), 14–39.

12 *A string of naval campaigns would be fought* Guilmartin (1980), 16–41, 81–83.

12 *Although the Spanish had succeeded* Guilmartin (2002), 126–151.

13 *The galley itself would remain* Guilmartin (1980), 1–6.

13 *After French corsairs began intercepting these shipments* Walton (1994), 44–55.

13 *During the reign of King Philip II* Martin and Parker (1988), 67–78, 93–102.

14 *After the Spanish-led victory over the French* For an account of the Pavia campaign see Konstam (1996). For an account of the Franco-Spanish conflict see Oman (reprinted 1991), 337–341, and Parker (1998).

14 *Many Protestants—Huguenots—responded by waging their own war* See Cordingly (1996), 19–25. For a general account of Huguenot corsair activity during this period see Konstam (2007).

15 *This powerful French warship* Soop (1992), 11, and Landström (1961), 144–145. James (2004) contains a useful appreciation of French naval power during this period.

15 *The Dutch relied on these men* Martin and Parker (1988), 249.

15 *This culminated in the destruction of a Spanish treasure flota* Phillips (1986), 3–6. For a general account of Dutch privateering actions during this period, see Konstam (2007).

15 *Just as important to Dutch national interests* For an account of the development of the Dutch East India Company see Boxer (1977). Also see Cook (2007).

16 *He ordered the building of the first European "super ship"* Oppenheim (1896 i), 14–15. Also Anon, *Notes* in *MM* (1923), vol. IX, 83–89; M. W. Prynne, *MM* (1968), vol. LIV, 115–128; Alexander McKee, *The Influence of British Naval Strategy on Ship Design, 1400–1850*, in Bass (ed.) (1974), 227–229, and Hutchinson (1994), 24.

16 *The foundation of an English national navy* See Oppenheim (1896 i), 1–44. Also Nelson (2001), 26–35.

17 *The Tudor Navy Royal really came into its own* For a detailed history of the Tudor navy during the Elizabethan era see Nelson (2001) and Moorhouse (2005).

17 *By the second decade of the seventeenth century* Lavery (1983), 12–16.

18 *This animosity drew the Scots into an alliance* Macdougall (1998), 192, 207–208.

18 *After the king's death on the battlefield* Norman Macdougall, *The Greattest Sheip that Ewer Saillit in Ingland or France: James IV's Great Michael*, in Macdougall (ed.) (1991), 55–57.

18 *Ultimately this drive for regional naval supremacy* Glete (2), 116–120.

19 *The flagship of this new fleet* R. C. Anderson, *The Stora Krafvel of 1532* in *MM* (1924), vol. X, 388–389. Also H. Börjeson, *Note* in *MM* (1928), vol. XIV, 158–162.

20 *She was designed along the lines of the English* Prince Royal Soop (1992), 10–11.

20 *When the* Sovereign of the Seas *was launched in 1637* See *Autobiography of Phineas Pett*, NRS, vol. LI, 164–165; also R. C. Anderson, *The Royal Sovereign of 1637* in *MM* (1917), vol. III, 109–212.

Chapter 2. Knights of the Sea

25 *What records we have* See M. W. Prynne, *MM*, vol. 54 (1968), 115–128, for a catalog of these sources; also Mrs. Carpenter-Turner, *MM*, vol. 40 (1954), 55–72; *MM*, vol. 63 (1977), 6–7; Bass (1974); and Hutchinson (1994).

25 *However, we do have the description* Quoted in M. E. Mallet, *The Florentine Galley in the Fifteenth Century* (Oxford, 1968).

29 *An inventory drawn up at the time of her maiden voyage* Rose (1982), 114–117.

29 *In his description of the ancient sea battle of Actium* Sayers, William, "Chaucer's Description of the Battle of Actium in the *Legend of Cleopatra* and the Medieval Tradition of Vegetius's *De Re Militari*," in *The Chaucer Review* vol. 42, No. 1 (2007): 76–90.

30 *In June 1431 her mainmast was removed* Rose (1982), 141–142.

35 *We know a little about the building of these two ships* Oppenheim (1896 ii), 24–43.

35 *One of the first of Rodgers's records* Ibid., 47.

36 *Another interesting document claims* Ibid., 49.

37 *We really don't know for sure how big the* Regent *was.* Spont (1910), xxiv.

38 The Pageant of the Birth, Life, and Death The *Pageant* is held in the British Library. For a more detailed survey of the work see Edward Maude Thompson, *The Pageants of Richard Beauchamp, Earl of Warwick* in *Burlington Magazine* 1, no. 2 (April 1903): 150–164; Viscount Dillon, *Pageant of the Birth, Life, and Death of Richard Beauchamp, Earl of Warwick* in *English Historical Review* 29, no. 116 (October 1914): 760–761.

41 *When she first entered service* PRO: Letters and Papers, Foreign & Domestic, of the Reign of Henry VIII, no. 5721, f229.

42 *By the time the armament of the ships was listed again* Spont (1910), doc. 31.

44 *This was why* Ibid., doc. 53.

44 *However, French galleys regularly clashed* For a detailed account of galley warfare in the Mediterranean during this period see Guilmartin (1980).

45 *In 1495, three years after his coronation* Christiane Villain-Gandosi, *Medieval Ships as Shown in Illuminations in French Manuscripts in McGrail* (1979), 195–225; also Christiane Villain-Gandosi, *Les Types Navals de Moyen Age in Archaelogia,* vol. 114 (Paris, 1978), 112–124.

45 *Although the records are scanty* Villain-Gandosi (1978), 116–119.

45 *The main difference between the two* Ibid., 112–116.

46 *Known as the Burghley nef* The model is actually a salt cellar shaped like a ship. No. M.60–1959, Victoria & Albert Museum, London.

47 *Another powerful French warship* Spont (1910), xxiv, docs. 47, 68.

47 *an English naval officer who encountered her* Ibid., doc. 30.

48 *On April 7 Sir Edward Howard* PRO: Letters and Papers, Foreign & Domestic, of the reign of Henry VIII, no. 1, f1132.

51 *René de Clermont obviously told a different story* Ronciere (1923), vol. 3, 100.

52 *French accounts claim* PRO: Letters and Papers, Foreign & Domestic, of the Reign of Henry VIII, no. 1, f1403.

52 *The* Sovereign *came alongside the* Cordelière Spont (1910), doc. 33. See also docs. 36–39.

53 *The fighting was described as cruel* Ibid., doc. 36.

53 *Another version claims that a French gunner* PRO: Letters and Papers, Foreign & Domestic, of the Reign of Henry VIII, no. 1, f1404.

54 *Later it was suggested that Primauget* Alain Bouchart, quoted in Spont (1910), xxvi.

54 *The same French observer was even more graphic* Ibid., xxvi.

59 *Echyngham thought* PRO: Letters and Papers, Foreign & Domestic, of the reign of Henry VIII, no. 1, f1844.

59 *To prevent his symbol* Ibid., no. 1, f1844. Also see *MM,* vol. 65 (London, 1979), 242.

60 *Sirs, I assure you* Spont (1910), xl.

Chapter 3. The Shipbuilding Revolution

65 *In 1418 Henry V ordered* Henry V's letter to John Alcetre in 1419, which outlines these orders, is quoted in full in Myers (1969), vol. IV, and is summarized in *MM,* vol. VIII (London, 1922), 376, and Howard (1979), 16–18.

66 *There is even some debate* Howard (1969), 17–18. Also Gardiner (1994), 80–81.

69 *The "WA" carrack* The "WA kraeck" has been illustrated and discussed several times, including in Howard (1969), Rule (1982), and Gardiner (1994). An interpretation of the vessel also is provided in Landström (1961) and Archibald (1984).

70 *That was why in 1966* A full account of Alexander McKee's efforts in locating the *Mary Rose* and the subsequent archaeological investigation are given in Rule (1982) and McKee (1983).

72 *Carew shouted back that* Carew's memoir is quoted in full in *Archaeologia: Journal of the Society of Antiquaries, London,* 28 (1893) and Rule (1982), 37–38.

77 *The* Mary Rose *will therefore have shared* For a detailed discussion of shipbuilding during this period see Gardiner (1994), 151–168.

80 *In 1545 she carried no fewer than twenty-six heavy guns* Rule (1982), 26–27.

81 *Although other ships entered service* Cott., Caligula, E. vol IX, f64. See also Rule (1982), 25, 38; Nelson (2001), 61–62.

Chapter 4. The Great Rivals

83 *She was carrying Charles de Tocque* This account of the arrival of the French ambassador to Scotland and his meeting with King James IV is based on Macdougall (1998), 143. His report survives in "The Flodden Papers," published in Wood (1933), 68–72. Also see Macdougall (1991), 36.

84 *"the greatest scheip"* Pitscottie (1899), 79.

87 *Finally, on September 20* The Italian historian Polydore Vergil's early-sixteenth-century *Anglica Historia* has been translated by Hay (1950), 89.

88 *However, the Spanish ambassador, Don Pedro del Ayla* Quoted in Macdougall, 116.

92 *On May 26, 1503, a bonus was paid* Mackie (1953), vol. 2, 373.

93 *In August 1506* Quoted in Macdougall (1998), 233.

94 *Norman MacDougall, who wrote the definitive biography* Macdougall (1991), 37.

95 *"If any man believes that this description"* Pitscottie (rep. 1899), 252.

96 *Pitscottie was a little more accurate* Pitscottie (rep. 1899), 252. For details of the founding of the *Michael*'s guns see Dickson and Paul (1877–1902), vol. IV, 451–507.

99 *Among the ships riding uneasily*   This account is based on Lesley (republished 1830), 82, and Hall (republished 1809), 524–526. For a modern account of the engagement see Macdougall (1998), 239–241; Moorhouse (2005), 1–7.

101 *"There was a sore battle"*   Hall (reprinted 1809), 525.

102 *According to Hall*   Ibid., 525.

102 *Sir Walter Scott took this line*   His "Account of the Death of Sir Andrew Barton" was published in *Tales of a Grandfather* (Edinburgh, 1827). He in turn took some of his description from a popular poem, "The Ballad of Sir Andrew Barton."

106 *Maritime historians have come up with a formula*   A fascinating summary of the determination of the tonnage of sixteenth-century ships is provided by Andrew Fielding, formerly of the *Mary Rose* Trust, and is available on the organization's Web site (www.maryrose.org).

108 *The same detailed records*   PRO: Chapter House Books, vol. VI, f.53, 57–63. Also see Oppenheim (1898 i), 52–53; PRO: Letters and Papers, Foreign & Domestic, of the Reign of Henry VIII, no. 1 (2), f3018.

110 *The name of Henry's new warship*   PRO: Letters and Papers, Foreign & Domestic, of the Reign of Henry VIII, no. 1 (2), f3024.

110 *The ambassador of the Hapsburg emperor*   PRO: Letters and Papers, Foreign & Domestic, of the Reign of Henry VIII, no. 1 (2), f3018.

115 *As they sailed past Ireland's coast*   From the poem "Squyer Meldrum," recorded in Laing (1879), vol. 1, 162–166, and quoted in Macdougall (1991), 55.

117 *The two armies clashed along the length of Braxton Stream*   This account of the Battle of Flodden is drawn from Macdougall (1998), 247–276. See also Reese (2003) for a detailed study of the battle.

120 *Still, she remained a useful member of the Tudor fleet*   Survey quoted in Nelson (2001), 73.

Chapter 5. The Black Art of Gunfounding

123 *The Chinese are generally credited with the discovery*   An excellent summary of the development of gunpowder in China is provided by Needham (1986), vol. 7. More recently Kelly (2004) provides a useful examination of the early development of both gunpowder and projectile weapons.

124 *Like the Chinese before him*   McLain (1980) contains an extensive scientific and historical review of the composition of gunpowder through the ages. Also see Padfield (1973), 15.

124 *In the mid-fourteenth century, English royal accounts mention* Quoted in Kelly (2004), 28. Also see C. F. Ffoulkey, *The Gun Founders of England* (London, 1937), 14–20; and Blackmore (1976), 392.

125 *The first sailor to have the dubious honor* Augus Konstam, "16th-Century Naval Tactics and Gunnery," in Smith and Brown, eds., *Guns from the Sea* (London, 1988).

125 *An English naval inventory of 1410–1412 records* L. G. Carr Laughton, "Early Tudor Ship Guns" in *MM* (1960), vol. 46, 242–285.

129 *Within a decade a whole range of gun types* Blackmore (1978), 392.

130 *Making a gun out of wrought iron* Guilmartin (2002), 60–69, provides a useful summary of the types of gun construction available during this period. See also Ffloukes (1937), Beer (1991), and Blackmore (1978).

137 *Bronze guns came in a range of shapes and sizes* Blackmore (1978), 392–393, provides a useful selection of lists from ordnance accounts and artillery manuals, illustrating the changing nomenclature and appearance of ordnance during this period.

138 *Artillery Required by Army, 1513* PRO: E.36/15, f.33v., quoted in Blackmore (1978), 302.

139 *List of Ordnance* Blackmore (1978), 393.

140 *Armament of Henry VIII's Major Warships, 1512* PRO: Letters and Papers, Foreign & Domestic, of the Reign of Henry VIII, no. 1 (2), f.5721. See also Oppenheim (1896 i), 54–56.

140 *Armament of Henry VIII's Major Warships, 1545* PRO: Letters and Papers, Foreign & Domestic, of the Reign of Henry VIII (bound version), vol. XV, 196, quoted in full in *MM* (1920), vol. VI, 281. See also Oppenheim (1896 i), 54–56, and Howard (1979), 72.

Chapter 6. The Baltic Connection

143 *Apparently he was born in the German Baltic port of Wismar* For a more detailed examination of the life of Klaus Störtebecker see Konstam (2008).

146 *As the ships changed, so too did the seals* Gardiner (1994), 37–45; also Landström (1961), 70–79.

147 *The next change appeared in the mid-fifteenth century* Gardiner (1994), 48–56. The "W.A. Kraek" is illustrated in Rule (1982), 18.

147 *A Hanseatic ship from Lübeck* Howard (1979), 41. This vessel is a development of the vessel re-created in Landström (1961), 92–93.

148 *The magnificent* Carta Olaus Magnus The map was included in a book—*Carta marina et Descriptio septemtrionalium terrarum ac mirabilium*

rerum in eis contentarum, diligentissime elaborata Anno Domini 1539 Veneciis liberalitate Reverendissimi Domini Ieronimi Quirini—and was effectively rediscovered in Germany in 1886. An original copy is held in the John Bell Ford Library, a collection held by the University of Minnesota Archives, Minneapolis, MN, and a copy is on display in the Tankerness House Museum, Kirkwall, Orkney.

150 *Until 1658 the Danes controlled both sides of this strait*   Glete (2000), 114–115, 128–130.

151 *The first of these new ships*   Ibid., 118–119. For details of the gun wreck found in Nämdö Fjord see John Adams and Johan Rönnby, *Furstens Fartyg* (Uppsala, Sweden, 1996). An interim report of the excavation can be found on the Web site of the University of Southampton: www.cma.soton.ac.uk/Research/Kravel.

152 *When the* Elefant *was launched she became the largest ship*   R. C. Anderson, "The Stora Krafvel of 1532," in *MM* (1924), vol. X, 388–389. Also H. Börjeson, *note* in *MM* (1928), vol. XIV, 158–162.

155 *At first the Swedes had the advantage*   Glete (2000), 121–123. Also see Robert I. Frost (2000) for a general account of the war.

160 *The* Jesus of Lubeck   This description of the ship is based on that in the *Anthony Roll* of 1545, now part of the collection of Magdalene College, Oxford.

163 *John Hawkins is best remembered as one of Elizabeth's sea dogs*   Kelsey (2003) provides us with a detailed biography of this greatly underrated Elizabethan commander and naval administrator.

165 *The third expedition was when it all went badly wrong*   This account of Hawkins's last slaving expedition is drawn largely from Unwin (1960). See also Konstam (2008) and M. Lewis, *The Guns of the Jesus of Lubeck,* in *MM* (1936), vol. 22, 324–339, for another account of the engagement at San Juan de Ulúa, and a summary of the Spanish version of the battle.

169 *The* Jesus of Lubeck   The Spanish inventory of the guns and stores captured on board the vessel is quoted in Lewis, op. cit., 328–332.

Chapter 7. From Carrack to Galleon

174 *"he handled his ship like a cavalryman"*   Quoted in Walker (1981), 26.

176 *It has been argued that the galleon*   Gardiner (1994), 91–114.

177 *The reason that the Spanish so enthusiastically embraced*   The account of the corsair attack is drawn from Thomas (1993), 565–569, and Cordingly (1996), 19. See also Konstam (2008).

178 *While the conquistadors and the administrators*   Parry (1966), 244–245; Watson (2005), 39–40.

180 *The beauty of this flota system*   Watson, op. cit., 44–64.
180 *In 1554 the homeward-bound New Spain fleet*   Arnold and Weddle (1978), 5–14.
181 *The* San Esteban *was a small ship*   Ibid., 375–384.
183 *This was the size of the* Nuestra Señora de Atocha   Mathewson (1986), 20–21. See Mathewson (1985) for a detailed reconstruction of the vessel's last voyage.
185 *This represented the first departure*   Oppenheim (1896 i), 110–114; Nelson (2005), 80–81.
187 *The first of these was the 750-ton*   Elizabeth Jonas Oppenheim, op. cit., 120–122, 134–136. Her proportions are drawn from PRO; State Papers Domestic, ccxlii, 36 and Add. MSS, 9336, f.10, cited in Oppenheim, op. cit., 124.
188 *In 1570 Hawkins entered into partnership*   The proportions of the foresight are cited in Oppenheim, op. cit., 124. See also Nelson (2005), 98–101, for an extensive examination of Hawkins's race-built designs.

Chapter 8. The Invincible Armada

194 *Don Alvaro had already begun assembling the ships*   Usherwood (1982), 75–77; also Rodríguez-Salgado (1982), 28–32.
198 *The* San Martín *was also very crowded*   Rodríguez-Salgado (1982), 154–155. Also see Martin and Parker (1988), 32, 62–63.
199 *She was listed as being of 550 tons burden*   Oppenheim (1896), 124.
200 *I think her the odd [best] ship in the world*   Walker (1981), 76.
200 *In April 1587 Sir Francis Drake launched a major raid*   Nelson (2001), 124–130.
201 *Although both the Spanish and the English*   For a discussion of the ordnance carried in the two fleets see Rodríguez-Salgado (1982), 173–176; Martin and Parker (1988), 39–43, 50–56.
202 *Although the Spanish had started experimenting*   Martin and Parker (1988), 215–225.
202 *These* Mary Rose *gun carriages*   Rule (1982), 156–168.
203 *Worse, the organization of the gun crews*   Martin and Parker (1988), 55. See also Konstam (2001), 19–20.
205 *"We have time to finish the game"*   Unfortunately, there is no contemporary evidence to corroborate this colorful tale, although it remains a popular element of the myth surrounding Drake and the Armada. Also see McKee (1963), 89–90, and Walker (1981), 81.
206 *An English sailor later wrote*   Walker (1981), 90.
208 *The attack degenerated*   Martin and Parker (1988), 172.

209 *"The galleon 'San Martin'"* Usherwood (1982), 125–128. Also see McKee (1963), 138, and Martin and Parker (1988), 173.

210 *Don Alonso responded* Konstam (2001), 55.

214 *The* Mary Rose *was in the thick of the fighting* Ibid., 64.

214 *As Sir William Wynter put it afterward* Ibid., 65.

215 *Another witness claimed that* Ibid., 65.

Chapter 9. Phoenix from the Ashes

217 *He must have realized* This account of the Matanzas Bay engagement and its consequences is based on Phillips (1986), 3–7. Also see Boxer (1977), Walton (1994), Glete (2), and Konstam (2008).

220 *This process of introspection began* Phillips, op. cit., 19–33, 43–46; Gardiner (1994), 105–114.

221 *The Spanish began looking at the way their ships were designed* This account of the engagement off the Azores in 1591 is drawn from Rowse (1937), 300–320, and Nelson (2001), 180–192. Also see Earle (1992).

224 *Worst of all, the Spanish fleet* Nelson (2001), 182–183.

225 *A model of this new breed of Spanish warship* Landström (1961), 124–125.

226 *In December 1607 a royal decree* Phillips (1986), 29, 230.

226 *An example of this new type of flota galleon* Mathewson (1986), 20–21.

228 *The closest Oquendo came to issuing an order* Guilmartin (2002), 191. The account of the battle is drawn from Padfield (1982), vol. 1, 185–213, and Guilmartin, op. cit., 191–203.

230 *The* Duyfken *(Little Dove) was typical of these early Dutch East Indiamen* Mutch (1942), 12–15. The replica vessel was built in Freemantle, in Western Australia. For details see the Web site of the *Duyfken* 1606 replica *Foundation* (www.duyfken.org.au).

231 *Then there was the* Aemilia, *Maarten Tromp's flagship* The *Aemelia* is reconstructed in Gibbons (2001), 44. See also Giggal (1988), 14–15.

Chapter 10. Prestige over Practicality

233 *The whole country was stricken with grief* The account of the death and funeral of Queen Elizabeth I is drawn from Milton (2001), 184–196. The quotes by William Camden are from Thomas Smith's *Viri Clarissimi Gulielmi Camdeni Vita* (*The Life of William Camden*) (London 1691)— available through the Web site of the Philological Museum, part of the University of Birmingham (www.philological.bham.ac.uk).

235 *The Elizabethan fleet bequeathed to the new king* Oppenheim, 184–202. See also Nelson (2001), 211–216.

238 *It all began with a small boy's model ship* This account of the building of the *Prince Royal* is drawn from Phineas Pett's own narrative, published in Perrin (1917).

241 *The sheer scale of the new vessel was impressive* Oppenheim (1896 i), 186, 203–205; Howard (1979), 96–101; Lavery (1983), 47–48; Gardiner (1992), 12.

242 *To make the job even harder* Perrin (1917), 224–238.

244 *The design of the* Prince Royal *was innovative* Lavery (1983), 47–48. Also see Landström (1961), 350–351.

249 *The Swedish king was once quoted as saying* Quoted in Soop (1992), 13.

250 *On January 16, 1625, the two shipbuilders* Ibid., 14; Matz (1999), 122–128.

253 *Finally he sent a missive to Jakobsson* Matz, op. cit., 133.

253 *He decided to test his theory* Ibid., 133; Soop, op. cit., 15.

255 *The royal official Gabriel Oxenstierna claimed* Matz, op. cit., 141.

256 *An inquest was held in the royal* An account of the trial is provided by Kvarning and Ohrelius (1998), 25–33.

258 *Then in August 1956 the Swedish engineer* This account of the rediscovery, salvage, and conservation of the *Vasa* is drawn from Kvarning and Ohrelius, ibid.; Sloop (1992), 15–18; and Matz (1999), 153 et seq.

Chapter 11. Toward the Holy Grail

263 *A letter written by a courtier to King Charles I's wife* Cited in Green (1857), 217–219.

266 *Buckingham's commissioners even issued* Oppenheim (1896 i), 202–208, Penn (1913), 104–138.

267 *Buckingham's solution was* Penn, op. cit., 204–205.

268 *This time Buckingham had eighty ships* Ibid., 167–204.

272 *Some maritime historians claim* Sloop (1992), 9–11. Also see Landström (1961), 144–145.

274 *A later and even more spectacular example* Howard (1979), 222–223.

275 *In 1634 Admiral Sir John Pennington* Penn (1913), 251–252, presents this overbuilding as the essential difference between British and Dutch warships of the period.

277 *As late as 1636, Algernon Percy* Oppenheim (1896 i), 254.

278 *Since the accession of Charles I* Oppenheim (1896 i), 251–267.

278 *Speaking about his brief apprenticeship* Perrin (1917), 43–44.

Chapter 12. The *Sovereign of the Seas*

284 *In 1636 he told the Dutch ambassador* Penn (1914), 223–224.

285 *The murder of the Duke of Buckingham* Oppenheim (1896 i), 279–284.

286 *At least on paper, in 1634 King Charles* Ibid., 251–257.

287 *The* Charles *was built by Phineas Pett's son Peter* Ibid., 255; Howard (1979), 95–104. Howard also compares these Pett vessels with the *Leopard*, built in 1634.

288 *In early 1634 the two Petts were called* Perrin (1917), 256–258.

289 *The "new great ship" would have a burden of 1,466 tons* Oppenheim (1896 i), 260–263; Howard (1979), 103–104; and Callender (1930), 4–6. Callender also provides a useful biography of the two Petts and a history of the *Sovereign of the Seas*.

290 *The local estate was owned by the king* The quotation, drawn from a survey of royal estates conducted in 1569, is quoted in "The History of Brancepeth Castle Golf Club" (available at the clubhouse and online). See also Oppenheim, op. cit., 261.

291 *In early 1637* Perrin (1917), 293–294.

293 *It was there that King Charles* Perrin (1917), 324-327; Callender (1930), 13.

293 *It was later declared that* Perrin (1917), 341–342. Also see Lavery (1983), 17. Lavery also comments on the effectiveness of the *Sovereign of the Seas* as an operational warship.

295 *He started with the figurehead* This account is quoted in Callender (1930), 7–9.

298 *The* Sovereign *was rebuilt in 1659–1660* Oppenheim (1896 i), 338; Lavery (1983), 160.

Postcript. The Ship of the Line

302 *Captain John Smith, the mainstay of the Jamestown colony* Smith and Boeteler effectively rewrote Stuart naval tactics between them, advocating methods of ship handling that would remain in use until the First Dutch War. Also see Lavery (1983), 15–16, and Tunstall (1990), 11–16.

305 *They laid down that* These fighting instructions are reproduced in full in Corbett (1905), and in passim in Tunstall, op. cit., 16–21.

BIBLIOGRAPHY

Apestegui, Cruz. *Pirates of the Caribbean: Buccaneers, Privateers, Freebooters, and Filibusters, 1492–1720.* London, 2002.

Archibald, E. H. H. *The Fighting Ship in the Royal Navy, 897–1984.* Poole, Dorset, 1984.

Arnold, J. Barto III, and Robert Weddle. *The Nautical Archaeology of Padre Island: The Spanish Shipwrecks of 1554.* New York, 1978.

Arnold, Thomas. *The Renaissance at War.* London, 2001.

Aston, Margaret, ed. *The Panorama of the Renaissance.* London, 1996.

Bass, George F., ed. *A History of Seafaring Based on Underwater Archaeology.* London, 1974.

Beer, C. de. *The Art of Gunfounding.* London, 1991.

Blackmore, H. L. *The Catalogue of Armouries of the Tower of London. Vol. 1, Ordnance.* London, 1976.

Boxer, C. R. *The Anglo-Dutch Wars of the 17th Century.* London, 1974.

———. *The Dutch Seaborne Empire, 1600–1800.* London, 1977.

Caldwell, David H., ed. *Scottish Weapons & Fortifications, 1100–1800.* Edinburgh, 1981.

Callender, Geoffrey. *The Portrait of Peter Pett and the* Sovereign of the Seas. Newport, Isle of Wight, 1930.

Capp, Bernard. *Cromwell's Navy: The Fleet and the English Revolution, 1648–1660.* Oxford, 1989.

Caruana, Adrian B. *The History of English Sea Ordnance, 1523–1875. Vol. I, The Age of Evolution, 1523–1715.* Rotherfield, East Sussex, 1994.

Cederlund, Carl Olof. *Vasa: The Archaeology of a Swedish Warship of 1628.* Stockholm, 2006.

Childs, David. *The Warship* Mary Rose: *The Life and Times of Henry VIII's Flagship.* London, 2007.

Cipolla, Carlo M. *Guns, Sails, and Empires: Technological Innovation and the Early Phases of European Expansion, 1400–1700.* London, 1965.

Cook, Harold J. *Matters of Exchange: Commerce, Medicine, and Science in the Dutch Golden Age.* New Haven, Conn., 2007.

Corbett, Julian S., ed. *Fighting Instructions, 1530–1816.* Vol. 29, Naval Records Society. London, 1905.

Cordingly, David, ed. *Pirates: Terror on the High Seas from the Caribbean to the South China Sea.* London, 1996.

Davidson, James D. G. *Scots and the Sea.* Edinburgh, 2003.

Davies, Jonathan. *The King's Ships: Henry VIII and the Birth of the Royal Navy, 1509–1547.* Leigh-on-Sea, Essex, 2005.

Davis, Ralph. *The Rise of the Atlantic Economies.* World Economic History Series. London, 1973.

Deuchar, Stephen, ed. *Concise Catalogue of Oil Paintings in the National Maritime Museum.* London, 1988.

Dickens, A. G. *Reformation and Society in Sixteenth-Century Europe.* Library of European Civilization Series. London, 1966.

Dickson, T., and J. B. Paul, eds. *Accounts of the Lord High Treasurer of Scotland.* Edinburgh, 1877–1902.

Dodds, James, and James Moore. *Building the Wooden Fighting Ship.* London, 1984.

Dupuy, R. Ernest, and Trevor N. Dupuy. *The Collins Encyclopaedia of Military History, from 3500 B.C. to the Present.* New York, 1985.

Earle, Peter. *The Last Fight of the* Revenge. London. 1992.

Fossier, Robert, ed. *The Cambridge Illustrated History of the Middle Ages, 1250–1520.* Cambridge, U.K., 1986.

Fox, Frank. *Great Ships: The Battlefleet of King Charles II.* London, 1980.

Franzen, Anders. *The Warship* Vasa: *Deep Diving and Marine Archaeology in Stockholm.* Stockholm, 1961.

Frost, Robert I. *The Northern Wars, 1558–1721.* Modern Wars in Perspective Series. London, 2000.

Gardiner, Julie, ed. *Before the Mast: Life and Death aboard the* Mary Rose. Archaeology of the *Mary Rose* Series. Portsmouth, Eng., 2005.

Gardiner, Robert, ed. *Cogs, Caravels, and Galleons: The Sailing Ship, 1000–1650.* Conway's History of the Ship Series. London, 1994.

————. *The Line of Battle: The Sailing Warship, 1650–1840.* Conway's History of the Ship Series. London, 1992.

Gibbons, A. *The Encyclopaedia of Ships.* London, 2001.

Giggal, Kenneth. *Great Classic Sailing Ships.* London, 1988.

Glete, Jan. *Warfare at Sea, 1500–1650: Maritime Conflicts and the Transformation of Europe.* London, 2000.

Graham, Eric J. *A Maritime History of Scotland, 1650–1790.* East Linton, East Lothian, U.K., 2002.

Green, M. A. E. *The Letters of Queen Henrietta-Maria.* London, 1857.

Guilmartin, John F. Jr., *Galleons and Galleys.* London, 2002.

——. *Gunpowder and Galleys: Changing Technology and Mediterranean Warfare at Sea in the Sixteenth Century.* Cambridge Studies in Early Modern History. Cambridge, U.K., 1980.

Gush, George. *Renaissance Armies, 1480–1650.* Cambridge, U.K., 1975.

Haigh, Philip A. *The Military Campaigns of the Wars of the Roses.* Godalming, Surrey, Eng., 1995.

Hale, J. R. *Artists and Warfare of the Renaissance.* London, 1990.

——. *War and Society in Renaissance Europe, 1450–1620.* London, 1985.

Hall, Edward. *Chronicle; Containing the History of England* c. 1548. Reprint, London, 1809.

Harland, John. *Seamanship in the Age of Sail: An Account of the Shiphandling of the Sailing Man-of-War 1600, 1860, Based on Contemporary Accounts.* London, 1984.

Hattendorf, John B., and Richard W. Unger, eds. *War at Sea in the Middle Ages and Renaissance.* Woodbridge, Suffolk, U.K., 2003.

Hay, Denys. *Europe in the Fourteenth and Fifteenth Centuries.* London, 1966.

——. *The Italian Renaissance in Its Historical Background.* Cambridge, U.K., 1976.

——. ed. and trans. *Polydore Vergil; Anglica Historia.* London, 1950.

Hibbert, Christopher. *Charles I: A Life of Religion, War, and Treason.* London, 2007.

Howard, Frank. *Sailing Ships of War, 1400–1860.* London, 1979.

Howarth, David. *The Men-of-War.* Time-Life Seafarers Series. Amsterdam, 1978.

Hutchinson, Gillian, ed. *Medieval Ships and Shipping.* The Archaeology of Medieval Britain Series. London, 1994.

James, Alan. *The Navy and Government in Early Modern France, 1572–1661.* London, 2004.

Jones, J. R. *The Anglo-Dutch Wars of the Seventeenth Century.* Modern Wars in Perspective Series. London, 1996.

Jones, Mark, ed. *For Future Generations: Conservation of a Tudor Maritime Collection.* Archaeology of the *Mary Rose* Series. Portsmouth, U.K., 2003.

Kelly, Jack. *Gunpowder: Alchemy, Bombards, and Pyrotechnics.* Stroud, Gloucestershire, U.K., 2004.

Kelsey, Harry. *Sir John Hawkins: Queen Elizabeth's Slave Trader.* New Haven, Conn., 2003.

Kemp, Peter, ed. *The Oxford Companion to Ships and the Sea.* Oxford, U.K., 1976.

Knecht, Robert J. *The French Civil Wars, 1562–1598*. Modern Wars in Perspective Series. Harlow, Essex, U.K., 2000.

———. *French Renaissance Monarchy: Francis I and Henry II*. Harlow, Essex, U.K., 1984.

Knighton, C. S., and D. M. Loades. *The Anthony Roll of Henry VIII's Navy*. London, 2000.

Koenigsberger, H. G., and George L. Mosse. *Europe in the Sixteenth Century*. London, 1968.

Konstam, Angus. *The Armada Campaign, 1588: The Great Enterprise against England*. Oxford, 2001.

———. *The Complete History of Piracy*. Oxford, 2007.

———. *Elizabethan Sea Dogs, 1560–1605*. Oxford, 2000.

———. *Historical Atlas of Exploration*. New York, 2000.

———. *The History of Shipwrecks*. New York, 1999.

———. *Pavia, 1525: The Climax of the Italian Wars*. Oxford, 1996.

———. *The Renaissance War Galley, 1470–1590*. Oxford, 2002.

———. *Spanish Galleon, 1530–1690*. Oxford, 2004.

Kvarning, Lars-Ake, and Bengt Ohrelius. *The* Vasa: *The Royal Ship*. Stockholm, 1998.

Laing, David, ed. *The Poetical Works of Sir David Lyndsay*. Edinburgh, 1879.

Landström, Björn. *The Ship: An Illustrated History*. New York, 1961.

Lavery, Brian. *Maritime Scotland*. London, 2001.

———. *The Ship of the Line, Vol. I: The Development of the Battlefleet, 1650–1850*. London, 1983.

———. *The Ship of the Line, Vol. II: Design, Construction, and Fittings*. London, 1984.

Lemee, C. P. P. *The Renaissance Shipwrecks from Christianshavn: An Archaeological and Architectural Study of Large Carvel Vessels in Danish Water, 1580–1640*. Ships and Boats of the North Series. Roskilde, Denmark, 2006.

Lesley, John. *The History of Scotland from the Death of King James I in the Year 1436 to the Year 1561*. Reprint, Edinburgh, 1830.

Levi, A. H. T. *Cardinal Richelieu and the Making of France*. London, 2000.

Loades, David. *The Tudor Navy: An Administrative, Political, and Military History*. Cambridge, U.K., 1992.

Loades, D. M., and Charles Knighton. *Letters from the* Mary Rose. Stroud, Gloucestershire, U.K., 2002.

Lockyer, Roger. *Buckingham: The Life and Political Career of George Villiers, First Duke of Buckingham, 1592–1628*. London, 1984.

Lynn, John A. *The Wars of Louis XIV, 1667–1714*. Modern Wars in Perspective Series. London, 1999.

Macdougall, Norman. *James IV.* East Linton, East Lothian, U.K., 1998.

———, ed. *Scotland and War, A.D. 79–1918.* Edinburgh, 1991.

Macintyre, Donald, ed. *The Adventure of Sail, 1520–1914.* London, 1979.

Mackie, R. L., ed. *The Letters of James IV, 1505–13.* Edinburgh, 1953.

Mallet, M. E. *The Florentine Galley in the 15th Century.* Oxford, 1968.

Marsden, Peter. *Sealed in Time: The Loss and Recovery of the* Mary Rose. Archaeology of the *Mary Rose* Series. Portsmouth, U.K., 2003.

Martin, Colin. *Full Fathom Five: Wrecks of the Spanish Armada.* London, 1975

———. and Geoffrey Parker. *The Spanish Armada.* London, 1988.

Matthew, Donald. *Atlas of Medieval Europe.* Oxford, 1983.

Matthewson, R. Duncan III. *The Search for the* Nuestra Señora de Atocha. Key West, Fla., 1985

———. *Treasure of the* Atocha. New York, 1986.

Matz, Erling. *Glorious* Vasa: *The Magnificent Ship and 17th Century Sweden.* Värnamo, Sweden, 1999.

McKee, Alexander. *From Merciless Invaders: The Defeat of the Spanish Armada.* London, 1963.

———. *How We Found the* Mary Rose. London, 1983.

McLain, J. H. *Pyrotechnics.* Philadelphia, 1980.

Milton, Giles. *Big Chief Elizabeth: How England's Adventurers Gambled and Won the New World.* London, 2000.

Moorhouse, Geoffrey. *Great Harry's Navy: How Henry VIII Gave England Seapower.* London, 2005.

Moote, A. Lloyd. *Louis XIII: The Just.* Berkeley, Calif., 1991.

Morris, Roger. *Atlantic Seafaring.* Auckland, N.Z., 1992.

Mowat, Sue. *The Port of Leith: Its History and Its People.* Edinburgh, 2003.

Muckelroy, Keith, ed. *Archaeology under Water: An Atlas of the World's Submerged Sites.* Maidenhead, Berkshire, U.K., 1980.

Mutch, T. D. *The First Discovery of Australia.* Sydney, 1942.

Myers, A. R., ed. *English Historical Documents.* London, 1969.

Needham, Joseph. *Science and Civilisation in China.* Cambridge, U.K., 1986.

Nelson, Arthur. *The Tudor Navy: The Ships, Men, and Organisation, 1485–1603.* London, 2001.

Oman, Charles. *A History of the Art of War in the Sixteenth Century.* 1937. Reprint, London, 1991.

Oppenheim, M. *A History of the Administration of the Royal Navy and of Merchant Shipping in Relation to the Navy from 1509 to 1660.* 1896. Reprint, Brookfield, Vt., 1988.

———. *Naval Accounts and Inventories of the Reign of Henry VII.* London, 1896.

Padfield, Peter. *Guns at Sea*. London, 1973.

———. *Tide of Empires: Decisive Campaigns in the Rise of the West*. Vol. 1, *1481–1654*. London, 1979.

Parker, Geoffrey. *The Army of Flanders and the Spanish Road, 1567–1659: The Logistics of Spanish Victory and Defeat in the Low Counties*. Cambridge, U.K., 2004.

———. *Europe in Crisis, 1598–1648*. Oxford, 2001.

———. *The Grand Strategy of Philip II*. New Haven, Conn., 1998.

———. *The Military Revolution: Military Innovation and the Rise of the West, 1500–1800*. Cambridge, U.K., 1988.

———. *The Thirty Years War*. Abingdon, Oxfordshire, U.K., 1996.

Parry, J. H. *The Spanish Seaborne Empire*. The History of Human Society Series. London, 1966.

Pastor, Xavier. *The Ships of Christopher Columbus*. Anatomy of the Ship Series. London, 1992.

Penn, C. D. *The Navy under the Early Stuarts and Its Influence on English History*. 1913. Reprint, London, 1970.

Pérez-Mallaína, Pablo E. *Spain's Men of the Sea: Daily Life on the Indies Fleets in the Sixteenth Century*. Baltimore, 1998.

Perrin, W. G. *The Autobiography of Phineas Pett*. Vol. 54, Naval Records Society. London, 1917.

Peterson, Harold L. *Round Shot and Rammers*. South Bend, Ind., 1969.

Phillips, Carla Rahn. *Six Galleons for the King of Spain: Imperial Defense in the Early Seventeenth Century*. Baltimore, 1986.

Phillips, Gervaise. *The Anglo-Scots Wars, 1513–1550: A Military History*. Woodbridge, Suffolk, U.K., 1999.

Pitscottie, Robert Lindsay of. *The Historie and Cronicles of Scotland*. 1728. Reprint, Edinburgh, 1899.

Powell, J. R. *Robert Blake: General-at-Sea*. London, 1972.

Reese, Peter. *Flodden: A Scottish Tragedy*. Edinburgh, 2003.

Ritchie, Robert (a.k.a. Angus Konstam). *Historical Atlas of the Renaissance*. New York, 2004.

Rodger, N. A. M. *The Command of the Ocean: A Naval History of Britain, 1649–1815*. London, 2004.

Rodríguez-Salgado, M. J., ed. *Armada, 1588–1988: An International Exhibition to Commemorate the Spanish Armada: The Official Catalogue*. National Maritime Museum. London, 1988.

Ronald, Susan. *Pirate Queen: Elizabeth I, Her Pirate Ventures, and the Dawn of Empire*. Stroud, Gloucestershire, U.K., 2007.

Roncière, C. de la. *Histoire de la Marine Française*. Paris, 1923.

Rose, Susan. *The Navy of the Lancastrian Kings*. Vol. 123, Naval Records Society. London, 1982.

Rowse, A. L. *Sir Richard Grenville of the* Revenge. London, 1977.

Rule, Margaret. *The* Mary Rose*: The Excavation and Raising of Henry VIII's Flagship*. London, 1982.

Rundle, David, ed. *Encyclopaedia of the Renaissance*. Oxford, 1999.

Simon, Edith. *The Reformation*. Amsterdam, 1967.

Smith, R. D., and R. R. Brown, eds. *Guns from the Sea*. London, 1988.

Soop, Hans. *The Power and the Glory: The Sculptures of the Warship* Wasa. Uddevalla, Swed., 1992.

Spont, A. *Letters and Papers Relating to the War with France, 1512–1513*. Vol. 10, Naval Records Society. London, 1910.

Stewart, Alan. *The Cradle King: A Life of James VI & I*. London, 2003.

Stirland, Anne. *The Men of the* Mary Rose: *Raising the Dead*. Stroud, Gloucestershire, U.K., 2005.

Sugden, John. *Sir Francis Drake*. New York, 1990.

Taylor, Frederick. *The Art of War in Italy, 1494–1529*. 1921. Reprint, Leigh-on-Sea, Essex, U.K., 1993.

Thomson, George Malcolm. *Sir Francis Drake*. London, 1973.

Throckmorton, Peter, ed. *History from the Sea: Shipwrecks and Archaeology from Homer's* Odyssey *to the* Titanic. London, 1987.

Tierney, Brian, and Sidney Painter. *Western Europe in the Middle Ages, 300–1475*. New York, 1978.

Tunstall, Brian. *Naval Warfare in the Age of Sail: The Evolution of Fighting Tactics, 1650–1815*. London, 1990.

Unwin, Rayner. *The Defeat of John Hawkins: A Biography of His Third Slaving Voyage*. London, 1960.

Usherwood, Stephen, ed. *The Great Enterprise: The History of the Spanish Armada as Revealed in Contemporary Documents*. London, 1982.

Usherwood, Stephen, and Elizabeth Usherwood. *The Counter-Armada 1596: The Journal of the* Mary Rose. Annapolis, Md., 1983.

Waley, Daniel. *Later Medieval Europe: From St. Louis to Luther*. London, 1964.

Walker, Bryce. *Armada. Time-Life* Seafarers Series. Amsterdam, 1981.

Walton, Timothy R. *The Spanish Treasure Fleets*. Sarasota, Fla., 1994.

Ward, A. W., G. W. Prothero, and Stanley Leathes. *The Thirty Years' War*. The Cambridge Modern History Series. Vol. IV. Cambridge, U.K., 1934.

Warren, John. *Elizabeth I: Religion and Foreign Affairs*. London, 2002.

Watson, Paul Barron. *The Swedish Revolution under Gustavus Vasa*. Honolulu, 2005.

Williams, Patrick. *Armada*. Stroud, Gloucestershire, U.K., 2000.

Wilson, Timothy. *Flags at Sea*. London, 1986.

Wood, James B. *The King's Army: Warfare, Soldiers, and Society during the Wars of Religion in France, 1562–1576*. Cambridge, U.K., 1996.

Wood, M., ed. *The Flodden Papers, 1507–1517*. Edinburgh, 1933.

Woodman, Richard. *The History of the Ship: The Comprehensive Story of Seafaring from the Earliest Times to the Present Day*. London, 1997.

Young, Alan R. *His Majesty's Royal Ship: A Critical Edition of Thomas Heywood's* A True Description of His Majesties Royall Ship. AMS Studies in the Renaissance. New York, 2006.

CREDITS

INDEX

Page references in *italics* refer to illustrations and tables.